Norma and Ann

May the God who speaks
give you all you need to hear
and respond.

Mark Bayler

Nine Ways God Always Speaks

Tyndale House Publishers, Inc.
Carol Stream, Illinois

Mark Herringshaw &
Jennifer Schuchmann

nine

ways

GOD

ALways

speaks*

* Offer only available in certain states

Visit Tyndale's exciting Web site at www.tyndale.com

Visit the authors at www.sixprayers.com

TYNDALE and Tyndale's quill logo are registered trademarks of Tyndale House Publishers, Inc.

Nine Ways God Always Speaks: Offer Only Available in Certain States

Designed by Jacqueline L. Nuñez

Published in association with the literary agency of Alive Communications, Inc., 7680 Goddard Street, Suite 200, Colorado Springs, CO 80920.

Library of Congress Cataloging-in-Publication Data

Herringshaw, Mark.
    Nine ways God always speaks : offer only available in certain states / Mark Herringshaw, Jennifer Schuchmann.
        p. cm.
    Includes bibliographical references (p.   ).
    ISBN 978-1-4143-2226-1 (hc)
    1. Prayer—Christianity.   2. Spirituality.   I. Schuchmann, Jennifer, 1966-   II. Title.
BV220.H43 2009
248.3'2—dc22   2008049075

Printed in the United States of America

15   14   13   12   11   10   09
 7   6   5   4   3   2   1

CHannels

101.0 Hearing Voices 1
102.0 Circumstantial Evidence. 27
103.0 Prophet Sharing 57
104.0 *His*-story 85
105.0 You Must Be Dreaming 119
106.0 The Nature Channel 157
107.0 Infectious 187
108.0 Pushy Little Weenie 219
109.0 Inhaling the Bible. 255
110.0 You Might Think I'm Crazy, But 291

Acknowledgments 321
Notes 325
About the Authors 333

CHANNEL 101.0
HEARING VOICES

SOME THINGS are TOO GOOD TO BE True:
  living to be 101
  winning the lottery
  hearing God speak

Despite the fact that these things are out of the ordinary and even unlikely, they happen every day to people all over the world. With a healthy diet, exercise, and regular checkups, it's possible that you could outlast your genes. Buy enough scratch-off tickets, and eventually you'll get lucky. But hearing God speak? Is there anything you can do about that?

We think so.

And so do others.

Many others.

One of them was Mrs. Murphey. Whenever God spoke to Mrs. Murphey, it usually signaled a painful or traumatic event in her family. As her son Cecil recalls, this particular time was no different.

My brother was maybe five feet two and weighed around one hundred pounds. He was a career man in the Navy, and he worked belowdecks. One night my mother had a dream that his ship had hit something, and when my brother went into the compartment to try and shut it off, he got trapped. This all happened in my mother's dream. She was agitated, but there was nothing she could do. There was no way for her to communicate with her son, and besides, who would believe her anyway?

A few weeks later, she was at a prayer meeting at our church in Davenport, Iowa. It was a mostly fundamental church, not the kind that believed in visions from God. But while she was there, she was gripped by a panic that what she dreamed was happening right then. She interrupted the meeting and said, "My son is drowning. You have to pray for him right now!"

The whole group stopped what they were doing and prayed for ten or fifteen minutes. A sense of peace came over my mother, and she told them they could stop. It was over.

About two weeks later, we got a letter at the house. It was from my brother, and he told us that he had almost drowned. The ship went aground, and one compartment started to take on water. My brother and several others went to close it off. In the confusion, the others left the compartment, locking my brother in.

He said that the water kept rising until it was above his neck and almost at his mouth when one of the guys said, "Where's Murph?" They figured out he was in the compartment, and they returned to rescue him.

Though the dream and the events surrounding it took place nearly a half-century ago, Cecil Murphey still remembers the details. His mother was known for having dreams that predicted terrible events—events of which she couldn't have had prior knowledge.

Cecil recalls a second dream, in which his mother learned about a divorce in the family (at a time when divorce was very rare) before the couple announced it. In still another dream, she was warned that another brother of Cecil's was dying of lung cancer before he had been diagnosed. Cecil believes his mother heard from God.

Is it possible for God to speak through dreams?

Cecil believes that God also speaks to him—just not through his dreams.

Off the top of his head, Cecil can quickly tell nearly a dozen stories of when God has spoken, helping him to perceive future events, make decisions, or gain insight into situations that he wouldn't have been able to except through divine knowledge.

He describes hearing God's voice inside of himself like an "anointed intuition."

> I feel a sense of conviction so powerful that I would die before I'd turn away from it. Say what you want, I can tell you I've been a Christian for fifty years, and I've never been wrong any time I had one of these

strong convictions. If I had to give up the conviction or die, I'm ready to die for it; it's that clear to me.

Does God speak that clearly to you?

101.1 crazy talk

Perhaps God has spoken to you in the past and you'd like to experience that kind of communication again.

Maybe you've never heard from God personally—but you long to.

Or could it be that you are skeptical that God speaks at all?

One reason people say they don't pray more is because they feel as if nothing happens when they pray, that God isn't listening, or worse, that he is not there at all.

A one-sided relationship isn't worth much.

If we're expected to talk to God through prayer, shouldn't we know whether he will talk back? And if he will, how we will hear him?

So does God speak to you?

Think carefully before you respond. People are likely to make judgments about you based solely on how you answer this question.

In the mid-eighties, Jennifer was a high school sophomore actively investigating the claims of Christianity, but she hadn't yet made a decision as to their veracity. While riding in a car with a guy from school, she had a disturbing conversation, so disturbing that twenty years later she can't recall the context or the guy, just the conversation. She remembers he was smart, cute, and she had a crush on him. And he was a Christian. Though cute and smart are good boyfriend traits, she wasn't so sure about the Christian part,

especially when he happened to mention that God spoke to him.

I clearly remember that he said, "God told me . . ." and all I could think was, *This guy must be crazy*, and I didn't mean crazy in some fun-loving way. I meant crazy in a certifiably deranged sort of way. People who hear God's voice do crazy-people things like shoot their mother or drown their kids in a bathtub.

I have to admit, I was nervous riding in a car with someone who thought he was hearing God speak, but like I said, he was cute. So I asked him about it.

"God speaks to you?"

"Yes."

"Do you hear voices? Do you hear a deep voice like in the movies?"

"No, not really—"

"Well, what does his voice sound like?"

"Well, it's kind of—"

"Wait. Do other people hear him when he speaks to you?"

I wasn't sure how I wanted him to answer that question. If God spoke only to him and no one else heard God's voice, then this guy was not boyfriend material; he was drown-our-future-kids material. But if he said that other people also heard God speak to him, like eavesdropping on a conversation at a restaurant—Cute Guy and God discussing football scores—then it was even weirder.

Was this guy a member of some strange cult?

Had he been drinking?

Or was it possible that God *really did speak* to him? Was he speaking to everyone? And if so, why didn't I hear him?

Fortunately, Cute Guy interrupted my thoughts with an explanation.

"No, it's not like God says things out loud to me like Charlton Heston shouting through a megaphone. It's more like it's a passing thought that comes into my head from out of nowhere. It's more like a feeling than an audible voice."

"Then how do you know it's God?" I asked before peppering him with questions about what he heard, how he heard it, and if he was taking any prescription drugs.

I left that conversation more curious and a little less skeptical. But if God really spoke to people, why wasn't he speaking to me? And could I get him to start? I wasn't yet convinced that he directly communicated with people. And I knew I wouldn't believe it based on someone else's reports. If God wanted me to believe that he really does speak, he'd have to speak to me personally.

Perhaps this is your story too. You're not sure that God communicates with us here and now. Or maybe the thought of the God of the universe talking personally to *you* creeps you out. Maybe you don't even believe that God exists— let alone that he speaks.

Or could it be . . . you have a great deal of head knowledge or scriptural knowledge about how God communicates but you don't have much in the way of personal experience?

Maybe you've grown up in the church or around religious folks who discuss how God talks to us, but you're not convinced that God talks—*to you*.

Maybe you're chuckling as you read this because you *know* that God speaks and that God speaks to you personally. But maybe your expectations of how and when he speaks are limited by your experience.

Regardless of your story, your preconceived ideas, even your experiences, what if your thoughts on God communicating with you (or not) are wrong? Or maybe not expansive enough?

What if there's a whole lot more to it than what you've seen so far?

What if God does speak?

What if he is speaking right now?

101.2 IT'S NOT ABOUT CHURCH

As a young boy, Mark was comfortable with the God language that spooked Jennifer. As the son, grandson, and great-grandson of preachers, Mark truly believed that God spoke personally to people.

In church.

Literally, *in church*.

Growing up in his father's congregation, Mark thought he knew exactly how God spoke—through the singing of traditional hymns, Scripture reading, and fiery preaching.

Mark knew what to do to receive a personal message from God. You put on a coat and clip-on tie and, together with your parents and two sisters, piled into the family's Oldsmobile Vista Cruiser, drove to the church, and solemnly entered the sanctuary. Once inside, you passionately participated in the singing and actively listened and responded to the preaching. Then at the end of the liturgy when the altar call of repentance came, you went forward, kneeled on the carpeted step, and wept. That's where God spoke to you—during the 11:00 a.m. service on Sundays and the evening services on Sundays and Wednesdays.

Although he was only eight, Mark understood this was the thing he needed to do to put himself in a position to hear God. What Mark didn't know was that God also spoke to little boys in their neighbors' living rooms—while their clip-on tie was still at home in the closet. Wearing a T-shirt, jeans, and Converse high-tops, Mark heard God speak.

And he didn't even have to kneel.

Twin Lakes Baptist Church was the largest evangelical congregation in Santa Cruz, California. Each year they sponsored an annual vacation Bible school—ironically named, since it was a vacation from neither Bible nor school.

Neighborhood children, like Mark, gathered in local church members' homes to do crafts (making Jesus and his disciples out of Popsicle sticks), to eat snacks (Rice Krispies Treats in the shape of an ark), and to hear flannelgraph stories from the Bible (think clip-art PowerPoint presentation replaced by cutouts on a flannel-covered bulletin board).

> I remember the woman had just finished telling a Bible story, the one about Jesus calling Zacchaeus down from the tree. I had heard that story countless times before, but this time when she finished, I began to feel something strange in the bottom of my stomach. I felt nervous, but there wasn't anything to

be nervous about; I was just sitting on the couch with my friends.

But then I began to think of a bunch of things I regretted. Nothing important, just trivial eight-year-old stuff like picking on my sister or lying to my mom. But I began to dwell on the specifics of each incident, and I felt ashamed. I could feel my cheeks burn, and I couldn't figure out why.

My friends didn't seem to notice. They didn't seem to be feeling what I felt. But to me, I felt as if a fifty-pound sack of guilt had been thrown on my back.

The woman telling the story noticed. She came over and asked if she could pray for me. I remember crying because I felt so bad. She spoke some simple words from the Bible and asked me to repeat them after her. When I did, something changed.

Immediately those feelings of shame and guilt evaporated. I felt as if I had been swallowed by a warm ocean of love and pleasure. In that moment of euphoria, I heard God speak.

The voice wasn't audible, but to me, it was real. It happened forty years ago, and though I can't remember the exact words he said, God told me that he loved me. But more than that, he said, "I have an adventure planned for you."

Any eight-year-old boy would be thrilled with an adventure, but one from God? I was positively pumped. I knew I'd heard from the Creator of the universe, that he knew my name, and that he had an adventure planned for me. This was so unlike anything I heard at the altar at church that I couldn't wait to tell my dad. I ran the entire four blocks back to my house. As I ran, I thought, *My feet aren't touching the ground.*

Is hearing from God reserved only for tie-wearing, head-bowing church boys? Or is it possible that eight-year-old Mark, with glue-stained fingertips and Rice Krispies on his shirt, really heard from God?

Mark believes he did, but frankly there's no proof.

If evidence were required, the woman leading the event could testify to the change in Mark's countenance. But she wouldn't be able to swear on a Bible and say she heard God speak to him. She, like Mark, might believe it happened, but she'd never be able to prove it.

That's the problem, isn't it?

If you've never experienced God communicating with you, there's nothing anyone can say or do to make you believe it's possible.

But if you've experienced God in this way, there is a deep conviction that it happened—regardless of how weird the circumstances. It's like *knowing* you're innocent when all of the evidence seems to point to your guilt. There is nothing anyone can say or do to make you deny it. You'd give your life for what you know to be true.

Perhaps that's why there's still so much controversy over a seventeen-year-old girl who sacrificed her life for what she knew to be true.

101.3 LITTLE GIRL HEARING VOICES

Jeanne was born in a small village in northern France at a time when girls didn't learn to read or write. But Jeanne had a devout mother who taught her sacred lessons, and as a result, Jeanne was known for her gentleness, charity, and holiness.

One day, while tending her father's sheep, she heard what she described as "a worthy voice"[1] and saw "a great light that came in the name of the voice."[2] Jeanne credited this voice to the archangel Michael and to two early Christian saints, Catherine and Margaret. Jeanne was not yet a teenager when she received her first vision; she cried when the voices left because they were so beautiful.

Her visions continued. In time, they became quite specific and directive. *They* wanted *her* to rescue France. At the age of seventeen, Jeanne d'Arc, known to us as Joan of Arc, heeded the call of those voices.

She cut her hair short and persuaded her uncle to give her a horse, a dagger, a tunic, trousers, boots, and a boy's black cap. She mustered a six-man escort and made them swear an oath to take her safely to Chinon.

Though yet uncrowned, Charles VII lived in the castle at Chinon and sat on the royal throne while the Hundred Years' War divided France. Charles had been declared illegitimate by none other than his own mother. Charles was weak, without money, and incapable of reaching Reims for his own coronation. France had no true king.

The country was a mess. Charles's own wimpish persona left him impotent to resist England's army. But learning of the young girl who had visions, Charles felt a glimmer of hope and decided to test her.

Before she arrived, Charles asked one of his nobles to take the throne while he hid among the ranks of his courtiers. When Joan arrived, she barely looked at the man on the throne. Instead, she walked up to Charles and curtsied to him as the king.[3] Still, Charles wasn't convinced. Only after she told him exactly what he had prayed for while alone in the palace chapel did he trust her.

Despite his faith in her claims, Charles subjected her to the scrutiny of his theologians. After passing their tests, she received a sword, a banner, and the right to command the king's troops.

Joan and her army marched to Orléans in 1429. At first, the leaders of the French military didn't want to follow her command, but they quickly found that nothing went well when they ignored her orders, and all went well when they heeded them.

God told Joan that her victory sword—a blade with five crosses cut into the steel—was buried in the church of Sainte-Catherine-de-Fierbois. When Joan announced this, knights were dispatched to search the church. They found the weapon just as Joan had prophesied.

Then, in the heat of the battle, Joan was wounded in the shoulder and carried from the field. One of her knights cut the head of the arrow off. She removed the shaft herself and, despite her wounds, went on to lead her army to victory in the liberation of Orléans. A few days later, in Reims, Charles was anointed as Charles VII, king of France.

The voices spoke again, this time to warn Joan that she would be captured by her enemies. "Then let me die quickly without a long captivity," she pleaded. The voices told her not to be frightened but to resign herself for what was to come next.

On May 23, 1430, Joan was at Compiègne, fighting the Duke of Burgundy. She was captured and turned over to the English, who sent her to church officials, where she was put on trial for heresy. Charles VII didn't lift a sword to save her.

Cauchon, the bishop of Beauvais, prosecuted her case. His tactic was vicious scorn. The voices, he claimed, were not God's guidance, but the devil's. Unmoved, Joan refused to deny her counsel.

At the age of nineteen, Joan was convicted. On May 30, 1431, she was burned alive at the stake with a paper cap on her head, on which was written, "Heretic. Relapsed. Apostate. Idolatress."

Despite her trial, many thought she was innocent. When a couple of English soldiers laughed, one English noble, terrified at the scene before him, turned and said, "We are undone; we have burned a saint."[4]

The controversy that existed in Joan's life continued long after her death. But Joan's mother was as strong-minded as her daughter and wouldn't let the case rest. Working with King Charles VII, she insisted the case be submitted to the pope. Twenty-four years later, a new trial opened in Paris.

In 1456, Joan was pronounced innocent by Pope Callixtus III.

In 1909, she was beatified by Pope Pius X in the first step of her canonization into the Catholic church.

Finally, in 1920, Pope Benedict officially declared her a saint.

Did Joan hear God's voice?

Obviously, church leaders disagreed.

Those present at her trial and at her death had differing opinions.

Six hundred years later, historians still argue whether the young girl actually heard the voice of God.

Some say she was mentally ill. Some say she was suffering from delusions as a result of a disease. Some, like the bishop of Beauvais, say it wasn't God she heard, but the devil.

As authors of a book on hearing God speak—which we guess makes us unofficial experts—we'd like to go on record with our opinion. We would like to say conclusively . . . we don't know.

There is no way for us to prove that Joan of Arc heard God's voice or even the voices of his divine messengers. There is no way for us to prove that she didn't. But *Joan* believed she heard God. More importantly, she acted on her belief in a way that not only changed the course of history, but resulted in her willingly sacrificing her life for what she believed.

We know that some people may be willing to die for something they believe is true. But no one is willing to die for something he or she *knows* is false. The fact that Joan believed she heard from God, and then sacrificed her life in defense of that belief, is the strongest evidence we have that Joan believed God spoke to her.

Understanding a bit of Joan's controversy makes it easy to understand why there is so much passion surrounding another teenage girl who also had a vision.

101.4 LITTLE GIRL HEARING VOICES—TAKE TWO

We don't know if she was smart or beautiful, but we know she was poor—a peasant girl in a small and humble town in the Middle East. The town was so insignificant that at the time people were quoted as saying, "Can anything good come from there?"[5]

Though her name, Mary, was a common name in first-century Palestine, by all accounts she was uncommonly good. At least that's what people thought until she started hearing voices. Voices that said some pretty wild and far-out things like, "You're going to have a baby even though you've never had sex." And "Oh yeah, your elderly cousin is pregnant too."

The details of her visions and the accompanying events are recorded for us by a doctor who wrote it all down in a letter. Though there were eyewitness accounts circulating at the time of the events, that wasn't good enough for Dr. Luke. From the beginning, he cautiously investigated everything and wrote his findings in a careful account so that the recipient of his letter could be *certain* of the truth.[6] Two thousand years later, the Gospel of Luke is part of the best-selling book in the history of the world.

Mary was engaged to a man named Joseph. Like many brides-to-be of her time, Mary was probably in the middle of her prewedding chores—addressing hand-engraved invitations, finalizing details for a honeymoon at Joseph's dad's house, and mending her best dress to wear on the special day—when an angel appeared:

> "Greetings, favored woman! The Lord is with you!"[7]
> "Don't be afraid, Mary," the angel told her, "for you have found favor with God! You will conceive and give birth to a son, and you will name him Jesus. He will be very great and will be called the Son of the Most High. The Lord God will give him the throne of his ancestor David. And he will reign over Israel forever; his Kingdom will never end!"[8]

Could this make sense? After all, Joseph was a descendant of the great King David. But a throne? And Son of the Most High? And oh yeah, one other thing . . . Mary asked the angel, "But how can this happen? I am a virgin."[9]

Yes, the obvious.

The angel spoke as if Mary were already pregnant. For a poor Jewish girl, it was stupefying to think of her son on a throne or her boy as the Son of the Most High. But being pregnant? Well, for such a good girl, that was *impossible.*

The angel replied, "The Holy Spirit will come upon you, and the power of the Most High will overshadow you. So the baby to be born will be holy, and he will be called the Son of God."[10]

It's not unusual for a virgin bride to be nervous about her wedding night. She'd have all kinds of questions: How would it feel? Would it hurt? Would she know what to do? But imagine a young girl being told that she was going to be impregnated when the Holy Spirit came upon her.

In addition, Mary had to be afraid of what those closest to her would say. This was an offense for which she could be stoned. What would Joseph do?

If Mary was confused before, she had to be out of her mind with fear by now.

But the angel gives her something else to think about:

> What's more, your relative Elizabeth has become pregnant in her old age! People used to say she was barren, but she's now in her sixth month. For nothing is impossible with God.[11]

This gave Mary something to hang her head scarf on. If indeed Elizabeth were pregnant, it would be a miracle, because Elizabeth was, well, really old. It would be nothing short of God's intervention if Elizabeth were with child.

Perhaps that is what gave Mary the confidence to respond, "I am the Lord's servant. May everything you have said about me come true."[12]

So did Mary hear from God via his messenger Gabriel? She believes she did . . .

. . . like Mark, who believed he heard God not in a church but in a living room.

. . . and like Joan, who believed the voices enough to let them guide her.

Dr. Luke goes on to say, "A few days later Mary hurried to the hill country of Judea, to the town where Zechariah lived. She entered the house and greeted Elizabeth. At the sound of Mary's greeting, Elizabeth's child leaped within her, and Elizabeth was filled with the Holy Spirit."[13]

Mary's faith in her supernatural encounter caused her to pack up and go visit her cousin in the hills. When she arrived, any doubts she had were dismissed. Beyond all rational explanation, her aged cousin was pregnant.

> Elizabeth gave a glad cry and exclaimed to Mary, "God has blessed you above all women, and your child is blessed. Why am I so honored, that the mother of my Lord should visit me? When I heard your greeting, the baby in my womb jumped for joy. You are blessed because you believed that the Lord would do what he said."[14]

Never mind the formalities of hospitality. There's no "Oh, it's been so long. How long are you staying?" Or even a "Can I get you something to drink?" Elizabeth doesn't waste words: "We're both pregnant. With little miracle babies!"

Buoyed by Elizabeth's faith, Mary is reassured. This is confirmation that she isn't crazy, that she heard what she thought she heard.

So how does Mary react? Well, she starts babbling about how good God is and how much she loves him:

> Oh, how my soul praises the Lord.
> How my spirit rejoices in God my Savior!
> For he took notice of his lowly servant girl,
> and from now on all generations will call me blessed.
> For the Mighty One is holy,
> and he has done great things for me.[15]

If you translate this from the original Greek into 1970s Northern California preteen boyspeak, it's basically the same thing Mark thought on the way home from hearing God speak in the neighbor's living room: *My feet didn't touch the ground the whole way home!*

But not everyone would have believed what Mary was saying.

The residents of Bethlehem may not have known where electricity came from, but they knew where babies came from, and it wasn't the Holy Spirit. Imagine the taunting she must have taken as she stood next to her school locker, confiding this secret to her BFF.

"Yeah, right. . . . If you didn't *do it*, then how'd you get knocked up? Hey, everyone, listen to what Mary says happened to her. Go ahead, Mary; tell everyone the part about the Holy Spirit."

Even Joseph was skeptical.

And you can understand his doubts. Right?

After all, here's a guy who has chosen Mary to be his wife, not for her dowry but for her character. Then she tries to tell him some crazy story about God speaking to her, evidently to justify a reality that has only one commonsense explanation. Joseph would be stupid not to rethink his decision to ask this woman to bear his children.

Matthew records Joseph's story this way: "Joseph, her fiancé, was a good man and did not want to disgrace her publicly, so he decided to break the engagement quietly."[16]

What we love about this is—*he doubted.*

Because, frankly, many of us do too.

We identify with him.

He is real to us in his struggle to believe.

In fact, we identify so strongly with Joseph's doubt that when he eventually overcomes it, we can take courage and overcome ours.

> An angel of the Lord appeared to him in a dream. "Joseph, son of David," the angel said, "do not be afraid to take Mary as your wife. For the child within her was conceived by the Holy Spirit. And she will have a son, and you are to name him Jesus, for he will save his people from their sins."[17]

When the vision ended, Joseph was a believer. And we can prove it. Here's how:

"When Joseph woke up, he did as the angel of the Lord

commanded and took Mary as his wife."[18] But (and here's the kicker), "he did not have sexual relations with her until her son was born."[19]

See?

Proof.

Proof that Joseph heard from God.

If a man hears a voice and then doesn't have sex with his new wife as a result of hearing that voice, it means the dude is convinced that something big happened.

How else could you explain a testosterone-filled newly-wed bearing the brunt of the nasty rumors that swirled around them? Joseph must have been absolutely certain that he had heard from God.

If Joseph heard from God, it only makes sense that Mary did too.

101.5 STORIES THAT STICK

Most of us haven't experienced something so dramatic and life changing. It's hard to imagine that such a thing could be real.

We know that you're likely to read a story or two in this book that you don't believe. You'll explain away the events in some rational or scientific way. But there will also be at least one story you can't explain—a story that defies your logic and experience. That account will stick with you.

Like your tongue returning to a piece of popcorn wedged between your teeth, your brain will return to that story and try to make sense of it. In the process, you tell others, hoping they can add insight or understanding that will make it go away.

Perhaps that's what Mary's story was like.

The Bible says that Mary treasured the things that were happening and pondered them in her heart—but that was after Jesus was born. Until then, could the events have been a sort of spiritual irritant?

There are lots of details about her pregnancy Mary could have included, like her first trip to the doctor and how cute Jesus looked on that first ultrasound. She could have included more details about the birth, like the fact that the donkey kept braying, and it was really driving Joseph crazy, or the fact that she asked him to sterilize the manger, but they forgot to bring disinfecting wipes. But she didn't share those details. And Luke didn't record them. These kinds of things are easily dismissed and forgotten.

The details that Mary dwelled on, the story that she told over and over, was the story of those visions, of meeting Elizabeth and receiving confirmation of her circumstances, and of Joseph's disbelief until he also had a visitation. Those were the details that stuck in Mary's teeth—the ones that she returned to, pondered, and treasured in her heart.

So she told the story of the vision—at Jesus' birthday parties, his bar mitzvah, his graduation from carpentry school, and to the twelve buddies he roamed the countryside with. That stuck-piece-of-popcorn story was passed on until someone like Luke heard the story, investigated it carefully, and wrote down his conclusions so we could believe what he came to believe.

That it is true.

Do you believe it is true?

Or are you still picking at your teeth?

Are there other God stories that have you stuck?

What if you could actually experience such stories for yourself?

How would that change what you think about how God communicates?

It's not likely you will have a virgin birth or lead an army into battle. But what if God did something equally improbable for your time and circumstances? Would that allow you to consider whether he could have done something similar for someone else?

If God can speak to others, then it's possible God can speak to us. By hearing the stories of God in another person's life, we become more aware of God's voice in our own.

Ultimately, the proof we need that God speaks is hearing God speak *to us*.

To have that listening experience, we need to be open to all the possible ways God speaks. We need to better understand how God communicates with us and others.

It sounds like a circuitous argument, but if we ever hope to understand it, perhaps we need to step into the middle of it.

101.6 we're surrounded

You're already in the middle of it.

Right now you are being bombarded with hundreds of thousands of electronic signals. You can't see them, but they're constantly swirling around you. Each signal has a specialized frequency. The electronic current has variations depending on whether it's for an AM or FM radio, UHF or VHF television, cell phone, cordless phone, walkie-talkie, Wi-Fi, pager, or satellite signal.

At any time, you can tap into just about any signal you want. All you need is the proper decoder.

Want the signal sent out by the American Broadcasting Company? Take your decoder and choose a channel that amplifies and decodes the signal into a television picture. For most of us, this means turning on the TV and using the remote to find our local ABC affiliate.

Want to talk to your mom? Pick up your handheld signaling device, enter a series of codes that will then be transmitted into an electronic frequency, and somewhere in Omaha your mom's phone will ring. (Assuming, of course, that Mom lives in Omaha.)

Want to trade chapters with your coauthor when one of you is at a Caribou Coffee in Minneapolis and the other is at Alley Beans in Canton, Georgia? With a couple of keystrokes, and through the magic of a connected computer, an electronic exchange of information takes place in less time than it takes to order a latte.

What if communication with God worked similarly?

What if there were divine signals constantly swirling around us?

Is it possible that, like an electronic signal, we can tune into certain channels and hear God speak?

What if he is speaking to you *right now*?

Are we in the right place to decode his frequency and make sense of his signal?

Or is it possible our receivers need to be tuned to the correct spiritual channel to hear what he is saying?

If so, what might these spiritual channels look like?

When you pack up the car to embark on a multistate road trip, sometime after you fasten your seat belt and before you put the car in drive, you tune the radio to your favorite station. For miles, the music and the banter keep your mind occupied. But at some point, the signal begins to get a little fuzzy. It's harder to hear than when you left home. Eventually, you hear only static, you can't hear anything at all—or your station is overtaken by a different, stronger signal. If you want to continue listening, you'll have to fiddle with the dials until you tune in to another station. Your favorite preset station is no longer working for you.

Sometimes that happens in life.

Before Mark's encounter with God in the neighbor's living room, Mark's spiritual receiver was only on at church. It was only after God's signal was strong enough to overcome the static in Mark's life that he figured there was more out there than his preset channels were picking up. Mark learned that God wasn't only on the AM station on Sunday mornings; he was also on the FM country channels and the rock-and-roll stations.

To know God, we have to hear from him. But hearing from him doesn't mean we have to spend our lives in a Benedictine monastery, climb a mountain and meditate, or even wait for the pastor to speak during the Sunday service. But it does mean that we have to tune in to the channels on which God speaks. And maybe even give up our preset channels to discover new ways of communicating.

We've identified different channels on which people claim to have experienced the presence of God. As you read the following chapters, tune in to different channels—signs and circumstances, the words of other people, history, dreams and visions, nature, your emotions, your conscience, and Scripture—and perhaps you will hear him in ways you never have.

Are these the only channels?

Not likely.

But these are the airwaves that seem to carry the most traffic.

And let's just get this out on the page: both of us authors believe that God speaks to us. Not in a Charlton Heston voice but in other ways—including the stories in this book.

God speaks,

and

sometimes we even hear him.

It's not always like we expect; sometimes it's downright surprising. Unexpected. Confusing. Frightening. Peaceful or disturbing. Both of us have learned a few things from our initial encounters with hearing God speak—and we believe he does.

But it's equally important that you know we're not Kool-Aid drinkers—we don't believe everyone who claims to hear God speak actually does.

As friends and cowriters, we've shared intimate details of our spiritual lives, we know each other's strengths and weaknesses, but frankly, we can still have doubts about each other's stories. As we should have. These kinds of things aren't provable. We eye the stories in this book as skeptically as we eye each other's stories.

The paradox is this: Sometimes we're all skeptical of another person's story. But we're never skeptical of our own. Mary gave up her reputation for her belief that she heard God. Cecil Murphey was willing to give his life. Joan of Arc did. When we have such a convincing experience, we can move past our own skepticism and begin to believe others' stories.

Hearing God speak is a personal thing. In this book,

we have no plans to convince you that God is speaking to you or even speaking at all. You will be convinced only when you experience it. You may read this book and doubt whether these stories happened as we describe them. We even have some doubts as we write them. But the question isn't whether God speaks to Mark or to Jennifer, to Joan or to Mary, or to any of the other people mentioned in this book. The question is, Does God speak to you?

We believe he does. And as you read this book, we'll be your guides on a listening journey that shows you how he does.

CHANNEL 102.0
CIRCUMSTANTIAL EVIDENCE

"IT'S a SIGN FROM GOD!"

People apply those words to everything from a phone call to a natural disaster. When confronted with a coincidence, do you immediately assume that God's behind it? And if you think he is, do you think he's trying to tell you something?

Is it possible that some things *just happen*?

Or is everything a sign from God?

In August 2007, Deb Serio, a high school teacher from Forest, Virginia, discovered that a slab of concrete in her driveway contained a sealant smudge resembling the face of Jesus.

Was Concrete Jesus some kind of pavement prophet?

Was it a sign from above?

Deb, a churchgoing Lutheran, considers the smudge little more than an odd occurrence—not a sign or miracle. "There are some people who need this kind of thing to sort of start them on their faith journey. I don't," she said. "That's why

I don't mind parting with it." She sold it to a winning eBay bidder for $1,800. After the sale, the slab was removed from Deb's driveway and shipped to the unidentified bidder.[1]

It seems that Deb believes the face of Jesus is a sign only if you need it to be.

• • •

In 2004, a ten-year-old toasted cheese sandwich said to bear the image of the Virgin Mary sold on eBay. The owner grossed $28,000.[2] Is the mother of Jesus in a cheese sandwich also a sign if you need it to be?

Perhaps the winning bidder thought so. The past-its-sell-by-date sandwich was bought by Goldenpalace.com, an online casino. Representatives of the casino considered the decade-old lunch a slice of pop culture. They planned to send their toasted-cheese trophy on a world tour before reselling it and donating the proceeds to charity.[3] (We can only hope they didn't send it coach, where it could easily be confused with airline food.)

• • •

Apparently, Holy Communion during Mass isn't the only time you can eat the body of Christ. While cooking breakfast for his family, Mike Thompson of Beachwood, Ohio, was astounded to see the face of Jesus appear on his pancake. In February 2006, Mike posted the Holy Pancake on eBay with an opening bid of $500. The bidding soon reached $14,999 and was headed higher when eBay pulled the sale, claiming Mike had violated posting rules.[4] Too bad he missed that sign.

Mike, Deb, and the original cheese-sandwich owner all claim their findings were not a sign. We respectfully disagree.

When Deb walked down her driveway and stared at the face of Jesus in the concrete, whether she admits it or not, she saw a sign. When the ten-year-old cheese sandwich went up for auction, it was also a sign. And when Thompson stared down the spatula into the flour-and-water face of Jesus in his pancake, he definitely saw a sign.

Each of these individuals saw a sign,

the same sign—

a dollar sign.

There are countless stories of individuals who have seen dollar signs, but the question is, Are any of these dollar signs also *signs from God*?

Is it possible that seemingly chance events—a haphazard splattering of sealant, the random melting of cheese, or the peculiar patterns of pancake batter—add up to something greater than what they seem?

Is God trying to tell us something through these seeming coincidences?

102.1 IT'S a SIGn?

Rob had wanted to be a state trooper for as long as he could remember. When an opportunity to take the required test came up, Rob "prayed and prayed for the job." He remembers saying to God, "If this is what I am supposed to do, help me get this job."

Rob made it all the way through the application process— tests, physicals, background checks, all the way to the very end—but the offer never came.

He was disappointed. Very disappointed. But with classic

Midwestern stoicism, he tried not to show his hurt pride and the sadness he felt. He didn't understand why God wouldn't allow him to get the job he desired. He figured it was a sign from God that he wasn't supposed to have it, even though he had no idea why.

A few months later, Rob's mother-in-law was diagnosed with cancer, and less than *three weeks* from the date of her diagnosis, she died. During those final weeks, his wife, Deb, attended to her mother's every need. The grandkids made her laugh and brightened her last days. The whole family was able to care for her.

If Rob had gotten the state trooper job, his family would've been living in a different city. Deb would've had long drives back and forth (if she could have gone at all). The kids wouldn't have experienced those last precious days with their grandmother, and it would've been an emotionally chaotic time for the whole family.

Now Rob believes that God used the circumstances of not getting the job as a way of telling him to stay put. Failing to become a state trooper, said Rob, was just God's way of saying, "I know what's best for you, and I love you enough to do what's best. Even when it hurts."

Did God speak to Rob through his circumstances?

. . .

Jennifer could point to conversations, circumstances, and opportunities that all seemed to suggest she should be a writer. But it wasn't what she wanted, so she chose to see the signs as nothing more than coincidences. But after a string of these seemingly fluke occurrences, she wondered if they weren't as random as they initially appeared.

Could they be some kind of sign?

After considering the possibility, she sat down at her desk, and for the first time, humbly prayed for God's will—even if that meant doing what she didn't want to do. Just then, she received an e-mail from an editor with an unexpected writing assignment.

A coincidence?

Or a sign from God?

. . .

Driving to work early one morning, Susan was distracted. She had overslept, the dog took too long to do his business, and now she was late. She felt crabby and self-absorbed. As she entered I-35E toward St. Paul, the radio played, but she wasn't really listening.

A song by artist Mark Schultz came on. Susan remembers bits of the lyrics of "I Am," followed by things like "the bright, morning star" and "breath of all creation."[5] Frankly, in her distracted state, she wasn't paying much attention. But subconsciously, the lyrics began to melt her icy attitude. She began to think that maybe it wasn't all about her. She glanced toward heaven as an acknowledgement of the God who created her. Without warning, a car turned into her lane.

As Susan stepped on the brake, the car slid into place ahead of her. Directly in her line of vision, the license plate said, "I AM."

Susan believes she received a sign, a divine connection from the God of the universe, interrupting her negative thoughts to remind her of what is really important. She saw it as a sign "not of a God who is far off, but of a God who is near." Does God really communicate through license plates?

Rob wasn't praying for an explanation—just a job.

Jennifer was ignoring circumstances.

Susan wasn't asking for a reminder.

Each individual was a little bit lost. They weren't necessarily asking for God to speak.

Yet they saw something divine in their circumstances—they each saw a sign from God.

. . .

In a cynical effort to identify true signs from fake signs, Dean Booth sells a God Detector for $4.95, plus shipping and handling. On his yo-god.com Web site, he makes this pitch:

> How many times have we heard it said, "Oh Lord, give me a sign!" Alas, too often the reply is vague and ambiguous: the phone rings at an opportune time, a feather falls from out of the blue. . . . We all want to know if God exists; maybe He just needs a reliable method to let us know He's here. The "Yo-God" God Detector gives God a way to send a simple, unambiguous message of His presence.

Instructions for using the detector include

> purchase and register a Yo-God God Detector;
> set out your God Detector anywhere in your home, church, or office;

offer a simple request or prayer that God reveal
    Himself through the detector;

check your God Detector daily or weekly for any
    indication of movement; and

report any movement of the detector at this
    Web site.

To date, more than 3,500 people have purchased and registered God Detectors. As of November 2008, no one had
reported a verified God signal using the detector.

Proving . . .

nothing.

Or perhaps proving that Booth has detected a way to
separate suckers from their $4.95.

Booth implies that God's refusal to verify himself
through the Yo-God Detector is a sign that he is either
indifferent, impotent, or nonexistent. But other explanations exist. Maybe the cardboard sign with a spinnable
arrow isn't sensitive enough to detect God's presence.
In the same way that licking your finger and sticking it
in the air can't precisely determine wind speed, could it
be that detecting God isn't as simple as a negative or an
affirmative?

Is your sign a sign from God?

Yes!

No?

Maybe there's another option?

102.2 THE MIRACULOUS E-MAIL
The following "miraculous" story began circulating on the
Internet in July 2001:

On a Saturday night several weeks ago, this pastor was working late and decided to call his wife before he left for home. It was about 10:00 p.m., but his wife didn't answer the phone.

The pastor let the phone ring. He thought it was odd that she didn't answer, but decided to wrap up a few things and try again later. When he tried again, she answered right away. He asked why she hadn't answered before, and she said that it hadn't rung at their house. They brushed it off as a fluke and went on their merry ways.

On Monday, the pastor received a call at the church office, which was the same phone that he'd used that Saturday night. The man he spoke with wanted to know why he had called on Saturday night.

The pastor couldn't figure out what the man was talking about. Then the man said, "It rang and rang, but I didn't answer." The pastor remembered the mishap and apologized for disturbing him, explaining that he'd intended to call his wife. The man said, "That's okay. Let me tell you my story.

"You see, I was planning to commit suicide on Saturday night, but before I did, I prayed, 'God if you're there, and you don't want me to do this, give me a sign now.'

"At that point my phone started to ring. I looked at the caller ID, and it said, 'Almighty God.' I was afraid to answer!"

The reason why "Almighty God" showed on the man's caller ID is because that church's name is Almighty God Tabernacle!

Five years later, a copy of this same e-mail was forwarded to Jennifer's eleven-year-old son's brand-new e-mail address.

"Mom! You gotta hear this. You're not going to believe it," Jordan said, reading the contents aloud. "I'm gonna send this to all of my friends!" (For those who wonder how spam e-mails stay alive year after year, you only need to watch the habits of tweens with new e-mail accounts.)

"Yeah, it's cool," said Jennifer, "but do you believe it really happened?"

"Probably not."

Seeing a teaching opportunity, Jennifer slid into the chair next to Jordan at the keyboard. "When you get something like this that seems too good to be true, you should verify it before you send it out." She pulled up Snopes.com, a Web site that verifies the content of urban legends.

She found what she was looking for. The *miraculous* e-mail was listed on the site, and a researcher had concluded it was false. Jennifer pointed to the screen, "See, it didn't really happen."

"That's okay," said Jordan as he regained control of the keyboard.

In disbelief, Jennifer watched as he forwarded the e-mail to all his friends.

Most of us would agree the details of the e-mail aren't believable. Yet even posting a thorough investigation of the fake e-mail lacked the proof some believers needed. Alongside the results of the investigator's findings, one inspirational Web site posted a series of questions challenging the veracity of the research. Those who commented defended the story as true—though they didn't have proof the church existed.

Regardless of the evidence (or lack thereof), some people were desperate to believe the incident happened exactly as described in the e-mail. To them, proving the truth of the e-mail was more than a confirmation of an unlikely set of events set in motion by divine powers; it was an affirmation that God was involved in the here and now. If they could prove God cared about the suicidal man, it would be a sign that God also cared for them.

Those were desperate people clinging to a seemingly absurd sign.

Jennifer didn't want that for Jordan. She called him back into the room and pulled up the new Web sites she had discovered that pointed to the truth: this e-mail was a fake.

"Yeah, I thought so," Jordan said as he picked up a book and headed out of the room.

"But if you don't believe it, why did you send it to all of your friends?"

He stopped in the doorway, turned, and smiled. "Because it's a cool story, Mom. Even though I know it's not true, it seems like the kind of thing God *would* do."

Jordan saw it as a sign.

Not *from* God, but *of* God.

Not a yes or no on a God detector, but as a third option—a reminder that God works in mysterious ways, even if he wasn't responsible for this specific way. To Jordan, it was a sign that God *has* in the past, and *can* in the future, use ridiculously absurd circumstances to send a message of his love to all who will listen, *whether or not God was responsible for this one.*

Jordan chose to believe in something bigger than the

e-mail. He chose to believe that God wants to, and does, communicate with us no matter what it takes.

And that is Jordan's choice.

What would you have chosen?

102.3 ROAD SIGNS

Jesse was a drug addict who had given up on himself. He paid for his habit the only way he knew how: by becoming a drug dealer in his home state of Minnesota.

Jesse's mother prayed for her son every day and called him almost as often. "Jesse, God has a plan for you," she told him. "He wants to tell you about your destiny. He's never given up on you, and neither have I."

Sitting in the passenger seat on the road to yet another drug deal, Jesse glanced at a passing billboard. It said, "Jesse, we need to talk."

Jesse strained to get another look as they drove past the sign. "Did you see that?" he asked the driver.

"What?"

"That sign. Turn around. Go back!"

"It's just a stupid cell phone ad or something," said his partner in crime. He kept driving.

But Jesse wouldn't let up.

After a few more blocks of nagging, the driver relented. He made a U-turn and drove back. There was no mistaking it. The sign clearly said, "Jesse, we need to talk."

The once skeptical driver was spooked. "Wild, man," he said.

"It's God," Jesse said. "My mom's been praying that God gets at me. That's him. He's after me. And he wants to talk."

Was seeing the billboard just a set of coincidental circum-stances? Or was it a sign from God?

Anyone who lived in Minnesota during that time would have immediately identified the billboard as an attempt to get another Jesse's attention. At the time, ex-wrestler and B-film star Jesse Ventura was the governor. A lot of people wanted to talk with him.

But none of that mattered to Jesse.

In his mind, the billboard was meant to get *his* attention. Today he tells anyone who will listen, "Hey, God wants to talk to you. And he won't give up until you listen."

Jesse had been hearing the same message from his mom for years, but when he saw it in a different context—tow-ering twenty-five feet above the ground—it had personal relevance.

No wonder Jesse interpreted that coincidence as an intentional gesture—a sign—from God.

A coincidence?

Possibly.

But it became a sign from God when it got Jesse's attention.

· · ·

M. Night Shyamalan's film *Signs* tells a haunting story of the power of faith and our ability, and sometimes inability, to interpret the signals God sends us. In the film, Graham Hess is a former Episcopal priest who loses his faith after his wife, Colleen, is killed in a horrific traffic accident. Hess now lives on a family farm with his children, Bo and Morgan, and his brother, Merrill.

One day mysterious crop circles appear in Hess's cornfield. In time, the same patterns begin to appear all over the world. There are signs of an impending alien invasion, and it becomes clear that Hess's farm is under surveillance. Hess sees alien creatures lurking about his property.

When an alien attacks the family and releases a poisonous gas against them, Hess suddenly recalls his wife's dying words: "see" and "swing away." In a moment of revelation, Graham realizes a redemptive purpose behind his wife's tragedy. She had given him a code of action. Hess tells Merrill to swing away. Merrill grabs a baseball bat and attacks the alien. Noticing several glasses of water left about the room by his niece, Merrill swings and shatters them, showering the alien with water and glass. The water burns the creature's body and kills him.

Meanwhile, the poisonous gas appears to have killed Morgan, who is not breathing. But Graham realizes his child is suffering an asthma attack. The attack closed his lungs, preventing him from inhaling the poisonous gas. Moments later Morgan's lungs expand, and he gasps for breath.

The final scene shows Graham preparing a Mass. In the horrid events he endured, he has found signs that God has not left him alone. His faith is restored.

The signs had been there the whole time. But like Jesse's billboard revelation, only when the crisis arrived did these same signs have context and meaning for Graham.

What if signs from God are always there?

What if they are waiting for us to recognize them and to give them context and meaning?

If so, is it possible that *everything* is a sign?

102.4 DO NOT EXIT

In December of 2001, Chris and Sherry, along with their two children, were driving back home after spending Christmas holidays with family. The couple was talking when Chris nonchalantly mentioned that he had applied for positions in the film departments at various universities. In the conversation, one of the schools he mentioned was Baylor University in Waco, Texas. Sherry was surprised but didn't comment. After all, she knew Chris had applied elsewhere, and so far, nothing had come of it.

But the thought haunted Sherry. Days later, she found herself in a Ruby Tuesday restaurant sharing the news with her best friend, Andi. "I distinctly remember telling her, 'I am *not* moving to Waco, Texas.'" Though Sherry hadn't wanted to move to Virginia almost a decade earlier, this was different. The family now called Virginia home, and as she told Andi, she had no plans to move.

Weeks later, Sherry and Andi were scrapbooking at Sherry's when the phone rang. It was a professor from Baylor calling to officially offer Chris an interview. "I felt something well up in me physically and emotionally, an excitement about this possibility," recalls Sherry, who had no intention of being excited about the idea of moving to Waco. "God spoke to me in this situation by completely changing my heart and mind about this job. I had been adamant about not moving from Chesapeake and adamant about not moving to Waco."

Seeking more information, Chris posted a message to his online screenwriters' group. Brian, a fellow member, replied. Not only did Brian work for Baylor, but he taught in the same department for which Chris was interviewing. If Chris got the job, it was possible that he would be given some of Brian's classes, yet his new online friend remained warm and welcoming. Brian happily shared information about the position. Sherry recalls, "I took his kind reception of Chris as a sign that this was where Chris was to go." With her approval, Chris flew to Waco and interviewed for the job.

As if to confirm her change of heart, Sherry began noticing things. "I started seeing signs everywhere—a street that I'd passed a hundred times before but never noticed was called Baylor Drive; a construction company had their name, Waco Construction, listed on the side of the truck. And even though we lived in Virginia, every license plate from the state of Texas somehow crossed my path."

Chris toured the Baylor campus, where he remembers taking special notice of Scripture engraved on the side of the seminary building. After he got home, the pastor of Chris and Sherry's church discussed the same Scripture in a Bible study meeting. Chris and Sherry report that this was the first time their pastor had ever attended that particular Bible study, which gave his choice of Scripture even greater significance to them.

Four weeks later, Chris heard from Baylor. If you guessed that he was offered the job, you guessed wrong. Chris wasn't offered the job.

"We were devastated," said Sherry. "Not because of the loss of the job, but because we were certain that we'd heard from God." Sherry remembers the confusion and frustration that followed. "We accepted the news, but I couldn't shake the feeling that we were supposed to go to Baylor."

Chris said, "For a long time, I couldn't understand why I didn't get that job. We were so sure, and then . . . nothing.

It was strange and disheartening. I am not sure, in fact, that I didn't lose faith at that point. But Sherry and I decided that even though *we* were sure about Baylor, we had to let it go in order to move on. So we did."

. Chris and Sherry resigned themselves to the idea that they had not missed what God was saying, but rather that he was preparing them for something down the road. Sherry remembers telling Chris, "We might be forty or fifty or sixty, but at some point we are going to Baylor."

The Hansens believed they had received a sign from God. In fact, they believed they had many signs from God.

But in retrospect, did they?

Or was this a case of paying attention to every green Camry on the road as soon as you drive your new one off the dealer's lot?

If God uses circumstances as some sort of divine sign, when is a sign a *sign*? And when is it not?

102.5 SIGN HERE?

We ask for signs. Believers, nonbelievers, skeptics, suicidal men, and preachers ask for them:

> Should I ask this girl out?
> Should I take this job?
> Should we make this move?
> Should I sign up?
> Should I quit?

These questions and others like it are all followed by, "God, just give me a sign!"

At times, we've *all* asked for signs.

Thousands of years ago, it was no different.

Once again, Israel was under attack. This time it was from Midianite raiders who lived east of Israel in the desert north of the peninsula of Arabia. The Midianites were an Arabian tribe, and the secret of their military success was new technology—domesticated camels. Camel riding enabled the Midianites to raid Israelite border towns and then escape across the wilderness. As their booty increased, so did their boldness. The Midianites eventually conquered and occupied Israelite cities and began spreading their reign of terror deep into the heart of Israel.

By chapter six of Judges, the crisis had become unbearable. Israel began pleading with God for rescue. They publicly repented of their waywardness and asked God to send someone to rescue them.

The Bible is filled with examples of God choosing the "wrong" man and sending him out with a "bad" plan, and the choice of Gideon to go up against the Midianites was no exception.

When the messenger of God finds Gideon, he's in a large hole in the ground attempting to thresh wheat. Threshing wheat is usually done on a hilltop where the winds can help separate the kernels from the chaff. But Gideon is so afraid of the enemy stealing his crops that he's hiding.

The angel of God greets the lad with, "Mighty hero, the LORD is with you!" Gideon isn't sure he can trust this divine messenger and asks if the Lord is with him, why do the Midianite marauders keep stealing from them?

That's when he's told that *he* is the answer.

Gideon himself is to fight off the Midianites.

But Gideon objects. "I'm no superhero," he argues. "I'm

the youngest in my family, and my clan is the least in our tribe."

He was right, of course. He wasn't qualified. Gideon was a timid, inexperienced, unskilled youth with little influence and not much prospect for success. Just the sort of leader God commissions for his toughest cases. Before Gideon can say more, the angel promises God will be with him.

But Gideon is unsure and asks for a sign. If the Lord will really be with him, could this angel please hang out under the tree while Gideon goes and prepares an offering? The angel agrees, and Gideon prepares and returns with the food. In a great display that included Gideon setting out the food, pouring broth on top of it, and the angel consuming it in a fireball, Gideon becomes convinced that God is with him.

Sign one? Check.

Gideon takes a few tentative steps of faith. He sets his own house in order. Then he begins to muster an army and prepare battle plans. But once again, he grows nervous. *Was that really God?* How could he be sure?

"God, I need something visible." Again Gideon asks, "I need proof that the voices in my head are really from you, not the lamb-and-lentil soup I had last night for supper. I need a sign." Gideon proposes a rather bizarre test of circumstances, something that seems to rule out all possibility of chance.

Literally, he cuts a deal. He lays out a sheepskin on the ground of his threshing floor and plans to leave it there overnight. Gideon tells God that if the fleece has dew on it but the ground is dry, he will interpret that as a sign from God.

The next morning, the ground is dry, but the wool has absorbed a bowlful of water.

Sign two? Check.

"God, don't be angry with me, but I need to be sure," Gideon bargains. "Can we do this again? I mean, someone could have spilled a Coke on the wool or something. I need to be sure. Can you do another sign, and this time make sure the wool is dry and the ground is wet with dew?"

Once again, the wool and ground were exactly as he specified.

Sign three? Check.

"Okay," says Gideon. "You win."

After "fleecing" God, the reluctant warrior proved himself by obeying God. Gideon assembled an army of thirty-two thousand men. God asked him to reduce the army to ten thousand.

Gideon sent twenty-two thousand home.

Then God asked him to reduce the numbers further, leaving Gideon with a mere three hundred soldiers in his army. Miraculously, with only three hundred exhausted men, Gideon rescued Israel from the Midianites.

We hear the story of Gideon, and it seems to have multiple meanings. Depending on the biases of the preacher teaching this mystifying story, the moral ranges from "ask God for a sign" to "believe God without asking for a sign."

Here's another possibility: what if the story *is the sign*?

Signs by nature are an inexact language, sometimes subject to interpretation and always open to controversy. For centuries that is what believers have done; they've seen their own convictions mirrored in God's response to Gideon. We read our own circumstances like tea leaves—we see what we want to see—and conclude that God was involved (or not).

Perhaps the story of Gideon is more than a story of signs. Perhaps Gideon's story *is the sign*—a sort of biblical Rorschach test.

. . .

In 1921, Hermann Rorschach began using a series of ink smears on paper as a tool for psychoanalysis. He showed the papers to patients and asked them to talk about what they saw. Over the years, his method has been refined. There are now ten official Rorschach ink blots. Five are black ink on white paper, two are black and red ink on white paper, and three are multicolored. The patient is given a chance to examine each paper and to explain what they see while the test administrator notes everything the patient says or does.

To some, a blot may be a double ice-cream cone. To another, it may be a bloody knife. The counselor then draws conclusions regarding the patient's mental state, based on their stories.

Do signs like those in the story of Gideon serve as some sort of spiritual inkblot test?

Is it only a sign to those who believe it is a sign?

Possibly.

Maybe that's why Jesus was reluctant to perform signs on demand. He knew signs wouldn't change anyone's thinking. In the Gospels, when Jesus is asked to deliver a sign, he refuses[6] and even goes so far as to question those who needed a sign to believe in him.[7]

In the Gospel of John, the writer attributes a miracle as a divine sign intended to get people to believe.[8] But both John and Jesus seem to know that a divine sign is little more than an attention-getter, a party trick for the faithful. Those who already believe become adamant in their belief. Those who didn't believe before rarely believe for long once the signs are gone.

Yet there are other times when Jesus willingly obliges a man who needs a sign. Thomas, the doubting apostle, needed a handout to help his faith. After his resurrection, Jesus appeared to the others, but Thomas wasn't there. Thomas *heard* the details of the blessed appearance, but he wanted proof. He wouldn't believe Jesus had risen from the dead until he not only *saw* Jesus' nail-scarred hands but could *touch* those hands himself. Jesus obliged. Doubting Thomas needed a sign, and the risen Jesus gave it to him.

Why is God so willing to wet sheepskins for Gideon, and why is Jesus so willing to hold out his hand to Thomas?

What's the difference between those who are privileged to see signs and those who aren't?

. . .

When was the last time you got excited about a piece of aluminum with directional arrows that pointed one way for Interstate North and another direction for Interstate South? Have you ever gotten excited about a green and white reflective traffic sign? Maybe when you were lost, and the sign pointed which direction to go; but beyond the sign's content, you probably didn't notice it much.

Perhaps signs are just that.

Signs.

Directional indicators that point to a destination.

When you put a street sign on the floor of a warehouse, instead of near a road, it is meaningless, useless to anyone who looks at it.

Maybe that's why, when we hear someone else talk of their "sign from God," it sounds kind of goofy to us. Like maybe they didn't really get a sign; they're just reading too much into the circumstances.

Yet when you ask people about the signs they've received from God, they have one of two reactions: either they say God never gives them signs or they say something like, "I know this sounds weird, but . . ." Then they tell you an unbelievable story they are absolutely convinced was a sign from God.

What if in all the time we spend asking for, interpreting, and studying signs, we're missing the point?

What if signs weren't meant to be analyzed?

What if they're just meant to give directions?

That makes sense when we think of what signs do. They point us to where we want to go. When we're on the right road, we don't stop to think about directional signs. The memory of them quickly fades as we near our destination.

But when we're lost, we remember with great urgency and conviction the last sign we saw. That last marker takes on greater significance than any other because it was the last thing to point us toward our goal. We return to that same sign as a way of making sure we're on the right road.

We *look* for signs when we're lost and we need direction.

We *see* signs of God when we go *looking* for signs.

Jesse's billboard was along that stretch of road long before he drove by there, but even before his car trip—in fact even before the sign was erected—Jesse's mom had been pointing out the way to God, and Jesse didn't see it.

Does God send signs to all who ask?

Does he send signs to those who are lost?

Could it be that the signs are already there; we just don't notice them until we're lost or asking for directions?

102.6 EXIT AHEAD

Sherry and Chris were confused and frustrated. Despite Sherry's initial unwillingness to consider a move to Baylor, Sherry had experienced what she thought were clear signs from God telling her to move to Waco. But Chris wasn't offered the job.

Months passed, and nothing changed. Later that fall, four-year-old Emma told her mother that she had prayed "that those people in Texas will let my daddy teach at their school." Once again, Sherry interpreted the circumstances as a sign from God. "We hadn't mentioned Baylor or Texas in months, and I wondered if God was speaking through Emma, using her to prepare us, but the academic year started, and there was no call."

Another sign?

Another dead end.

Sherry and Chris had another baby. Their third child, Olivia, was born with health problems. She was so sick that they didn't know whether she'd survive. Having lived in Virginia for so long, they had a close group of friends and church members who were able to pray with them, take care of the kids, and assist in every way possible.

By May 2004, more than two years after the initial Baylor signs, Olivia made it through her health crisis. Chris and Sherry, recovering from the upheaval in their lives, were hoping for normalcy—when the phone rang.

It was Baylor wondering if Chris would consider coming back for another interview.

"I called my mom, who is as close to God as anyone I know," said Sherry, "and I said to her, 'You won't believe who called us today.' She replied, 'Someone from Texas?'"

There were so many other people her mother could have guessed—doctors calling about Olivia or long-lost friends—but Texas? How did she know? It had been more than two years since that first interview.

Three weeks later, Chris went for an interview.

"All our friends sadly commented, 'Y'all are moving this time,' but I couldn't let myself get my hopes up," recalls Sherry.

Ten days later, the phone rang again. Chris was offered the job.

Yet, like Gideon, Sherry began to doubt. "As much as I knew we were supposed to go before, doubt crept in, and I actually wondered what we were supposed to do. I know all of my friends were thinking, *How many signs do you need?*"

The next day Sherry found herself in the car, listening to a song from the Sandi Patty's CD *Artist of My Soul*. Sherry remembers a particular line from the song that caught her attention, "Silence my fears so that I may hear from you."

"Every time I heard that line I wept. When I got home that evening, Chris said, 'So, what are you thinking?'" Through her tears, Sherry said, "We're moving to Texas."

"God spoke to me," said Sherry later. "He spoke through

that song and told me that my problem was fear—fear of the unknown, fear of things changing. God had spoken so clearly, again. I knew what we were supposed to do. Fear was the only thing standing between me and Texas."

Later that night, Sherry picked up her copy of *The Power of a Positive Mom*. "I hadn't read it for weeks, since the night before Chris flew to Texas for the interview. I opened up the book and started reading, and much to my surprise, I read this line: 'Perhaps you remember the "running craze" of the 1980s. I was a student at BAYLOR UNIVERSITY at the time.' Okay, it wasn't in all caps, but it didn't need to be. I started laughing out loud. It was like God was saying, 'Have I made myself clear?'"

Like Gideon, God had given Sherry and Chris signs along each step of their journey. "I could go on and on about how we found a house the first day we looked, or how the principal of Emma's school lived across the street from us and was the first person we met, but suffice it to say, God continued to show us that we were right where he wanted us."

When signs seem to point to a dead end, people get hung up. They question whether they saw the sign, whether the sign was intended for them, or whether it was a sign from God at all.

God's signs gave Chris and Sherry direction, but it was their faith that kept them on the road to their destination.

102.7 SIGNS OF FAITH

It's true that we're more likely to see signs when we're looking for them. But that's not really the question, is it?

The real question is this: Does God use random

occurrences as signs, or are the signs we see just a human explanation for coincidental circumstances?

Maybe signs are helpful only if you already know where you're going.

Remember the e-mail about the suicidal man getting a phone call from the Almighty? Was that a sign from God?

According to Jordan, it didn't matter. Whether the story was true, his belief wasn't found in the proof of the event but in the faith that God could: believing God *can* use caller ID seemed as good as God actually *using* caller ID. To Jordan, the sign wasn't pointing to a set of circumstances that never took place; it was pointing to a God who will do anything—send an e-mail, make a chance phone call, or send his Son to die—to save us.

Jordan's destination wasn't the veracity of the e-mail; it was the truth of God.

Perhaps he was pointed in the right direction.

You should know that Jordan sent that e-mail to his friends almost two years ago as we write this. The timing is important because of what happened next.

As we were finishing this chapter, we received an e-mail from Karen Danz. Karen is sixtyish with large, laughing eyes. She's one of the funniest people you're likely to ever meet. She's a cutup, but she's no nutcase. A secretary at Mark's office, she juggles incoming calls for a seven-thousand-member church on two campuses. She never misses a call, and she never loses her sense of humor.

Karen is famous for e-mails like this:

> It is that time of the month when, once again,
> I threaten and beg, and my face turns red, and the

veins in my neck start to stand out. You got it! I need interoffice envelopes, and I need them now. Whoever is sitting on them, please put them in the mail room, or I will have to come after you, and it won't be pretty.

But that wasn't the e-mail we received. Karen heard we were writing a book about the ways God speaks to us, and she sent us this e-mail:

> I am not sure if you are aware of the fact that I have a criminal history (white-collar crime—governmental agency). From the time I was formally charged until I was finally sent to Shakopee, my depression hit an all-time low—as you can imagine. Every time I had a court date, I sank deeper and felt I had been totally abandoned.
>
> My relationship with God had been on a hit-and-miss basis. I was raised in a Christian home but was taught to believe God was to be feared—not loved like the best friend a person could ever have or as someone who was there for you 24/7. I was scheduled to go to court three times. Each time before I was to go, I contemplated suicide.

Karen planned to overdose on prescription medications. She didn't want to leave a mess for her husband Bob and the boys to clean up. She wanted something quick and clean, so all she had to do was go to sleep.

> The first time, I stood at my kitchen sink with pills in my hand. Bob was working. As I raised my glass of

water to my mouth, the telephone rang. Startled and distracted, I went to answer the phone. No one was on the other line. We didn't have caller ID in those days—sure wish I would have. I would have loved to have seen the phone number. Anyway, I put the pills back and proceeded to do something else.

The second time, once again the day before I was to appear in court, I stood by the sink again, pills in hand, running the water. The doorbell rang. Of course, not wanting to disappoint someone who felt a need to talk, I put the glass down, still hung onto the pills, but answered the door. You guessed it—no one was there. I looked around outside because no one could have left that fast.

The third time, I was going for sentencing, and I was at an all-time low but trying to act as if everything would be all right for the sake of Bob and my boys. Bob had run to the store to get something. I put the pills in my mouth and raised the glass to drink, and a voice—this thunderous voice—seemed to come from nowhere and called, "KAREN!" I tried to ignore it, but it was booming in my kitchen and was so loud I was sure my neighbors could hear it. I put my glass down and looked around in disbelief. There was no one in the house besides me. The voice in a loving, scolding way said, "Don't do it. Trust in me. It's a permanent solution to a temporary problem!"

I spit out the pills, rinsed my mouth, and ran around the house to see who would be playing such a mean joke on me. No one was there. But somehow I knew—there was something or someone who loved me so much that they were not going to let me go through with my plan. I had a sense that he, she, or it had other plans for me.

I truly believe the voice was God's. He wanted me to know I was not alone. No matter what had happened or was about to happen, I would not go the distance alone, and I have never thought about committing suicide since. Things don't always go my way—but I know they are going God's way, or he would let me know. I have never heard a voice like that before and probably won't again until it is my time to be with him forever. I don't fear the unknown like I used to, and when I look back on the whole experience, I have to say there were far more blessings than disappointments.

We [Bob and Karen] both see God at work every day in our lives. We might not be rich, but we have been richly blessed.

Karen M. Danz
Thursday and Friday receptionist
North Heights Lutheran Church

Is *believing* God can use caller ID as a sign the same as God actually *doing* it?

Perhaps it depends on where you're going.

Where are you going?

Are signs of God pointing the way?

We started by asking, Are coincidental signs and circumstances one of the channels that God uses to communicate with us?

We had already written 70 percent of this chapter,

including the story about the God Almighty e-mail, and we were trying to decide how to wrap it all up. We wanted to leave the reader with the same sense of wonder that we feel when circumstantial events, improbable coincidences, or random signs line up in such a way to convince us that God has his fingerprints on them, and that he is confirming our way.

The e-mail from Karen arrived when we were trying to decide how to end this chapter.

We took it as a sign.

CHANNEL 103.0
PROPHET SHARING

IT WAS CAROL'S THIRD TIME to the prison, and she feared it would be her last.

The prison chaplain and two female Sunday school teachers from her church had been involved in prison ministry for years. Although Carol was new, it didn't take long for her to get the drill. As they neared the secured hallway, they entered one at a time. They each exited through the secured doorway at the other end. The chaplain went first, followed by the other women. Finally, it was Carol's turn. When the door buzzed, she entered the monitored hallway. Like the previous three, she walked to the end, where she waited for the second door to open. But the buzzer didn't sound. Carol tried the knob. The door remained locked. She turned to the guards behind the glass partition.

A prison guard pointed at her.

"You," the female guard mouthed.

Carol was surprised. *What could she want?* The guard should have recognized the chaplain, known who they were and why they were there.

"Me?" asked Carol.

"You. You wait there," the prison guard mouthed, waving the other three off. Carol stared through the glass while her two friends and the chaplain kept walking. Finally the guard opened the door to the office and said, "Sit down. I want to talk to you."

Carol sat. She watched as the guard continued her business, buzzing other people through the hall, making notes on her clipboard, and monitoring the visitors that passed. Confused, Carol wondered what she could have done. They had taken everything from her when she passed through the initial security stop. She had turned over her purse, jewelry, belt, and cell phone. Carol realized she didn't even have her driver's license. She couldn't possibly be less of a threat.

Finally, the petite guard looked Carol in the eye and said, "You're a Christian, aren't you?"

Later recalling the question, Carol said, "I didn't know if I was being held because of this or not, so I went all Judas on my friends and said, 'Well, so are they!'"

"I know that," said the guard, "but are you?"

"It was one of those moments I could have totally blown," said Carol. "I panicked. What I wanted to say was, 'What do you want to hear? What will get me out of here?' But what I said was, 'Yeah, why?'"

"Because I have a question for you," said the guard. Carol braced herself, not knowing what was coming next. "How do you know when God is talking to you?" the guard asked.

Carol froze. "I'm thinking, *Boy, did you choose the wrong person. You just let a chaplain and two Sunday school teachers go through the door and you stopped me? You've got to be kidding. I've been a Christian for less than three years. I know nothing. I don't have the degrees they have, the experience teaching Sunday school, or the knowledge of the Bible. Of all the people you could have asked, you stopped me?*"

Carol turned it back on the guard: "Can I ask you a question? Why did you stop *me*? You know Chaplain Baird, and you know these other two women; they've been coming here for years."

"Yeah."

"So why didn't you ask them?"

"I don't know. Something told me you'd be the easiest to talk to."

Carol blurted out the first thing that came to mind, "That's how you know God's talking to you." She went on, "Clearly, there were *other* people you could have asked but you asked *me*."

They spoke for a few minutes, and Carol promised to bring the guard a book the next time she came. Carol didn't ask why the guard wanted to know, and the guard didn't offer anything else.

Released from the room, Carol went to find her friends. By the time she found them, she began to have doubts about her conversation with the guard. "I'm not sure I did the right thing," she said.

One of the Sunday school teachers spoke up. "It was God's plan that you were the one to answer her question. If I had answered it, I would have given her a long theological discourse involving Bible references and quotes from C. S. Lewis. You were the person God intended."

Carol's friend was right. God couldn't care less about qualifications—theological or otherwise—when he wants someone to speak for him. Before Jesus, no one spoke for God with greater authority than Moses. And he had a speech impediment.

God stutters?

Seems so—when Moses was speaking for him.

When God speaks to us, or perhaps through us, it is often in surprising and unexpected ways. Carol surprised herself by being in a place where God could use her words. Then God used her friend's words to speak to Carol.

103.1 PLAYING HOLY SPIRIT

Many people believe God speaks by sending some nosy, judgmental church lady to fix them without knowing who they are or caring about their problems.

Is that what you believe?

If hearing God speak through other people brings to mind your spouse's nagging, your father's disappointment, or your preacher's list of dos and don'ts, you aren't thinking of God-speak; you're thinking of manspeak.

But how do you know the difference?

"Playing Holy Spirit" is a phrase used to describe the action of one Christian giving unwanted advice to another and salting it with divine authority.

> "I don't mean to play Holy Spirit, but I think you
> should find a new job."

"I don't mean to play Holy Spirit, but do you really
think you should keep smoking?"

Let's just say up-front that when God speaks through
other people, it's seldom in this way. Jesus didn't scatter
advice like birdseed. He didn't give Matthew specific directions to quit his job, even though his sin as a tax collector
was so bad that, according to some translations, it had a
separate category of sinfulness.

It seems Jesus wasn't interested in bossing people around.
Instead of exact instructions, he gave general principles that
were left completely up to the listener to implement.

"Follow me."
"Go and sin no more."
"The last shall be first."
"Blessed are the children."

His advice was so vague at times that people often didn't
know what he meant by it. Sometimes they even had to get
up and do something to figure out what it was he was trying
to say.

They had to follow him to figure out what it meant to be
his follower.

They had to act to figure it out.

Personally, Mark and Jennifer believe that God speaks
through people. In fact, we've each heard God speak that
way. But we also acknowledge that sometimes it's hard
to know when it's God and when it's someone with well-
meaning advice or wise-sounding words.

So how can we be sure it's God?

103.2 OUT OF THE MOUTHS

God's messages can sneak up on us. As Jesus warned, sometimes God hides things from the wise and learned and reveals them to—and through—children.

On more than one occasion, he pulled a child up on his lap and said that they, not the religiously educated, would be first in the door of the Kingdom of God.[1] But children don't always understand or comprehend the things they repeat. Is it possible to speak for God, not knowing you're being used and not understanding what you're saying—or why?

We've all heard stories of kids who said one thing but meant another. Are we like children when we speak for God?

If you knew Curtis, you might think he had always been the perfect father. He loves his wife, is active in church, and is always involved in his children's activities. Though he is a busy attorney, he finds time to volunteer at his kids' school. But it wasn't always that way.

It was a Friday afternoon, and I was returning from the airport. I'd been on the road, busy with cases and lawsuits around the country. I was making a big splash and making good money. My trips took me away for days at a time. On that occasion, I had been out all week.

As I pulled into the driveway and got out of the car, I could hear my two-year-old daughter, Lily, playing on the swing set in the backyard. I walked around to say hi, and she smiled and asked me to push her higher. After a few minutes, we heard a jet flying overhead. She jumped off her swing and pointed up at the jet, turning her head toward me and saying, "There's Daddy."

Of course, my heart was broken. But it affirmed what I had been struggling with. What were my priorities?

Lily was communicating a message from God to her father, though she didn't understand what she was doing or the message she was communicating.

"People don't announce that they have a message from God and blurt it out," said Curtis, who has never heard God speak audibly, but only through circumstances or through other people. Having that conversation with Lily, reading a couple of books suggested by his wife, and experiencing a few circumstances that were a little too coincidental slowly made him realize that God was trying to tell him something:

> It all led to a series of decisions to change the way I lived. I sold my practice in Indiana. My family moved to Georgia to help start a ministry to high school kids. A few years later, I restarted my law practice, working with local churches and individuals in all aspects of their lives.
>
> I don't travel on cases any more. I'm engaged in my children's lives, and I have a deeply intimate bond with my wife. I heard from God, and through these inspired life changes, I have been blessed.

Like Lily babbling, how often do we speak and not realize that God is speaking through us?

. . .

Cynthia's church needed a new teacher for the ladies' Sunday school class. As a homeschooling mom, Cynthia knew she couldn't handle the responsibility of teaching every week by herself. She agreed to do it only if she could find a co-teacher.

"I asked a friend if she would teach with me," said Cynthia. "She told me to think about which book of the Bible I wanted to start with and asked me to call her later."

A few days later, Cynthia called her friend. Not wasting time with small talk, the friend immediately asked, "What do you want to teach?"

"I intended to say 'Ephesians or Philippians,'" said Cynthia, "but I stumbled over my words and couldn't talk for a second. Finally, I said, 'Philippians.' Well, that is exactly what my friend needed to hear. She had prayed that if God wanted her to teach with me, I would say 'Philippians.' I couldn't say the words I intended to say. Instead, I said the word she needed to hear."

Cynthia didn't know why she choked on her words or even the meaning of leaving out the book of Ephesians, yet God used it for his purposes.

. . .

Art Within is a Christian theater company in Atlanta that presents plays with Christian themes but few, if any, direct references to the Bible. After viewing a play about three men trapped in an apartment in which some unexpected things happen, a patron asked the director for further explanation.

"I understood the Resurrection scene," she said, "but I didn't quite catch the meaning of the Garden of Gethsemane scene. Can you explain it to me?"

The director wracked his brain. He knew the woman personally and knew she was not a believer. Yet he also knew there had been no allusion to either the Resurrection or the Garden of Gethsemane.

"I think you'll get more out of it if you discover it for yourself," he told her, knowing that whatever she'd seen wasn't the scene he'd put there.

Something takes place in the space between the speaker's mouth and the listener's ears. And that is the space where God works.

Mark often sees this when preaching. After church, an emotional congregant will tell Mark how personally inspiring the sermon was, often quoting things back to Mark that were never said.

Apparently, God can speak through others—like Cynthia's tripping over her words, Lily's confused declaration of her dad's location, or the actors of Art Within—even though they don't realize what is happening or understand what *he* is saying. Often, the speakers may not even know that they are communicating divine messages.

But occasionally . . .

they do.

103.3 SPEAK UP

Mark rose early on Saturday morning and realized there was no milk in the house. With company that would soon wake and want breakfast, Mark knew a trip to the store was in order. He threw on sweats, a shirt, and a baseball cap and headed out.

The aisles were sparse, and the workers were few as the night crew was finishing their shift before the day crew arrived. Mark grabbed a gallon of milk and a package of blueberry muffins. As he walked to the front of the store, he looked for open checkout lanes. There was only one. He got in line behind a man with a cart filled with boxes of donuts. The man noticed Mark's glance. "Garage sale," the man said, pointing to his load.

Mark looked up, and his gaze landed on the check-out lady. Clearly, she had worked all night. Exhaustion and boredom draped over her like a heavy blanket. She appeared to be in her mid-fifties. Life had been difficult, that much was certain. Mark glanced at her name tag. "Macy," it read.

He shifted on his feet, thinking of nothing in particular. Then from somewhere deep inside, a voice interrupted his indifference. "Tell Macy that I think she is beautiful."

Mark coughed out loud.

"Not a chance," he argued to the inner voice. "I'd get slapped. Or worse, I'd get slapped with a sexual harassment lawsuit! I'm not telling a fifty-year-old grocery clerk she's beautiful."

Garage Sale Guy packed his donuts into the cart and headed toward the door. Mark set his breakfast items on the conveyor belt. Macy avoided his eyes and maneuvered the milk and muffins through the bar-code reader and waited for his payment.

Mark fumbled for time as he continued arguing with the voice in his head. "I don't even know her. I'm married, and

I'm a pastor. What would it look like if I said something like that?"

"$5.49," Macy said. Her voice sounded worn from cigarettes and screaming.

"Tell her I think she's beautiful," the voice said again.

"I can't." Mark felt sad—a helpless regret that comes when you buckle to your fears.

The voice fell silent.

All Mark could hear was the Muzak playing over the store's speaker system—some tired hit from the seventies. He reached into his wallet.

Macy waited.

"All right," the voice broke in with a tinge of irritation. "Then I will."

One song ended, and immediately a new one began. It was Joe Cocker crooning, "You are so beautiful, to me."

Mark handed Macy the money, stuffed the food in a bag, and slouched toward the door.

He'd missed his chance, and he knew it.

Speaking is a volitional act, and God gives us the privilege of participating in his work, but he doesn't *need* us to speak for him when he wants to get his message across.

He can do it himself, thank you very much.

. . .

Simon Peter the fisherman was never reluctant to speak. In fact, he had the opposite problem: He often spoke before he knew what he was saying. Sometimes he was way off base. Sometimes, he was brilliantly right.

Impulsive is the word we use to describe him, but Jesus

used a different one—*rock*. The New Testament word is *Petros*, translated for us as *Peter*.

Peter and several other students of Jesus accompanied their teacher on a retreat to a town north of Galilee, Caesarea Philippi. The village had been built at the foot of Mt. Hermon, near the headwaters of the river Jordan. For centuries the area had been considered sacred. It was a good place for an important question.

"Who do you believe I am?" Jesus asked his disciples.[2]

Peter piped up. "You are the Messiah, the Chosen One of God." There had been rumors and backroom mumblings, but until now no one had actually come out and said, "Jesus, you da man-God!"

When the disciples heard Peter's unabashed proclamation, they must have choked on their matzo bread. But there it was, out on the table and on the record.

Jesus responded by saying, "Peter, this isn't your idea. You didn't think this up. God revealed it to you. You have spoken, in your words and from your mouth, the words of God."[3]

Wow, what a heady compliment. Peter the Prophet. Now the others really wished they had been the ones to speak up. A few probably wondered why God wasn't speaking to and through them. Jesus went on to affirm Peter further, to say that he would carry a key leadership role in the coming Kingdom. Peter was in a groove—he was speaking for God.[4]

Then the conversation took a surprising, troubling direction when Jesus told his ambitious followers that he was headed to Jerusalem, where he would be arrested and killed by religious leaders.

The disciples were aghast. Jesus had admitted he was

the Messiah and given Peter major kudos for being the first to say it—even telling him that he had spoken God's own words. Now Jesus says that the religious leaders are going to kill him? Furthermore, he's going to walk into Jerusalem, right into their trap?

Again, Peter spoke for everyone present: "No way. We won't let this happen. You aren't going to be killed."[5]

As quickly as Jesus praised Peter, he admonished him. He turned to Peter and said, "Get away from me, Satan! You are a dangerous trap to me. You are seeing things merely from a human point of view, not from God's."[6]

The same man who was encouraged for speaking God's words was suddenly reprimanded for being the voice of Satan.

Was what he said really so bad?

He was just trying to be a good friend, telling Jesus that he had his back, that he wouldn't let anybody hurt him.

Does that sound so evil as to be from the mouth of Satan?

But Jesus saw it differently. He knew Peter's words were a temptation. Instead of heading into trouble in Jerusalem, Peter's words were an invitation to stay with his buddies, avoid the Cross, and bathe in the sunshine of Caesarea. Hang with his homeys until trouble passed. Jesus knew these were not the words of his Father.

How?

First, Jesus knew the words were tempting. And he knew the source of that temptation. Three years earlier, Jesus spent forty days in the desert being tempted. Second, Peter's words were contrary to the purpose for which Jesus was called. Jesus was clear on what his job was, and he wasn't about to let himself be distracted.

How do we know when someone is prophetically speaking God's words versus Satan's? Apparently, it isn't enough that the advice or message seems good. Peter's words sounded like the kind of thing one friend would say to another friend. There must be another way to determine whether it is a message we heed.

103.4 Lyrical Stairway to Heaven

Sig described himself as a practical atheist. He wasn't hostile to religion, but he failed to see how religion provided realistic answers to the big questions in life. During spring semester of his freshman year in college, the computer science major would leave home to head for class. But instead of going to class, he would travel out of town to sit by a creek all day and read. When he returned home, he'd crank his cheap stereo and continue his "deep thoughts" while listening to Elton John, the Eagles, America, or Styx.

"Drifting" is how Sig described that time of his life. "I only liked tracks whose words I could understand," said Sig. "Sometimes I would find a song I liked and play it over and over, dozens of times an hour, while I tried to make mental sense of the chaos that was my life. The song 'Stairway to Heaven' became one of my favorites."

Sig was reading books by C. S. Lewis and Billy Graham—he admired Lewis's clear thinking and Graham's convictions—even though he found them both wrongheaded. He was fascinated that those two authors, wildly divergent in style and content, each found Jesus fundamental to their ideas about morality as well as human purpose and personal identity.

"I wanted to have a sensible reason for living day to day,

and by degrees I was starting to wonder if that reason might not be a person rather than an idea or philosophy. At last, I reached a point of understanding that Christianity entailed a decision on my part to believe in Jesus, not intellectually, but personally, by trusting and choosing to follow him."

Sig describes what happened next:

> One day in the midst of countless repeats of "Stairway to Heaven," listening to the same words that I had heard probably two hundred times, I heard something new. At first, I thought the stereo speakers had gone quirky, because the volume, depth, clarity, and every aspect of sound quality improved. It was as if the stereo system had a disconnected speaker wire that suddenly reconnected briefly and brought out the full force of the music as I had never heard it before—for the duration of a single line: "The piper's calling you to join him."
>
> Without knowing how I knew, God was calling me to join him—and I knew the way to do so was to trust in Jesus. I was so perplexed that I replayed that part of the song over and over, hoping to reproduce the acoustic effect. I couldn't.
>
> Later that spring, while sitting in a lawn chair beside the creek, I said yes to the invitation of God to come to Jesus.
>
> Years later, I began to hear about the spiritual or unspiritual leanings of different musicians, and I was told—often with a judgmental attitude that questioned my faith—that Led Zeppelin was a "devil-worshiping band." Whether or not this is true, I never tried to

ascertain. Honestly, it didn't matter to me then, and it doesn't now.

When the book of Hebrews opens with the declaration that God has spoken "at many times and in various ways,"[7] I can confirm this from my own experience. If God spoke to me through words produced by those who hate him for the purpose of spreading lies from hell, then no ways of communicating are beyond his capability.

In Sig's hands were books by distinguished Christian authors, yet God spoke through a rock-and-roll band?

Is that possible?

If Peter once spoke for Satan,

it's possible that a rock band could speak for God.

. . .

Street preachers and loonies both claim to speak for God. But maybe it isn't the speaker who decides. After all, Peter didn't know what he was saying when he spoke God's words or when he spoke Satan's. In both cases, Jesus *knew* for whom Peter spoke.

Did he know that because he was God?

The members of Led Zeppelin had no idea they were singing an invitation from God to Sig through stereo speakers. And as Lily pointed up to the plane, Curtis's heart broke at the obvious sign that he'd been gone too long.

Maybe it's not that the speaker *speaks* for God, but that the listener *discerns* God's voice. That is, maybe recognizing God's voice doesn't happen in the broadcast but in the reception.

This makes sense, doesn't it?

If a crazy person said that he or she speaks for God, it's the listener who immediately dismisses his or her words. But if a child said something crazy, like "My daddy is in that plane" when her daddy is standing beside her, isn't it also the listener who hears a deeper meaning behind the words?

The burden of discerning God's communication isn't on the speaker; it's on the listener.

103.5 confirmed

Dan left his job in anticipation of landing a position at a nearby college. When the job didn't materialize, he needed to save money and could no longer afford his rent at Paul's house. Dan had lived with Paul and his family for a year, so Paul was saddened by the news that Dan was moving out. Paul offered a suggestion.

"Dan, let's put the burden for this where it belongs—with God. You tell him that you are planning to pack up and leave on Friday [it was Wednesday], and if he has another plan, he has your number."

They prayed for God's plan to become obvious. If nothing happened, that meant it was God's will for Dan to move out.

Paul reports what happened:

"Dan went downstairs to make a call. He clicked over when someone called in. It was the lady from Bethel University, offering him the position he understood had already been taken."

Dan was stunned at the timing and clarity of God's voice.

But honestly, would the same call have taken on such divine significance if Dan hadn't been listening for it?

Would the call still have been God speaking if Paul and Dan had not just prayed to hear God's voice?

. . .

Mary DeMuth is a successful writer with five books in print and four more on the way. But she was having a bad day. "I felt terribly small as a writer after reviewing the edits on my book," said Mary. "Though I agreed with my editor, I felt inadequate after reading all that feedback. I labored over that book, only to find flaws that needed to be worked out. I guess I was hoping for a 'brilliant!'" Instead, Mary had a lot of questions and more than a little self-doubt.

"I'd also been wrestling with a friend's misunderstanding and judgment of my heart," said Mary. "No matter what I did to clear the air or prove my innocence, I couldn't make my friend see my heart or understand my motives."

Mary went to church that morning and prayed about her discouragement. During worship, she felt the Lord speak. "I know your heart. I know the situation. I see it all. But your friend is too wounded to see that. Rest in me and give grace to your friend who doesn't understand yet."

"His words came out of the blue," said Mary. "They were specific to some recent fears and old wounds, and salved my heart like only Jesus could. I raised my hands a little higher, tears of thankfulness in my eyes. *God sees me*, I thought. *He sees. And he understands.* But yet, I needed a little more confirmation, so I dared to pray, 'Please show me *specifically* that you see me.'"

After the services, a woman Mary didn't know stopped

her to talk. Mary attends a large church, and only her closest friends know she is a writer. The woman told her that she was reading Mary's first novel, *Watching the Tree Limbs*. "I can't put it down," the woman said. "The way you write is beautiful. Thank you."

Not only were the words encouraging to Mary, but she said, "they were proof that God sees me, and Jesus is real."

Basking in the encouragement, Mary went to her usual spot and waited for her son. Another lady approached. "You don't know me, and I don't know you," she said. "But God wouldn't let me walk by you without telling you how much you are loved by him. He has placed you on my heart to pray for you, and I don't even know your name. Be assured that he is mindful of you."

Mary thanked her and marveled at God's swift, double-punched answer to her small prayer. "I left church knowing again that Jesus is so very real. And that he loves me enough to whisper encouragement in my ear during worship and lead two strangers to stop and give me the words I needed to hear."

Confirmation comes in different ways. For Mary, it was from strangers.

• • •

For Amber, the prophetic words she heard were confirmed, not by strangers, but by her parents.

Patricia and David tried to be quiet as they got ready for work. Amber was home on a break from college, and they believed she was sleeping in the next room.

Quite unexpectedly, David said, "I feel Amber's going to

meet someone pivotal this coming summer, maybe even her husband."

Patricia stopped what she was doing and looked at him. "I've felt that way, too, for several weeks now."

Surprising them, Amber walked in, tears in her eyes. "You guys," she said, "God has told me the same thing."

They all hugged. "This is a warning or a promise," Patricia told Amber, "and only you and God will know which."

The end of school came. That summer, Amber flew from their home in Chattanooga to work at her assigned ministry location in Washington, D.C. She lived with a pastor's family and spent the entire summer working with children in a local ministry. At the end of the summer, she returned home. There were no further revelations.

A week later, she returned to college in Nashville. Once there, she reconnected with Henry, a young man she'd known only as a friend. She discovered that Henry was from the D.C. area, so they had much in common. Amber soon learned that the pastor's family she had stayed with were serving at the church Henry's grandfather had founded years before. That meant the children she ministered to in inner-city D.C. were the same children Henry had ministered to many times. He and Amber knew the same kids by name.

Over time, Henry and Amber fell in love. They married in 2002.

Today he is a youth pastor and she is a children's pastor, and they live in Washington, D.C.—the same place where they had both ministered to those inner-city children.

And now they also minister to two children of their own.

One way to know God is speaking is through his confirmation. Sometimes it comes through other people, through seeing prophetic words play out in our lives—as with Mary and Amber. We can also receive confirmation through Scripture.

But there may be another category: crowd confirmation. Sometimes God seems to give the same words, ideas, or thoughts to different, unrelated people, all at the same time. A simultaneous groundswell of people saying the same thing can confirm that he is at work.

103.6 MOVEMENTS

Throughout history, renewal has often come as a result of a simultaneous movement. The same idea grows concurrently in many places. The movement builds until the changes affect the direction of modern Christianity. We often think of reforms or corrections to the church as being led by one man, but a deeper look often reveals that many people and cultural factors seemed to come together at the same time.

Recently, evangelical Christians have been reawakening to the issues of social justice: concern for the environment, feeding the hungry, and caring for the poor. This trend isn't sparked by a single individual. Instead, the ideas seem to come from many directions: individuals and churches, as well as cultural and government leaders. In each area, they just followed the conviction of their heart. But soon, others caught their passion, and a worldwide movement began.

When Jennifer was trying to interest editors in her first book on how to leave an eternal legacy, she met with Steve, an editor at a small publishing house. He told Jennifer there had been a lot written on the subject recently. He mentioned books he knew of that were just about to be released, as well as songs hitting the Christian charts, recent news stories, and magazine articles. He said he'd seen this pattern before.

Steve gave examples of books his publishing house had worked hard to produce, only to see his competitors bring out books on the same topics. The release dates of all the books were within months of each other.

Knowing the lead time to write and publish a book was years, not months, Jennifer asked Steve if he thought there was some sort of leak—did someone working at his publishing house inform other publishers what they had coming out?

"No, I don't think that's it at all," said Steve. "I think God raises up the same idea in different people—artists, writers, musicians, etc.—all at the same time, and some of them act on it."

This was a new thought for Jennifer, who had always seen the publishing marketplace as a competitive business. If one publisher had a successful book about *purpose*, four other publishers released books about *purpose*. But now she reconsidered whether it was a profit-seeking motive or a God-following obedience that simultaneously flooded the market with similar projects. If God wanted a message out to his people, it would only make sense to first give his message to the people who could best spread it.

Could it be there is a real correlation between profits and prophets?

103.7 CALLING ALL PROPHETS

There were only a few prophets in ancient Israel. And those who were genuine prophets were often quite peculiar. The image of a prophet from the Old Testament is one of an eccentric. Speaking for God at that time in history was dangerous to one's health and seemingly to one's sanity.

Hosea was driven by a revelation that he should marry a prostitute.

Isaiah walked naked for three years to make a point.

Poor Jeremiah—he did little else but weep most of his pitiable life.

Prophet was not a career the ambitious aspired to. Recruited by God, they had the rare privilege of communicating intimately with him. They shared his ideas and passions. But this was more than their mortal psyches could handle. Prophets often turned into something hardly recognizable as human. No actuary worth his salt would insure an Old Testament prophet.

John the Baptist continued that tradition in the New Testament. He was the model prophet. A bit over the top. Wild looking. Bizarre diet. Hairy shirt. And the subject of a lot of finger-pointing.

Then things changed. In Acts 2, Peter announced God's promise from the book of Joel that *all* God's people would hear and speak the voice of God.

This was also Paul's charge in his first letter to the young church in the Greek city of Corinth. Toward the end of the letter, in chapters 12 through 14, Paul urged all Christians to speak God's Word to one another. In fact, he called it prophecy. No longer is this the domain of odd fellows; it is the business and calling of all followers of Jesus.

Everyone will prophesy?

103.8 DO YOU HEAR WHAT I HEAR?

We watch a news story about a mother who kills her children. She says she did it because God told her to.

A mass murderer says that God told him to kill female joggers.

The adulteress says God told her to leave her husband and marry her lover.

We're confident that God didn't say these things.

But how do we know for sure?

As the Jesus and Peter story taught us, we can't always trust the messenger. Just because a person claims to speak for Christ, that doesn't mean Christ said it.

Even the best intentioned—like Peter—can unknowingly speak out of both sides of his mouth. And a person's claim to have heard from God isn't proof that he did. Mouthpieces for the divine rarely know when they are being used that way.

In nearly every story in this chapter, the person who spoke a message from God didn't realize she was speaking for *him*, or if she did, she didn't have a complete understanding of what it meant. And yet, though the listener may not have been given all the details, it was clear that God was trying to tell her something, and then she chose to act on it (or not).

What does that mean for those of us who want to hear God's voice?

Could it mean we need to *know him* to hear him? Just as a bird-watcher who knows what a Golden-Winged Warbler sounds like is more likely to spot one, those listeners who know what God's Word sounds like are more likely to recognize it when they hear it.

God is speaking through other people *all the time*.

We need to always listen in a way that we can discern his voice when we hear it.

Perhaps God has already spoken to us today.

Did you hear his words?

Or did you miss them because they sounded like words from your boss, your mother, or your best friend?

Could it be that we miss hearing from God, not because we weren't listening *hard enough*, but rather because we couldn't discern *his words* from the thousands of other words, images, advertisements, and conversations that assaulted us today?

What if,

just for a minute,

we assumed God is speaking to us through other people, right now?

How would we know?

Of the hundreds of messages that we encountered today, how would we know *which messages were from him*?

We know God didn't tell that woman to kill her babies, the mass murderer to kill joggers, or the adulteress to run off with another man. We recognize the craziness, the immorality of these actions.

Yet, even when we think we're hearing from God, we sometimes think his words sound crazy. We doubt what he said or that he said it at all.

But here is what's really cool . . .

He is consistent with his character even in those moments when we doubt.

He patiently explains it again.

He sends a confirmation through Scripture, through others, through circumstances, or through results. Where he extends his words, he also extends his grace to provide a confirmation that he has spoken.

What would happen if we got as good at discerning wisdom as we are at discerning craziness?

How *much more* would we hear from him if we *knew* him better?

When we hear details of a friend's adventures, we say things like, "That sounds like her," because we know her well enough to know the kinds of things she would do or say.

What if we knew God that well?

Well enough to say, "That sounds like him!"

If hearing God speak through other people brings to mind your spouse's nagging, your father's disappointment, or your preacher's list of dos and don'ts, maybe you don't know him well enough.

We're best able to hear him speak, regardless of whose voice he uses, when we actively and intentionally know him better.

103.9 TRY, TRY AGAIN

When God speaks, he calls us by name.

Huh?

Does that mean we're going to hear Morgan Freeman's voice thundering our name through the clouds?

Not likely.

But God's words will be as personal to us as our name.

We will recognize his voice. We will want to follow him.

In John 10, Jesus said

> The gatekeeper opens the gate for him, and the sheep recognize his voice and come to him. He calls his

own sheep by name and leads them out. After he
has gathered his own flock, he walks ahead of them,
and they follow him because they know his voice.
They won't follow a stranger; they will run from him
because they don't know his voice.[8]

The verse makes it sound so easy: we'll always know the
shepherd from the stranger. But we don't, do we? Even
those who were present when Jesus used the sheep metaphor didn't get it. Verse six says, "Those who heard Jesus
use this illustration didn't understand what he meant."

If they didn't get it, what hope do we have?

Maybe our hope is found in the next verse, "So he
explained it to them." In the verses that follow, Jesus talks
about how much he loves us and the sacrifices he is willing
to make on our behalf. In other words, when we didn't understand what God was saying, he sent Jesus to tell us. God
became fully human to improve the lines of communication.

What if,

just for today,

you assumed God was trying to communicate with you,
and that he wanted you to do something about it.

How would that change your day?

What if you made the same assumption every day?

How would that change your life?

For those times when we think we hear him and yet we
don't understand, what if we asked him to explain? It appears
as if he'd stop what he was doing and explain it all again.

Why?

Because he loves us.

We don't have to get it right the first time, but neither do we have to spend our lives in confusion and bewilderment. The first step to hearing God is knowing that he wants to be heard.

Like long-distance lovers with a bad cell phone connection, who keep trying despite the static, we know that God will truly do whatever it takes for us to hear his message. There is no fear that our lover is elusive, doesn't want to be heard, or doesn't want to talk to us.

God doesn't hang up and go away. Even when we don't get it.

If one channel doesn't work, he uses another.

We've joked about crazy people speaking for God, but the truth is, the whole thing is kind of crazy, isn't it? The most awesome and powerful being in the universe tries to personally connect with us mere peons. We can't even get a live voice on the tech-support hotline, but the Creator of the universe continues to redial when we get disconnected.

Knowing his character means knowing that he loves us enough to bridge the communication gap. He will do his part to explain it again and again and to love us even when we're frustrated because we don't get it.

Perhaps more than anything else, that's how we know he's the One speaking and not someone else. He continues to reach out even when we've given up.

He keeps trying because he loves us.

He will do anything to keep the conversation going.

And we have the history to prove it.

CHannel 104.0
HIS-STOry

AFTer nearly TWO WeeKS of visiting art museums in
northern Italy, waiting in line for hours to see the Vatican,
and walking through endless halls filled with priceless art,
the Bailey family arrived at Michelangelo's famous ceiling.
They stood outside the door of the most renowned ceiling in
the world as nine-year-old Danny whined, "But I don't want
to see the 'sixteenth chapel.'"

His parents understood his impatience with the sacred
art tour. They hadn't given him a context for understanding
the importance of the Sistine Chapel. As the line moved
forward, Janice explained why the ceiling was such an
important piece of art. Doug described how Michelangelo
lay on his back on scaffolding to paint it. They both pointed
out images Danny was familiar with, like the extended fingers, and taught him how to see the stories behind each of
the vignettes.

Suddenly the artwork came alive for Danny. He discovered animals and people. He recognized biblical characters and stories. Using his camera lens, he looked at the painting up close. Context aided his understanding.

Too bad the Baileys didn't learn the lesson they taught.

The next day, they set out to explore the Roman Forum and the ancient ruins near the Colosseum. The sun shone brightly in the June sky. As they walked toward the Forum from the Vittorio Emanuele II monument, the Baileys were excited about seeing the grand and majestic ruins they had heard so much about. They turned the corner and were surprised to see . . . rocks.

All around them stood piles of rocks. Some rocks had fallen from nearby crumbling structures, while others appeared to be randomly scattered. Pillars that once proudly crowned the exterior of important buildings now stood alone. A few arches and facades appeared to be intact, but they were worn and weathered, like battle-scarred gladiators. Walls were reduced to rubble. Ruins on the hillside had a hollow and vacant look. The Forum wasn't a tourist attraction as much as the aftermath of an earthquake.

After a few minutes on the main path, bumped by jostling tourists trying to create a better Kodak moment, Danny said what they were all thinking, "This is boring. It's just rocks!"

What was supposed to be a day of basking in the ancient sites of an eternal city turned into a half hour of rock gazing followed by two hours of souvenir shopping.

104.1 making connections

It wasn't until they arrived back in the States that the Baileys learned that they missed it. Like Danny in the Sistine

Chapel, they didn't see anything in the ruins because they weren't prepared to see anything.

Two years later, the Baileys returned to Rome. This time they were armed with a solid guidebook and the advice of other travelers who'd gone before them. With a map of the ruins, they started in one corner and took turns reading about the history of each place.

No longer did they see a deteriorating stone building; they saw the place where the Roman Senate had met. The arch was no longer a decaying architectural piece; it was a reminder of Constantine, who first brought Christianity to the Roman Empire. The brass doors, patina green with age, spoke of man's ability to create objects capable of surviving—more or less—two thousand years.

This time, the Baileys understood the connections between their modern lives and the lives of those who lived and worked in the ancient sites: the first form of representative government, the spread of Christianity, the influence of art, laws, logic, religion, and war. The rocks weren't just a part of *past history*; they were also a part of the family's *own current story*. Only after understanding the greater story could they understand their place in it.

Does God speak through history?

Does he use things of the past to connect to the present? Of course.

The Bible is filled with many historical examples from which we're meant to learn. The history of God's people is also *our story*. When we know more of God, we know ourselves. History informs us of who we are.

But perhaps the more interesting question is, Can God

speak here and now through things that happened then and there?

104.2 Personal History

Jennifer often hears God speaking at conferences. Whether through the presenters and speakers, other attendees, or even alone in her hotel room, she has a history of hearing God during those times, in those places. In fact, one such conference helped her learn from her own history.

I remember attending one of my first writers' conferences. I wrote what I thought was a decent children's picture book and was excited to have landed a critique session with Andrea Brown, who at the time was one of the only literary agents specializing in children's books. This was a lady who knew her stuff, and I couldn't wait to hear what she had to say.

She took a quick look at my manuscript and asked me why I wanted to write picture books. I gushed on and on about how much I loved to read them. Finally, she interrupted me and said, "But you don't have a voice for picture books. Picture books are comforting, warm, and intimate."

I looked at my manuscript about a toddler's messy meal and the bath to clean him up, and I knew she was right. "You have a voice for middle-grade novels," she continued. "You're funny and sarcastic; you need to write that instead."

She had nailed it. That wasn't a case of believing whatever the expert said. I *knew* she was speaking the truth. But I also knew that middle-grade novels were about food fights in the cafeteria, the nerd taking revenge on the jocks, and booger jokes. I didn't want to write books with booger jokes.

As I headed to my next class, I felt stripped of all my writing dreams. Maybe that's why I was ready to hear the advice given in the next session. The teacher advised attendees to look back through their writing career and follow their past success.

I reflected on my history and discerned some patterns. My publishing success came from adult non-fiction. In fact, it was so obvious, I was surprised I hadn't seen it before.

At that moment, God spoke to me through my own history. Now when I don't know what to do, I reflect on those words and that moment. I reexamine my writing history to see where God would have me go next.

For Jennifer, breakthroughs like those have happened so many times at conferences that now she expects to see God at those events.

Likewise, Mark expects to see God while hiking. Mark's past experiences include hearing God while alone in nature. Whether hiking, walking, or just hanging out, he has learned from his past to expect to hear God in the outdoors.

Is this just an example of expectations becoming reality?

Do we, Mark and Jennifer, hear God in these places because we *expect* to?

Or is this an example of people who've learned from our own pasts? Do we listen more actively because of our previous experiences?

Can we make our past work for our future?

If you're trying to hear God speak, perhaps you first need to tune in to the "history channel" and reflect on your personal spiritual history. Can you identify general themes in your history? places or times that God has spoken to you?

What happens when you revisit the channels where you heard God speak in the past?

104.3 CORPORATE HISTORY

Twenty years ago, Christians in Theatre Arts (CITA) was birthed as a ministry to support, educate, and provide networking opportunities for Christians who wanted to further explore the relationship between their faith and their theatrical talents. For many years, the organization experienced success in the growth of its membership, awareness in the culture, and respect in the artistic community. But in the past few years, numbers had dwindled at conferences, with less volunteerism and more debate about the future purpose and direction of the ministry.

Dale, the executive director, had grown weary. The ministry had accomplished much in the past two decades, yet the leaders were short on vision for the future.

In an effort to find direction, Dale gathered past and present board members for a weekend retreat. They were asked to spend time in prayer before they arrived. When the retreat began, the first question put before them was whether or not to cease operation. Said one board member about that trying period, "It was time for us to change our ways or close our doors."

To provide context for the discussion, surveys had been sent to all existing members. Surprisingly, 44 percent of those had been returned, most with positive encouragement to keep the organization alive.

The first question had been answered. But if the ministry was to continue, it needed a purpose for the future.

It was suggested that the board members start with a look at the past, at the original needs that compelled them to start the ministry. By examining the culture and context of their beginnings, they clearly saw the existing needs of that time and how God had blessed them to meet those needs. Though they were quick to point out they couldn't take direct credit for many of the changes that had occurred in the past twenty years, they had to acknowledge a strong correlation between CITA connections and the positive changes in the Christian theater-arts culture.

Churches now included drama and the theater arts as a regular and important part of their ministries. Christian dramatists had improved their skills in writing, acting, and production. There was a growing number of Christian artists who worked professionally in regional and Broadway theaters and who no longer felt they had to hide their faith. Seminaries and colleges had recognized the growing importance of this ministry and had begun to offer new educational opportunities.

Founding CITA members had been on the forefront of many of the cultural changes, and in their surveys they unabashedly attributed their actions to the support and relationships they developed through CITA's ministry. This reflection helped board members understand how valuable their ministry and networking had been during this important time of cultural change.

Reflection on the organizational and spiritual history of

CITA made it clear that the organization must continue. By examining the past, the board was able to discern important areas of future opportunity.

As CITA continues in new directions, they'll try new things that could alienate longtime members. They'll face new challenges. Growth may be slower than in the past. But with a history of obstacles overcome, results achieved, and impact made, their past will continue to speak to them—reminding them of what's important as they continue to move the ministry forward.

This cycle of historical introspection will repeat. The next time the organization finds itself tired and visionless, this board retreat will be an integral part of their corporate history—it will be a model of how to look back before looking forward.

Our history grows in layers and in meaning.

What does your past—your "history"—say about your future?

104.4 TUNING IN TO THE PAST

Annette felt as if her prayers weren't being answered. In an effort to get better at praying, she attended a prayer seminar at her local church.

During the workshop, the leader asked everyone to close their eyes and ask God to reveal three things that he appreciated about them. Annette closed her eyes and prayed, but she suspected that she already knew the answer. She had just spent months working on curriculum to be used by missionaries in third-world countries. The materials would help local Christian entrepreneurs start their own businesses and support not only their families but also their local churches.

Annette knew her efforts were something God would appreciate.

But as she listened for God to affirm her thoughts, something unexpected happened. The first thing she heard was, "You're a good mother." As she continued to listen, she heard . . .

well,

nothing else.

When the leader told them to open their eyes, Annette was convinced that once again she had failed at prayer.

The leader asked participants to share what God told them with the person sitting beside them. As luck (okay, God) would have it, Annette was sitting next to a pastor from her church. As Pastor Wilder rattled off the three things that God had spoken to him, Annette was near tears. How would she explain that she was a failure at prayer? that she hadn't heard three things? that she hadn't heard what she expected, and that the *one* thing she had heard wasn't even something she believed, because it was something she'd never say?

As she confessed her prayer failures, Pastor Wilder listened patiently and then said, "Isn't it amazing how God's priorities are different from ours?"

That was a new concept.

What if she weren't a failure at prayer?

What if she heard *exactly* what God *intended* her to hear?

Later, Annette reflected on how big God was in that moment.

Bigger than the prayer leader—God wasn't confined to a list of threes.

He was bigger than the seating arrangements, making

sure she was near Pastor Wilder, someone who would help her understand when she missed what God was trying to say.

And God was big enough to remind her that sometimes he works

with us

differently than we expect,

differently than our teachers teach us,

and differently than he works with those around us.

Even as you're reading this book, you might be feeling as if you're not hearing God right, that he isn't speaking to you in the same way he does to others, or perhaps you feel he isn't speaking to you at all.

Isn't it amazing?

He knows that's what you're thinking. But the thing is, he doesn't want you to be like anyone else.

He wants you

to be

like

him.

It's still easy for Annette to believe that God isn't speaking to her like he does to everyone else, but when she remembers this lesson from the past, she no longer feels inadequate. She feels loved for who she is and who she aspires to be.

Her present is different because of her past history with God.

What are the turning points in your spiritual history?

Is your future different because of them?

Historian Jean Jaurès said, "Take from the altars of the past the fire—not the ashes."[1]

God speaks through the fires in our past, but occasionally we're so busy digging through the ashes we miss the light of the flames that spark our future.

104.5 FAMILY HISTORY

Marie surveyed the crowded kitchen and family room. Eleven of her twelve children. Seven of their spouses. Two boyfriends, a girlfriend, and fifteen grandchildren. Including Paul and her, that made thirty-eight people for Christmas Eve dinner. Silent night, holy night? Not that night. And that's the way she liked it.

This Christmas would have new stories to carry to the future, but for the moment she reflected on stories from the past. . . .

One Christmas more than a decade ago, Tim, the seventh child in the family, received an abundance of socks and underwear. That was amusing enough, but it was even more so because each piece of underwear and each sock was wrapped separately. The whole family joined in the laughter as he continued to open package after package of undergarments.

Her son Rob's last year at home had become a memorable Christmas too. He earned a good salary and paid no rent, and his present to himself that year was a new stereo and television equipment. Though many of his siblings had already moved out of their parents' house, he bought a single gift for the entire family to share—a sugar shaker. Having to spoon sugar out of a bag onto his cereal each morning had frustrated him, and on Christmas he proudly placed on the table his unwrapped gift—earning himself the title of "Mr. Tightwad."

One year the older sisters gathered to play a word game. When it was Carrie's turn, she failed to realize she had the winning word in her hand—N-I-P-S. Carrie lost the game and was teased mercilessly by her sisters.

Marie wasn't the only one thinking of those Christmases past. Tim came into the room and sat next to his older brother.

"Did you get me a sugar shaker this year?" asked Tim.

"No, but I did pick up some underwear at a garage sale," Rob responded without missing a beat. "It's even color coded so you know which side goes in the front and which side goes in the back."

Those nearest the conversation groaned and then added their own one-liners, only to be interrupted by a small box flying across the room. It landed in Carrie's lap—its intended target.

"Hey, Carrie, I got you some candy!" yelled an unseen sister.

Carrie looked down to find a box of hard chocolate caramels. Of course, they were better known under their Nestlé brand name, NIPS.

"Nice," said Carrie as she opened the bag and shared it with the grandkids.

These silly and seemingly trivial events serve a noble purpose—they are the ties that bind this family together. Outside the walls of the Sullivans' house, jokes about these practical or embarrassing gifts would have no meaning. Yelling *nips* in a crowded movie theater wouldn't make the crowd break out in belly laughs. These words wouldn't unite a team, an army, or a country—but somehow they unite this family.

At the Sullivan house, the jokes about prior Christmases do more than bring laughs to Marie's kids; they also pass on values to the grandkids. The third generation is quick to learn that the practical is valued over the extravagant, that it's okay to laugh at others if you first laugh at yourself, and that sugar shakers don't make good stocking stuffers.

"In every conceivable manner, the family is link to our past, bridge to our future," said Alex Haley.[2] Each family has its own code or set of values shaped by the events, actions, behaviors, and words of their history. This history binds them together beyond the way their own blood unites them. In a way, we become the stories our families tell.

• • •

On December 27, 2006, in a rented banquet hall at the Lowell Inn in Stillwater, Minnesota, three generations came together to celebrate the fiftieth wedding anniversary of Howard and Joyce Herringshaw, Mark's parents. For the couple, it was a moment to look back at the years they'd shared together: the day they first met; their courtship; the wedding that took place in a little church in Portland, Oregon; the birth of their first, then second, and finally third child; and the chaotic child-rearing years that followed. And though they may not have been consciously thinking about it, the celebration was also a time for them to pass on the values they held dear.

After the meal, sixteen-year-old Ellie asked her grandma and grandpa to repeat the story of how they'd met. It was a story they had all heard before—a story that each one at the party could probably have told in detail, but Howard happily told it anyway. Under the table, Howard grabbed Joyce's hand. That story led to another, and then another.

As Joyce and Howard's son (and Ellie's dad) Mark listened to each story, he heard something more than the familiar tales. Though his parents' lives had been filled with joy, it also held times of sadness, sorrow, and struggle. As Mark listened to them retell the old stories, he recognized the grace of God through the difficult times. He listened as they described the blessings in their lives. They had joy and they had pain, but it was obvious they also had purpose and direction. Looking back at the tapestry of their lives, it was clear how God wove beauty and meaning within each event. Mark watched Ellie beg for yet another story, and he wondered if she saw the same things in her grandparents' lives as he did.

He also wondered, *How would God manifest himself in Ellie's life and marriage?*

To Mark, it wasn't a question of *if* God would be a part of Ellie's life; it was a question of *how*. Mark already had proof that God had been present for generations, and that gave him all the faith he needed to know that God would always be there.

History isn't limited to the books we read, the Renaissance art we see on the Vatican ceiling, or the ancient ruins of an impressive civilization.

Yes, God speaks through grand historical events—the Bible is full of them—but he also speaks through our personal family histories, reminding us of who we are and where we've come from.

Tradition.

Language.

Shared experience.

In a family, these things add up to something greater than the sum of their parts. They provide a *context*.

Context helps family members feel connected to a common history that started before them and will continue after them. It's a reminder that we're all a part of something bigger than ourselves, and that some part of us will pass into the future.

If Ellie paid attention that night, she saw examples of devotion, commitment, sacrificial love, and service to others. When Howard reached out to take Joyce's hand, it was an unspoken familial prayer that one day each grandchild would also know the kind of love experienced in their grandparents' touch.

History not only speaks backward, but when families are involved, it can also speak forward.

104.6 SPIRITUAL FAMILIES

But what if, unlike Ellie's, your grandparents aren't the hand-holding type?

What if, instead of family reunions, you have family court dates?

Whether your family is united by the serious, the significant, or the silly—or divided by the same—God speaks through your family history. For some, it may be a simple message to value your heritage. To others, it may be a message to change the direction of the future. Regardless of whether an earthly family reunion brings laughter or tears, we are part of a more important family.

A spiritual family.

And this one has a longer history of God speaking through it.

When we picture a spiritual family, many of us imagine noble scenes of Thanksgiving—white linen tablecloths spread over a long banquet table, with the saints gathered around. Paul sits near the head of the table, and when the moment is right, he tells his Damascus Road story. The apostles, seated together, take turns recalling their favorite moments traveling the countryside with Jesus. And Jonathan and David's conversation has to be interrupted to remind them to pass the potatoes.

If this is your picture, you're forgetting the other side of the table, where the crazy family members sit. The ones who don't use forks and who sometimes throw food.

Our spiritual family is as dysfunctional as any earthly family. Tim may have been embarrassed by the quantity of underwear he received for Christmas, but it's also likely that had Adam and Eve exchanged gifts that first year, they would have been embarrassed giving, and receiving, fig leaves. Imagine the stories this first couple told at their fiftieth wedding anniversary celebration.

"Hey, Eve, remember our first house in the Garden?"

"More apple pie, anyone?" Eve asks, changing the subject.

What if being a child of God means sitting at the Thanksgiving table next to Uncle John-the-Baptizer while he munches on grasshoppers? Or hoping Cousin Jacob, who stole his brother Esau's inheritance, doesn't steal your piece of pumpkin pie? Noah's sons smell like animals and tell stories about their dad getting drunk and passing out naked. And you'd have to keep asking the guy who sits across from you, "Now, which one are you, Elisha or Elijah?"

Once again, the stories would bring us closer. Though

we've heard them before, we'd beg to hear them again. "Hey, Mary, tell us again how Jesus changed the water into wine."

Like our earthly family stories, do these spiritual stories of our past serve to unite us?

Perhaps the Bible is more than just the history or rule book we often take it for. Could it be a collection of family stories meant to connect us?

What stories about our Father would make us want to be just like him?

And what would celebrating a family holiday with Jesus be like?

Would it look like the Last Supper?

104.7 Passover Through the Years

Jesus gathered his friends together for one last blowout party. There was food, conversation, and probably singing. The occasion was Passover, an annual celebration of the Jewish people to commemorate a real event that took place in history. The details of that event are in Exodus 12, but we'll summarize it here.

While the Hebrew people were in bondage in Egypt, God sent Moses to tell Pharaoh to free the slaves. Pharaoh refused. So God sent ten plagues as a sign he was serious. Each plague was a specific attack on one of Egypt's gods. Pharaoh's firstborn was considered the heir to divine status. So the tenth plague was the angel of death—sent to take the firstborn child.

Miraculously, God made a way for death to pass over the homes of the Hebrew families. Each family was told to sacrifice a year-old lamb, without defect, and spread its blood over the sides and tops of the door frames. Then they were to roast the lamb and eat it as preparation for travel.

That night happened as God said it would. The angel of death passed over the homes marked with the lambs' blood, sparing the Hebrew children. With Egypt in the throes of grief after losing all their firstborn children, Pharaoh released the slaves, and they began their journey back to their homeland in Canaan.

In Jesus' day, as now, Jewish families gathered together to remember and celebrate the Feast of Passover as a reminder of their deliverance from slavery. Eating the same meal their ancestors did, the family listens to the story again. Remembering ancient history is a way for Jews to connect with their past, identify with it, and let God do again in that present moment what he did so long ago. Though they may not be experiencing a literal slavery, maybe they seek a release from the bondage of an addiction or from a nagging fear.

Jewish philosophers view time not as a circle or as a line, but as a spiral that moves from one fixed point to another, like a stretched-out Slinky. Time has repeating patterns (like Passover), but it constantly moves forward. Remembering and reliving the past through repeating patterns—whether it's a Passover feast or any recurring commemoration—is a kind of time travel. It is a moment when God does it all over again for the first time.

When Jesus invited his disciples to a celebration in the upper room, they gathered together to remember what God had done in the past. But what they didn't know was that they were about to make history. At that moment in time, a new sacrificial lamb would be revealed.

All the traditional elements of Passover were present: songs, prayers, readings from the Scriptures, candle lighting, blessing of the wine, and washings. There was also the breaking of the middle of three matzos: the Afikomen, which means *the bread of affliction.*

> A great drama takes place with the Afikomen. Three matzos are placed in one pouch. The middle one is taken, broken, wrapped in white, hidden away, found, redeemed, and shared by all. This middle matzo has taken the place of the lamb in importance, as shown by the fact that everyone at the table must partake of it. Traditions associated with the Afikomen add to its drama. European Jews (Ashkenazi) believe it has the power to heal the sick. Oriental Jews believe it can calm a stormy sea.[3]

And though this breaking of the bread would have seemed very common to the disciples, Jesus did something that should have seemed strange to them:

> As they were eating, Jesus took some bread and blessed it. Then he broke it in pieces and gave it to the disciples, saying, "Take this and eat it, for this is my body."
>
> And he took a cup of wine and gave thanks to God for it. He gave it to them and said, "Each of you drink from it, for this is my blood, which confirms the covenant between God and his people. It is poured out as a sacrifice to forgive the sins of many. Mark my words— I will not drink wine again until the day I drink it new with you in my Father's Kingdom."[4]

Um, that had to be a little weird.

Usually they wrapped it in a cloth and hid it. Instead, Jesus said this was *his* body, and then mentioned something about a covenant and a sacrifice for sins. The disciples should have found this to be pretty disturbing. It was like Thanksgiving, only instead of serving pumpkin pie, Mom talks about her death.

Were the disciples disturbed by this proclamation?

Not much.

The next verse says, "Then they sang a hymn and went out to the Mount of Olives."[5]

Think about it another way: To the disciples, this event would have had the significance of a Christmas or anniversary spent with friends. It was a celebration. At the time, they didn't know it was Jesus' *last* supper. It is only through the lens of history that this particular feast takes on the significance of the Last Supper. Only in hindsight are the traditional elements of this holiday recognized as a metaphor for a much more significant spiritual event:

> The three original elements of the Passover were bitter herbs, unleavened bread, and the lamb. Bitter herbs speak of bitter bondage. Believers are to reflect at Communion and realize the bitter bondage of sin and the cure for that bondage—the Lamb, Jesus Christ. He was pure, sinless, without spot—just like that unleavened bread.
>
> When Christians remember Jesus at Communion, they remember that He—the second person in the Godhead—was taken, broken (or killed), hidden away in a tomb, and then raised from the dead. Believers

remember Him by taking a little piece of unleavened bread and eating it. It means *He came*. The Afikomen is back, not as the Passover lamb bringing physical salvation in Egypt, but as the Savior, the Passover Lamb who brought spiritual salvation to the world.[6]

This ancient Jewish feast, celebrated for thousands of years before Jesus, was given new meaning and fuller revelation by the Messiah. Now Christians reenact the elements of Passover in the Lord's Supper.

In Matthew 26, Jesus instituted Communion. He took unleavened bread, symbolic of His pure and spotless body, and the cup, representing His blood. The cup He took was the third cup, the cup of redemption. He did not drink the fourth cup, saying He would not drink it until he drinks it with us in His Father's Kingdom.[7]

Through the history of this single meal, God speaks to us— from the past—about our future. It is a living memory, a way to pull the past into the present.

One of the things that history tells us is that God has a way of messing with time. Though we've all experienced a sense of déjà vu, God seems to be able to predict future events in great detail thousands of years before they happen.

And sometimes he can do it in freaky ways.

104.8 PROPHETIC HISTORY

The town is abuzz. Their favorite son has arrived for a visit, and everyone wants to find a moment to slap him on the back and tell him they wish him the best on his new rabbinic venture. Jesus has come home to Nazareth.

It is the Sabbath, and everyone in town has gathered at the synagogue for the ritual singing of psalms, prayers, and the reading of the Scriptures. Jesus hasn't been traveling and teaching more than a few months when he returns, but already his reputation is spreading across Israel. There are rumors of amazing healings. Thousands flock to hear him teach, not only because he is a great storyteller, but because what he says is fresh and profoundly simple. Even children understand him.

But the people also gather to watch the fireworks.

The religious leaders, too, follow Jesus around—not as his disciples, but as his foils. They often heckle him from the back rows of his gatherings, challenging his authority and then accusing him of undermining Jewish law. But Jesus always has a way of turning the tables on them. And common people love to see their pompous leaders humbled a bit. Jesus is the best show in town.

Each week, when it is time to bring out the sacred Scriptures, a different man from the congregation is asked to read. The specific passage is predetermined—this week's reader begins where last week's reader finished. It is also customary for the reader to share a few thoughts after he finishes his reading. This day, Jesus is chosen as the reader.

Jesus stands before the group of familiar faces. The men are directly in front of him, most of them seated on the straw-covered floor. The women and children are behind a lattice screen, off to the side. As he unrolls the long strips of leather fastened to two finely carved wooden dowels, Jesus clears his throat and begins:

106

> The Spirit of the LORD is upon me,
> for he has anointed me to bring Good News to
>   the poor.
> He has sent me to proclaim that captives will
>   be released,
> that the blind will see,
> that the oppressed will be set free,
> and that the time of the LORD's favor has come.[8]

Then Jesus rolls up the Isaiah scroll, hands it back to the attendant, and sits down.

Silence.

Everyone in the room waits.

Is he going to comment? Where's the homily?

They stare at him.

The suspense mounts.

Then Jesus speaks, "The Scripture you've just heard has been fulfilled this very day!"[9]

What?

Did they hear him right?

Isaiah was writing about God's promise to restore and re-create the essence of the world. One day all things would be as they had been in Eden. The famous passage is a sacred vision for all Jews. The heart of this promise is that provision, pardon, healing, deliverance, and favor will all be the wondrous outcome of the full coming of the Kingdom of God.

Did Jesus just say these events were happening today?

Yep. He said it.

The residents of Nazareth are stunned and pleased. It is happening—the salvation that godly people have always longed for!

What had been promised as a future event is coming in the present.

History made and fulfilled in the very same moment.

With his very presence, Jesus pulls those historical words—spoken hundreds of years before—into the here and now and fulfills them before their eyes.

Prophecies from history have always been a key essence of Judaism. Just a few pages prior to the Isaiah 61 promise, speaking on behalf of God, Isaiah writes, "Everything I prophesied has come true, and now I will prophesy again. I will tell you the future before it happens."[10]

God's process is simple: Through prophecy, God says ahead of time what will happen in the future. By his powerful hand in history, he brings those events about. Then, after the fact, he reflects back and explains what it means.

As Jesus speaks, his birth has already fulfilled many prophetic promises in the Hebrew Scriptures: that he would be born in Bethlehem, of a virgin girl; that there would be a massacre of children at the time of his birth; that he and his family would escape to Egypt; and that he would be raised in Nazareth. These are but a few of the historical predictions Jesus' life validates. By the end of his life on earth, he would fulfill hundreds of Old Testament predictions.

In his book *Science Speaks*, Peter Stoner calculates the odds of Jesus' fulfilling just *eight* of the hundreds of messianic prophecies as one out of 10^{17} (a one followed by seventeen zeros). The odds would be about the same as covering the entire state of Texas with silver dollars two feet deep, marking one of the coins, and then having a blindfolded person select that one coin at random.[11]

So how does God speak through history?

Jesus.

Jesus is history come alive.

And for the people of Nazareth, in this moment in time Jesus gathers together all the prophecies and promises God has spoken in the past and calls them present and accounted for. Heaven has come to earth. It's begun, here and now. But in doing so, Jesus surprises and offends those attending synagogue.

"You don't get it," he goes on to say. "You think you know me, but actually, there are others who will grasp the magnitude of what I'm saying to you Nazarenes before you do."[12]

His hometown homeys are irate and deeply offended. *How dare he accuse us of blindness! Who does he think he is?*

The once-adoring citizens become a vicious mob. They rush at Jesus and pull him toward a cliff on the outskirts of town. They fully intend to push him off. But Jesus steps forward and passes through the crowd and out of town.

From that point on, Jesus moves from village to village fulfilling Isaiah 61: he brings provision for the poor, pardon for the guilty, healing for the broken, deliverance for the demonized, love for the alienated. But he never does much in Nazareth. They had been present when history turned, but they missed the moment.

It seems we can learn from history—or we can fail to learn from it.

As Norman Cousins said, "History is a vast early warning system."[13]

104.9 KNOWING YOUR HISTORY ISN'T ENOUGH

We all know someone who has gone through a series of bad relationships and continues to date the same kind of losers.

Maybe you know a woman who is intelligent, educated, and loving, but for whatever reason she finds herself attracted to the bad boys, the mama's boys, or worse, the guys who beat her, mistreat her, or cheat on her. Whether it is a celebrity, a sister, or a friend, you've watched as she's dated one loser after another. Men can have similar repetitive relationship problems. When we see those kinds of bad relationships, we have only one question: why don't they learn from their mistakes?

Television's Dr. Phil is notorious for featuring guests with messed-up relationships. He'll ask them why they continue to do things the same way and then listen patiently as they rationalize their behavior. When the guest has talked herself into believing she has good reasons for what she does, Dr. Phil will interrupt with, "So how's that working for you?"

It gets a laugh from the audience every time, because it's obvious—her life isn't working well at all.

We're all guilty of making mistakes. And most of us are guilty of making them again. Our past is often the best predictor of our future. Maybe this is when God speaks the loudest. The Bible tells us again and again that we can be forgiven for our past mistakes.

In the parable of the Prodigal Son, we're reminded that a father can forgive and a son can start over. When the innocent man who taught us that parable was hung on a cross, he still begged his Father to "forgive them, for they don't know what they are doing."[14]

Could it be that God speaks loudest through history when he wipes away *his* memory of *our* sins?

Wait.

God speaks through forgetting?

Possibly.

Though bringing the past into the present is difficult to wrap our minds around, it's even harder to imagine that God may forget. It's not because he is some aging old man or has early onset dementia. When he forgives, God chooses to forget the bad, the ugly, and the selfish things we've done as a way of showing how much he loves us.

The Bible is a story of Creation and the Fall. But it is also a story of redemption and restoration. God said that we don't have to live in our past. We can be forgiven, and our future can be different. This story is played out in each individual's life, as well as in the story of God's people in the Bible.

God's story doesn't begin or end with us, but it has relevance to us. We may not be facing the same biblical circumstances that we read about in his book, but it seems that God wants us to remember them, anyway:

> I don't want you to forget, dear brothers and sisters, about our ancestors in the wilderness long ago. All of them were guided by a cloud that moved ahead of them, and all of them walked through the sea on dry ground.[15]

We aren't in the same physical space as the ancient Hebrew people, but we do face our own wildernesses. We become lonely. Tired. Frustrated. Angry. Hurt. Sad. Scared. Directionless. Lacking in purpose or meaning.

Yet God's promise extends to us today. He guides us, not by a cloud, but by the "clouds" of the past. Just as the Passover Feast takes on new meaning when Jesus fulfills the promises implicit in the story, so can other ancient stories of the Bible take on new meaning when God uses them to speak to us.

As he said in the verse above, he doesn't want us to forget.

Yet . . . we want him to forget.

Not to forget *us* but all the things we've screwed up. That's where things get sticky. God asks us to remember the past and to learn from it, and we ask him to forget our past.

How can it be that we are to remember and he is to forget?

Like other biblical paradoxes—"the last shall be first" or "the weak shall be strong"—perhaps as we remember and learn from our past, God can forget it.

Actually, it makes sense.

If we can learn what we need from our past, God no longer needs to speak to us about it. As we learn from it, he's free to forget it.

Is that what grace is all about?

104.10 DUAL REALITIES

Is there more than one way to look at the past?

To the Jewish people, Passover has one meaning. Christians see multiple meanings in the same event. Does that suggest there could be an even deeper meaning? That, as we said earlier, history has layers?

C. S. Lewis was a serious historian. As a scholar of medieval European literature, Lewis had few peers. But despite his Cambridge/Oxford academic prowess, Lewis believed in something deeper than history. He believed in Providence.

One method he employed to communicate his philosophy of history was through his children's fantasy stories,

The Chronicles of Narnia. In *The Silver Chair*, the fourth book in a series of seven, Lewis argues that historical events can have deeper meanings.

The story begins when Eustace Scrubb and Jill Pole are whisked into Narnia and sent on a quest to find the missing Narnian prince, Rilian. Aslan, Narnia's lion king, gives them four signs that will guide their journey. Things soon go wildly amiss as the travelers fumble the first three of Aslan's signs—the third sign being, "You shall find a writing on a stone in that ruined city." They miss the sign completely until, by chance, they spot the words "under me" formed by the shape of ancient ruins. The words had been cut long ago by the king of the giants. He wanted to declare that his entire kingdom was in his control, so he inscribed "under me" into the architecture itself.

As the children and a gloomy but stalwart Marsh-wiggle named Puddleglum escape from the house of the giants, they fall through a cavernous hole, down into the mountain, and wind up literally under *under me*.

Through the rest of the story, the children are tempted to dismiss the idea that the accident was the sign they needed. It had its own historical context, they argued, thus it wasn't intended for them. Near the end of the tale, this skepticism is expressed by the Black Night (the enchanted Prince Rilian). Puddleglum fires back, "There are no accidents. Our guide is Aslan; and he was there when the giant King caused the letters to be cut, and he knew already all things that would come of them; including *this*."[16]

Is God like Aslan?

Was he there when the letters were cut and the words were written?

Did he know all things that would come of them?

The apostle Paul writes, "And we know that in all things God works for the good of those who love him, who have been called according to his purpose."[17]

Does that mean there are no accidents in history?

And that all history works *for good*?

Really?

104.11 HISTORY OF EVIL

Certain events in history cause people to question God. They look at 9/11, the Holocaust, the two world wars, famines, earthquakes, tsunamis, and other disasters and say, "How can there be a loving God?" or "Why wasn't God there?"

But even a modest view of history reveals that God was present.

> The Israelites were led out of slavery even if they preferred it to the desert. And it was God, through Moses, who led the way.
>
> Though many Jews died at the hands of the Nazis during the Holocaust, others were sustained by their faith or saved by those who acted in faith.
>
> Terrorists, floods, and earthquakes have taken the lives of innocent people; many lives have also been spared by what could only be described as divine miracles.

Looking back on historical events, it's easy to ask, "Where was God when it was so bad?" Maybe the wiser question is, "How bad would it have been without God?"

Just because you haven't heard God's voice in the evil events in history, that doesn't mean he was absent. If you want to know where God was, maybe it's as simple as asking him.

> "God, can you show me where you were during the Holocaust?"
> "Father, where were you when I was being neglected and abused?"
> "God, what beauty did you bring to the ugliness I experienced?"

If our view of the past is done through a lens of faith, it is possible to hear God speak now about what happened then.

Perhaps he even spoke then,

but we didn't listen.

104.12 Reason

It's easy when we enter a new situation—a church, a job, a neighborhood—to observe how things are done and conclude that we have a better way, that we can make the process more efficient or fix what's broken.

Occasionally, it's true. We have thought of something that the regulars haven't.

But it's also likely that the processes, procedures, or plans currently in place are there because they serve purposes we can't see. Maybe our vantage point makes things seem illogical or out of control.

As we have more experiences, and as we mature, we learn to see from other points of view. We're slower to offer our opinions. We realize that these are also intelligent, thoughtful people who've made reasonable choices based on factors that may be unfamiliar to us.

To hear God speak through history, we have to know him as eternal. When we compare our history to the history of a corporation, a family, a community, or to the history of God's people, we gain new perspectives. We learn that we're not the story but only a part of it.

In *Mind of the Maker*, Dorothy Sayers says she believes that God is best understood when we see the story he is telling. God, after all, is first and foremost a creator. A story-teller. We know him best when we recognize apparently random, chaotic events around us as a part of his story. When God tells us ahead of time the story he is crafting, we recognize it when it happens. And we see him in the process. We may have but a few lines in this great epic, but we recognize that we are in it.

God speaks through history to give us context for
where we are,
who we are,
and our part
in the story that he is telling.
History gives us purpose.
And meaning.
Security in knowing there is a plan
and we're a part of it.

History teaches us to trust that someone else is in control of the story and that though we don't always understand his choices, see him at work, or hear him speak, looking back, we can see that *he has been there*.

Maybe this is the greatest lesson of history. When God speaks from the past—whether from our recent history or ancient civilizations—maybe what he is saying is that it isn't all about us.

We don't have all the answers.

We don't have to.

History will come.

And go.

Like the Baileys in Rome, could it be that we need to see ourselves as passing through a greater history, a blip on an eternal radar screen?

We're not the focus,

not the star of the story.

But we remember that we are part of something greater.

Something that started before us

and goes on after us,

but without us will never be the same.

"No doubt all history in the last resort must be held by Christians to be a story with a divine plot," said C. S. Lewis.[18]

History is *his*-story.

And his story has a message.

"Trust me," says God.

> "I am good.
> I am in control.
> You don't have to understand.
> Just trust."

Things are as they are for a reason. Sometimes we can see and understand. Sometimes we're not in a position to see the reasons, or we don't have a context to understand them. But they do exist, whether we see them or not.

Through *his*-story, God is speaking an invitation—
not to rewrite the story
but to share a part in it.

CHANNEL 105.0
YOU MUST BE DREAMING

"MY HUSBAND OF ELEVEN YEARS thrust a gun in my face and threatened to kill me," said Nan.

She had every reason to believe it wasn't just a threat.

Most of us have had a dream so real that once we awoke it took a while to realize it was only a dream. But for Nan, it was exactly the opposite. She had no doubt that what was happening to her was real—because she'd dreamed that it would happen.

Nan recalls sitting on the edge of her bed that March day, watching her husband hurl his clothing into a suitcase. His anger intensified with every toss. Nan watched helplessly. The past few years of their marriage had been abusive. Afraid she would antagonize him further, she said nothing.

He slammed the dresser drawer shut. When he turned toward her, a sudden change came over his face. Slowly and deliberately, he moved toward the bedroom doors, locking first one, then the other. Next he moved to the windows and methodically locked each one. Nan watched as he disappeared inside their walk-in closet. When he emerged, he held a gun in one hand and a box of shells in the other.

"He looked directly at me, but his eyes were lifeless and cold. It was like he wasn't really in there."

Meticulously, he loaded each chamber. She could barely comprehend what was happening.

"With each dropping bullet, I measured what was left of my life. I felt the dream coming true. I knew my dream had been a warning from God."

Two weeks before, Nan had had a disturbing dream. "I dreamed my husband was angry with me and was pointing a gun at my midsection. In the dream, I was out of control, screaming hysterically. He yelled at me to shut up, but I continued screaming. Then I heard shots, clutched my stomach, and fell to the floor. I knew I was dying."

Incredibly, the dream was coming true. With the gun now fully loaded, he picked it up and aimed it at her.

"When he pointed the gun at me, I screamed hysterically, just like in the dream," said Nan. "When he shouted, 'Shut up!' I just froze. In my mind, I knew the outcome, so I started to silently pray, 'Please, Lord, I want to live. I want to see my children grow up. Please . . .'"

Nan knew she was out of time. She closed her eyes and prepared to die.

"It was then I heard an inner voice say, 'Tell him you love him.'"

It was an odd request, but one that Nan honored.

"I opened my eyes and said, 'I love you.' And I meant it.

I did care for him, although at that moment I also knew I would never live with him again."

His hand trembled, and she wasn't sure what would happen next. Then, as she watched, the hardness in his eyes softened, and he lowered the gun.

The immediate danger had passed—but the threat had not.

"It wasn't until later that I learned how close I'd come to dying. While lying next to me on the bed, he talked about the detailed plans he'd made to kill me. I truly believe the dream was a warning from God."

Later that weekend, Nan packed a few things for herself and the kids and left without his knowledge. She never went back.

Does God speak to us through our dreams?

Nan thinks so. She believes her dream was a warning.

Maybe it was also a rehearsal. Inside the safety of her dream, she did what came naturally—she screamed. She also saw what happened after that. Perhaps that preparation was what made her able to hear the voice of God during the actual traumatic event.

Does God do that?

Does he give us dreams to communicate things he wants us to know?

Is it possible that God speaks through our dreams the things we can't, or won't, hear during the day?

105.1 NOCTURNAL PROMPTINGS

It wasn't unusual for Kathy's young son to wake in the middle of the night with a bad dream or in need of some comfort until he could fall back asleep. He would stand at the foot of her bed and call out until she woke and he had her attention.

One night when Kathy heard her name called, she immediately sat up and looked toward the foot of her bed. She didn't see him in his usual spot. She blinked, and as her eyes focused, she looked around the moonlit room. No one was there.

"A prickle climbed the back of my neck when I realized the voice couldn't have been my son's. It called me, 'Kathy.' My son would have called me, 'Mom,'" said Kathy. She was fully awake by then. "I looked to the opposite side of the bed. My husband slept soundly, so I lay back down on my pillow."

Kathy knew someone had called her. Twice. But no one else was awake. She remembered the biblical story of Samuel.

Samuel was a young boy working for a priest named Eli. In the middle of the night, Samuel awoke when he heard his name called. He went to Eli to see what he wanted, but Eli hadn't called him, so Samuel went back to bed. This happened a second, and then a third time. On Samuel's third visit, Eli recognized that it was the Lord who was calling.

Eli instructed Samuel to go back and lie down, but if he heard his name called again, he was to say, "Speak, LORD, for your servant is listening." When Samuel did this, he heard the Lord speak, giving him a warning about what was to come.[1]

Lying in bed, Kathy thought it was worth a try. She silently prayed, *Speak, Lord, for your servant is listening.* She waited in the darkness for an answer, but sleep overcame her. That night she had a very vivid dream.

"In the dream, I spoke to a friend of mine as if I knew what was happening in her life. I was giving her words of wisdom that God had spoken to me. When I woke, I realized I had no idea what was happening in this woman's life. But because I remembered every word I'd said to her in the dream, I wondered if it might have some significance."

Kathy asked God, "Is this why you woke me up? So I would pay attention to the dream? Am I to tell her in real life what I told her in the dream?"

She immediately knew the answer, and it scared her. She was to tell the woman everything she heard. "What if I'm wrong?" asked Kathy. But she felt God urge her on.

"I called the woman. I told her that if the dream was only a dream, and I was wrong, to please forgive me. I relayed to her the same things I'd told her in my dream. There was a long silence. Did she think I was crazy? Was she going to hang up on me?"

Kathy waited.

Then from the other end of the line, a soft weeping broke the silence. The dream's message had meaning for the woman.

"When she told me her situation, it all made sense. I also understood that in order to reach out to one of his beloved children, a loving God had spoken to me in the darkness of my room, because my friend couldn't hear him through the darkness in her life," said Kathy.

Years later, surprisingly, neither Kathy nor the woman can remember the details of the woman's situation or of Kathy's dream. "She remembered that I'd called her," said Kathy, "but she couldn't remember what I'd told her. Maybe that's the point: what God spoke isn't as important as the way God chose to speak."

Through the dreams of someone else.

. . .

Jill woke suddenly in the middle of the night. The room was dark, and she was alone in bed. In her dream, she had seen a plane crash and burn, and then saw herself walking through the wreckage. Human bodies were buried in the debris. When she sat up and rubbed her eyes, she realized it was just a dream. But even awake, Jill was haunted by the images. Not knowing what else to do, she prayed.

Though her husband had been out of town for the past two days, Jill knew he was driving through the night and would be home in the morning. Feeling calmer, she pulled the covers up and went back to sleep.

It was still dark when Jill was awakened again, this time by her eight-year-old son, Matthew, shaking her arm.

"What's the matter, Matthew?"

"I had a bad dream."

Jill sat up and hugged him. Safe in his mother's arms, he told her the details.

"There was a man with a whitish robe and a long gray beard. He broke into our house. We chased him down the street, but I was scared."

With her husband not yet home, Jill rolled over and made room in the bed for Matthew.

"I had a scary dream too. Let's just give them to Jesus and go back to sleep." They both prayed, and then fell back to sleep for a few more hours.

That morning, as Jill stood in the kitchen making break-fast, she turned on the TV. The screen was filled with images from a breaking news story.

The date was September 11, 2001.

Are you kidding?

What was Jill supposed to do with that?

Unlike Kathy, who could give her friend the specific words of her dream, even if Jill and her son had realized their dreams' meaning, what could they have done? Could they have called the FAA and told them of their mutual nightmares? Or driven to the airport to see if they could find men with gray beards and white robes and make a citizen's arrest?

Did God really expect Jill and Matthew to stop the atroci-ties of 9/11? She was a Minnesota housewife with no aero-nautical or political connections. Matthew wasn't even a Boy Scout. And the Department of Homeland Security was not yet in existence.

No. Even if they'd understood the meaning behind their dreams, they would have been considered crazy. No one would have listened. Frankly, even after September 11, Jill is still hesitant to mention the dreams, because people are often skeptical.

So what's the point behind dreams like that?

What was God trying to say to Jill and her son through two such inexplicable dreams and their timing?

• • •

The church Wade Trimmer grew up in was so legalis-tic that by the time he was a teenager, he was over the whole religion thing. "I just kind of put my middle finger up, said, 'No, I don't think so,' and walked away from the church."

Years later, Wade returned. Although he became an all-out Christ follower, he would describe himself as a marginal church attender. "I am involved in the church, but I seem to stay on the margins of Western Christianity. This has given me room to look at things a little differently, because I am not so entrenched in the church's position."

Questions stuck with Wade for months as he asked God over and over to make things clear to him. One issue Wade struggled with was the purpose and the manifestation of the Holy Spirit. He wondered why churches seemed to recognize different levels of importance and different expressions of the same Spirit.

It was during this search for answers that Wade's wife woke him in the middle of the night. Before he was fully awake, she had gone back to sleep. He gently shook her until she awoke.

"What?" she said.

"Why did you wake me?" asked Wade.

"I didn't wake you. You woke me," she said, pulling the covers tighter.

"Before I could make sense of what happened and without thinking about it," Wade said, "I started praying for some woman I didn't know and had never heard of who lived in Connecticut. The woman had cancer. The details were that clear to me. And I was praying for her."

Wade thought he was crazy. He woke up his wife again and asked her if he was insane. "Have you seen anything in my life that makes you think I'm crazy? Because I feel crazy right now. I woke up and started praying for this woman in Connecticut who has cancer."

His wife assured him he wasn't losing it. "Maybe it's just the Holy Spirit," she said.

Over the next few days as he tried to process what happened to him, Wade began to think that this was an answer to his questions. Was this how the Holy Spirit worked?

"When someone needs prayer, maybe the Holy Spirit sends these messages out, and whoever receives them, receives them," said Wade, who never learned more about the woman he felt compelled to pray for. "Maybe this is how God engages us. He sends things down here, and whoever captures them, captures them, but he keeps talking and trying to engage us until we hear him."

If Wade is right, is that what happened to Jill and her son in the early morning hours of September 11?

Did the Holy Spirit prompt people to pray?

Were Jill and Matthew two people who responded?

105.2 GOD SPOT?

It's easy to dismiss our dreams as the manifestation of last night's pizza rather than the workings of the Holy Spirit. After all, who hasn't had a dream that didn't make sense or seemed to have no spiritual application? In fact, could it be that all our dreams are just some neurological misfire?

Experts say that our sleep consists of five separate stages. The first is a light sleep—we're easily awakened in this stage. In the second stage, we move to a somewhat deeper sleep. During these first two stages, our brain activity gradually slows down. Stages three and four represent our deepest sleep, at which time we experience our slowest brain waves—delta brain waves. Finally, about ninety minutes after we fall asleep, we begin the fifth stage, rapid eye movement or REM sleep. This stage is primarily characterized by eye movement that can be observed by watching the closed eyelids of the sleeping person. While we are in the REM stage, our heart rate and breathing increase, our blood pressure rises, and our body temperature is less controlled. Interestingly, our brain activity increases to the same level as when we are awake, yet our body is completely inactive, in essence, paralyzed.[2]

If the spiritually significant dreams we have could be explained, at least partially, as natural phenomena of our brain wiring, could any other—or even all—religious experiences be explained by natural causes?

Many scientists think so. They believe that all religious experiences, including dreams, are explainable as natural events that occur inside the brain. Jeffrey Saver and John Rabin argue that religious experiences are little more than delusions that actually originate from and are therefore created by the limbic system of the brain.[3]

In *The God Gene*, Dean Hamer identifies religious motivation and experience as artifacts of evolutionary advantage, and he explains religious affections as survival mechanisms.[4]

Scientist Michael Persinger even built a "God helmet" that stimulates portions of the brain, prompting the wearer to experience visions and other sensations of transcendence.[5]

In other words, these guys all believe that religious experience is a chemical or electrical reaction in the brain.

But not everyone agrees with these scientists. In their

book *The Spiritual Brain*, Canadian neuroscientist Mario Beauregard and his coauthor, Denyse O'Leary, present a scathing critique of the popular trends that try to explain religious mystical experiences as either electrical storms in the brain or artifacts of obsolete evolutionary accidents.[6] Citing their own research observing the brain patterns of Carmelite nuns as they recollect intense spiritual experiences, Beauregard and O'Leary debunk the idea that all religious feelings are organically explained.

For example, in separate studies using two different brain-scan technologies, groups of nuns were observed practicing a discipline called centering prayer. During this time, they were asked to recall their most intimate spiritual experiences. Both studies showed that the mere memory of a transcendent experience was enough to significantly change the nuns' brain activity. But, unlike the hypotheses of Hamer, Saver and Rabin, and Persinger, the spiritual brain activity was not limited to specific areas of the brain. Instead, the activity registered as that accompanying a whole-brain experience, using areas involved in processing perception, cognition, emotion, body representation, and self-consciousness.[7]

Beauregard and O'Leary concluded that there isn't one "God spot" located in the temporal lobe;[8] rather, they argue that the results suggest that mystical experiences are mediated by several regions and systems.[9]

These researchers go so far as to suggest that visions and other mystical events they observed are quite distinct from the brain activities observed during hallucinations, autosuggestion, or states of intense emotional arousal. They argue that their findings are *consistent with an actual experience* rather than with a delusion.[10]

In other words, when the nuns prayed, they weren't reacting to neurological firings. They were firing neurons when they prayed because they were reacting to something outside of themselves. Prayer wasn't coming from the inside out.

It was a response to something on the outside
that changed the inside . . .

105.3 Making an Appearance

What motivated Constantine's conversion to Christianity?

The year was AD 312, and Constantine was battling Maxentius for dominance in the Roman Empire. As the decisive battle grew near, Constantine saw something in the sky. Above the setting sun was a luminous cross bearing the words *By this sign, conquer!* The troops around him were awestruck, for they all saw the sign.

Though the details are disputed, most agree that the following night, Jesus appeared to Constantine in a dream. In the vision, Christ told him to make a likeness of the cross, and with the representation, to march on his enemies. At dawn, Constantine called his artisans, described to them what he had seen, and ordered them to make a standard bearing the image.

What they created became known as the labarum, a military standard bearing the Chi Rho—the first two letters of the word *Christ*. From the transverse bar of the standard hung a silk cloth, embroidered in gold and studded with precious stones. The cloth bore the images of Constantine and his two sons. At the peak of the cross hung a golden wreath surrounding the monogram: Christ.

Constantine defeated Maxentius and secured the empire

under his rule. He also declared Christianity the official religion of Rome. He played an important role in defining Christianity for future generations by clarifying who Jesus is and by pointing followers back to the Scriptures.

It seems that Christianity spread through the Roman Empire because of one man's dream.[11]

· · ·

For the past decade, the producers of the film series *More Than Dreams* have noticed a phenomenon occurring in the Muslim world. Here's how they describe it on their Web site:

> Men and women—without any knowledge of the gospel and without any contact with Christians— have been forever transformed after experiencing dreams and visions of Jesus Christ. Reports of these supernatural occurrences often come from "closed countries" where preaching the gospel is forbidden and where converting to Christianity can invoke the death sentence. A common denominator appears to be that the dreams come to those who are seeking to know and please God.[12]

The producers conducted numerous personal interviews and selected five true stories of former Muslims who now know Jesus as their Savior. Using high-definition video, they re-created these stories into a docudrama, producing each one in its original language so the stories can be used as a ministry tool in their country.*

---

* They also have a Web site: morethandreams.tv.

One of the stories featured on the site is of a man named Khalil.

Khalil began memorizing the Qur'an when he was young. He developed a love for the holy Scriptures. But Khalil became fanatical. He considered Christians his worst enemies, and he was involved in attacks on their churches and leaders.

Khalil joined an extremist group whose goal was to overthrow the government, and he was involved in several high-profile kidnappings. Eventually he got himself arrested, tortured, and imprisoned for two years. When he was released, he joined other radical Muslims until the local authorities discovered their plans. His group was forced to abandon their military options in favor of an intellectual battle.

Led by a man named Emir, the group decided to write a book proving Muhammad was the true prophet of God, and the Jewish and Christian Bible was a corrupted text. Khalil was chosen for the job. He objected, describing the research as the "most distasteful thing" he had ever done, but eventually he relented.

Khalil read the Bible and cross-referenced what he read with numerous Islamic books. His research surprised him. It showed the Bible was neither inaccurate nor corrupted. The Bible's teaching on forgiveness and unconditional love, especially as demonstrated through the life of Jesus, surprised him too. And he was stunned to realize that Jesus had warned his followers two thousand years ago that they would be persecuted.

Khalil realized he was now the one doing the persecuting. He began to understand why Christians didn't retaliate against the Muslims and why they chose to forgive. Though he hated reading the Bible, he fell in love with its message.

As he continued his research, he noticed a striking similarity between the attributes of God as listed in the Qur'an and the attributes of Jesus. Khalil began to have serious doubts. He had always loved Islam, but for the first time, he began to question whether Muhammad was the only way to God.

Eventually, Khalil showed all his documentation to his leader, Emir. As far as Emir was concerned, Khalil was now an infidel. He promised Khalil that he would kill him if he shared any of his heretical ideas with any other Muslim.

But Khalil wanted to learn more. He decided he would join a Christian church, but as a notorious Muslim zealot, no one would believe his interest. Christians, even pastors of local churches, refused to meet with him.

This caused Khalil to have more questions and eventually to doubt his own research. Maybe Christ wasn't the answer, after all.

Days later, Khalil stood making a phone call in a café when his attaché was stolen. Not only was his identity card inside, but also his research papers and his Bible. Everything he had written would be considered blasphemous. His life was in jeopardy.

Khalil returned home tormented. He began to repent for all he had done. Believing he was being punished by God for thinking that the Qur'an wasn't the Word of God and that Muhammad was not his prophet, Khalil repented.

He pulled out his rug to pray. But when he tried to kneel, he couldn't bend his knees or open his mouth to say one word of the Qur'an.

Broken, he sat down and said, "God, you know that I love you, and I know that you want me on the right path. God, I can't resist anymore. All that I did, I did trying to please you. Please pull me out of this darkness."

When Khalil slept that night, he had a dream. In the dream, a man came to him and said he was the one for whom Khalil had been searching, but Khalil didn't recognize the man. The man told him to look in the Book (the Bible). In his dream, Khalil explained that the Book and his papers were lost. The man replied, "The Book never gets lost. Get up and open your closet, and you will find it."

Khalil woke up and went to his closet. In it he found his copy of the Bible on a shelf.

He knew at that moment that the man in his dream was Jesus. Right then, he went to his mother's room and begged her forgiveness for how badly he had treated his family. The next morning, Khalil continued to ask for forgiveness from friends and strangers. He even begged for the forgiveness of Christian business owners whom he had robbed or mistreated.

Over the next few months, he grew in his new faith, eventually winning the trust of local believers. He found a church fellowship and was baptized. Even now, Khalil receives physical attacks and threats against his life, but he gladly endures them for the One who gave everything for him.

It's not hard to accept that God spoke through dreams to ancient people in the Bible, but it's much harder to accept a story like Khalil's, at least it is until you consider the fact that it bears much resemblance to a vision that appeared to another Middle Eastern man who also considered Christians his enemies. His experience isn't recorded on the same Web site as Khalil's; his story is recorded in the New Testament. There are many similarities between Khalil's encounter and that of Saul (who was later renamed Paul).

Maybe dreams and visions aren't just for ancient Bible characters.

105.4 BIBLICAL Dreamers

The Bible is filled with stories of people who experienced God-prompted dreams. Sometimes they even happen when the receiver is awake. Whether dreams or visions, the Bible is clear that they are from God.

Elihu describes it this way in the book named after his friend Job:

> For God speaks again and again, though people do not recognize it. He speaks in dreams, in visions of the night, when deep sleep falls on people as they lie in their beds. He whispers in their ears and terrifies them with warnings. He makes them turn from doing wrong; he keeps them from pride. He protects them from the grave, from crossing over the river of death.[13]

Though many consider Elihu a less-than-reliable source (due to some bad advice he gave Job), the Bible confirms what he said. There are countless stories of God speaking to his people through dreams and visions. Here are a few:

> Abraham had fallen into a deep sleep when a terrifying darkness covered him. Then he heard the Lord make a promise that Abraham's descendants would

be strangers in a foreign land and oppressed as slaves for four hundred years.[14]

Jacob dreamed that he looked into heaven and heard God say that he was the heir of his grandfather Abraham's covenant blessing. He was so overwhelmed by this experience that when he woke, he set up a memorial as an act of worship and gratitude.[15]

When God appeared to King Solomon in a dream, God told him to ask for what he wanted and it would be granted. Solomon asked for wisdom; he got that and much more, including great wealth and fame.[16]

And these experiences aren't limited to the Old Testament:

Matthew's account of Jesus' birth is peppered with significant dream encounters: Mary's miraculous pregnancy was confirmed to her future husband, Joseph, in a dream; the magi who traveled from a distant land to offer homage to Jesus were warned in a dream to avoid returning to Herod in Jerusalem; then Joseph received another dream warning him to flee to Egypt to save the new baby from Herod's wrath. And of course the whole thing started when Mary had a vision from an angel of God.[17]

Peter had a startling vision during an afternoon rest on the rooftop of the home where he was staying. In the vision, Peter saw animals lowered in a sheet from heaven. He heard a voice say, "Kill and eat them." Because Peter was an observant Jew and

didn't eat unclean animals, he refused. Then a voice
said, "Do not call something unclean if God has
made it clean."[18]

In addition to his Damascus Road experience,
Paul had other visions. One night while he was
traveling through Turkey, he had a vision of a man
from Macedonia, asking him to come and share
the message of Jesus with his people. Paul took
this as a message from God to move his ministry
westward.[19]

These experiences weren't limited to the spiritual elite. You
didn't have to have the title *apostle* or *prophet* to see or hear
God in a dream or vision.

On the Day of Pentecost (the day the Holy Spirit was let
loose), Peter stood up and quoted from the prophet Joel:

"In the last days," God says, "I will pour out my
Spirit upon all people. Your sons and daughters will
prophesy. Your young men will see visions, and your
old men will dream dreams."[20]

According to Peter, this promise—made hundreds of years
earlier—was fulfilled. From that point forward, God spoke
directly to men and women. Young and old. Rich and poor.

That covers you.

But let's be honest. It's not too difficult to think of someone having a dream that somehow seems spiritually relevant, but it's a whole *other thing* when someone says they
heard an audible voice or saw a vision of God while they
were awake.

And sober.

What would you say if someone claimed to have heard God's voice—out loud? Or felt his touch—physically?

105.5 In Person

Jennifer's son, Jordan, was four and sitting in front of the television, mesmerized by a cartoon. When she walked in, his concentration broke. "Did you call me?" he asked.

"No, I just came in to do the laundry."

"Did you call my name when I was in the shower?"

"No, I didn't say anything," Jennifer said as she picked up the laundry basket.

"Oh. Then it was God."

"What was God, honey?"

"When I was in the shower, somebody said 'Jordan, Jordan,' and it sounded like God."

Now he had Jennifer's full attention. She set the laundry down and looked him in the eye to see if he was playing some kind of trick. "What does he sound like?"

"He has a deep voice."

"Could it have been the thunder? There's a storm outside."

"Nope, it was God," he said confidently, his faith unshakable. "Besides, God doesn't sound like thunder."

He was sure he had heard God's voice.

Jennifer got nervous. *What did this mean?*

"Did he say anything else?"

"Nope, just 'Jordan, Jordan.'" With that, Jordan ended the conversation and returned to his cartoons.

Jennifer fidgeted with the laundry and tried to convince herself that he had heard the thunder, the TV, or even some sort of storm-related power surge. As she talked herself into other possibilities, it occurred to her that Jordan really had heard from God. Was she trying to shake his faith because hers wasn't strong enough to believe it?

Jennifer later said, "I realized I was trying to share my doubts. If God had spoken to him in the shower and Jordan believed it to be so, who was I to persuade him differently?"

. . .

Tyler was four, and Ryan was at the crawling stage when Trixie and her husband took the kids to visit their grand-parents. Though her mother-in-law kept an immaculate house, Trixie still scanned the area where the kids would be playing. She knew that Ryan's newfound mobility made even the most common household items hazardous. Tyler loved to play with his baby brother, but he was too young to be expected to keep Ryan out of trouble.

Before moving to the adjoining kitchen, Trixie made sure the door to the basement was securely closed. The stairs were steep, and she didn't want Ryan falling or Tyler running off downstairs.

Trixie was in the kitchen only a few minutes when she heard her older son's terrified scream. She looked toward the hall and saw why Tyler was screaming—Ryan was about to fall down the basement steps. The only thing that stopped him was Tyler's chubby little fingers grasping his ankles.

Though it was only a few feet, it felt like a mile as Trixie crossed the kitchen to get to the boys. She scooped them up and slammed the door, her heart racing as she thought about what could have happened.

"Is that man Jesus?" asked Tyler, who seemed puzzled by his mom's behavior.

"What man? Who are you talking about?"

"That man who was standing at the top of the stairs so Ryan didn't fall," said Tyler.

Tyler saw someone his mother hadn't. He saw Jesus keeping his brother safe, protecting him from a fall.

As adults, we're quick to think that this kind of thing can happen figuratively. "Yes, Jesus was with me," we say, meaning that we had a sense of comfort or peace during a difficult time. But we rarely believe it literally. "No, *really*, Jesus was standing at the top of the basement steps."

So how do we explain Jordan hearing God in the shower or Tyler seeing Jesus save his little brother?

The easiest explanation is that it didn't happen.

These were just kids, after all. It's pretty easy to explain away.

But what if something similar happened to an adult?

What if something like this happened to you?

Would you believe it?

. . .

Kim climbed into her dorm-room bed feeling like she needed a hug, but no one was there to give her one. A freshman in college, she was away from her family, wasn't getting along with her roommate, and had just broken up with her boyfriend. Finals were nearing, and school bills were due. She wasn't prepared for either. She felt completely alone.

Kim was in that drowsy state in which you're not quite awake, but you're definitely not asleep. Though she remained in bed, she remembers the sensation of being lifted and given a long, strong, bear hug that calmed her down. "I didn't open my eyes, not because I was scared, but because it felt so good. It was the kind of hug you get from a dad who makes it all better."

. . .

Betsy was pregnant with twins, and she wouldn't be able to carry them to term. The twins were sick (one twin was actually sharing the other twin's blood), and the in utero surgery to correct it had caused an infection. Betsy's temperature was 104.7, her uterus was contracting, and the doctors warned that if they didn't take the babies soon, she would die too. Betsy fought for more time. Or a different diagnosis. Anything for the outcome that would save the three of them. But the sicker she got, the more sure she became that she had to deliver the twins. She also knew that at twenty-four weeks, they wouldn't be viable. Betsy explains what happened next:

> At that moment, something came over me. There was a presence in the room, as if there was a hand on my soul and I heard, "It's going to be okay." I believe that God physically touched my body that day. It was a feeling I had never felt before and haven't since. I'd recognized his presence in my life, but had never known his touch until that moment.

Though losing her twins was indescribably painful, somehow God's touch helped to make it bearable for Betsy.

• • •

So, a couple of kids, a lonely college student, and a woman about to give birth to stillborn twins all *hear*, *see*, or *feel* God.

Perhaps they were confused.

Or were they needy, and they made something out of nothing to soothe their fears?

What you believe about it is up to you.

You can explain it away. That would be easy to do, considering each of their circumstances and heightened sense of emotion.

But what if their situations weren't so emotional?

Or if they weren't so dependent or needy?

Would that change the way you viewed their experiences?

What would you do if your coworker, a responsible, sane, contributing member of the office, came to you and said he knew your secret? And that it was God who told him?

105.6 Heavenly Business

"Shut the door, Mike," Charles said. His face was flushed and tense. He motioned for Mike to sit down opposite him. "Mike, I can't say much, but I want to ask you to pray this weekend. Our company is facing a grave challenge. It's very serious, and it will mean major changes. I just wanted to warn you."

Mike knew not to ask more. He and Charles had been friends for years, long before they each had joined this start-up company. It had been an exciting, exhausting ride, and until that moment, Mike had had every reason to believe they were not only going to survive, but thrive. He also knew Charles, and he knew Charles wouldn't say more.

As he walked to his car that Friday, Mike wondered if he'd have a job on Monday. He found himself feeling anxious and more than a bit angry with God. He and his wife had been certain that this opportunity was God's provision. Why this? Why now?

Mike was a praying man. Early in his adult life, he had developed disciplines that enabled him to pause throughout his day and hear clear and practical messages from God. Sometimes he heard things inside his soul. Sometimes he saw visions. So, later that weekend, he paused and asked God, "What's going on here?"

God quickly and tenderly responded that Edward, the founder of the company, had gotten a bad report from his doctor. That information wasn't enough for Mike, who feared not only for his own job but also for Edward's life. "Is there more?" he asked God.

Then Mike began to hear God speak through images and words—a vision. He saw a doctor's office. In the room sat Edward and his wife, Jane. He heard the doctor speaking to Edward.

"We have bad news, Edward. You have an especially aggressive form of lung cancer. Most people with this diagnosis die within three months. I'm sorry."

Mike was shocked. But the vision continued. The doctor gave specific details about the disease. Then God spoke directly to Mike, telling him five specific things he was to pass on to Edward, including a specific prayer pattern, information about his relationships, and comforting words for some of Edward's specific concerns. But sadly, what was absent from the vision was a promise of healing. In fact, Mike knew that Edward was going to die.

Sounds a bit like the television drama *Eli Stone*, in which Eli, the lead character, can't decide whether the visions he sees are because he is some kind of a prophet or if he's hallucinating as a result of a brain tumor.

But Mike didn't have a brain tumor. He just wasn't sure what he was supposed to do with what he saw. So he asked, "What am I supposed to do with this?"

The Lord clearly told him to go to work on Monday and share it with both Edward and Charles.

Mike's mouth went dry. How could he? What if this was all wrong? Much of it was personal. How does one start a conversation like that?

But it was clear.

Mike arrived at work early on Monday and waited nervously for Charles. When he arrived, Mike immediately recognized the same gray pall of anxiety he'd seen on Friday. The voice urged him on.

"We need to talk," Mike said as he followed Charles into his office.

"I know about Edward's diagnosis," Mike began.

Charles dropped his briefcase on the desk and stared.

"There is no way you could know that," he said. "He's told no one."

Mike told Charles what he saw in the vision.

Charles had no words. Everything, down to the minute details of the diagnosis, was exactly correct.

Charles then turned and dialed Edward's cell phone. "Ed, this is Charles. You've got to see Mike right away. He knows everything. And I didn't tell him. God did."

When Edward arrived, he summoned Mike into his office, and Mike repeated what he'd told Charles, including the actions the company should take and the prayer strategy Edward should follow.

Edward sat motionless and said nothing for some time. "Okay," he finally said.

Several months later, Mike awoke suddenly from a sound sleep. He looked at the clock. It was midnight. He had an overwhelming sense that he should pray for Edward. He lay in bed and quietly interceded for his friend and employer. As he prayed, another vision opened to him. He saw himself in a heaven-like place, and then Edward entered his vision for a moment. Edward looked surprised to see Mike there. Then Edward turned and was lost in the bliss.

As his vision faded, Mike knew what had happened. He got up from bed, went downstairs, and typed an e-mail to Edward's daughter. The e-mail said, "I'm so sorry to hear of the passing of your father. He was dearly loved. And now he is with Jesus." Then he sent the note. It was shortly after midnight. Later, Mike discovered that the time recorded on his e-mail was just moments after the time listed on Edward's official certificate of death.

It's one thing to have a strange dream in the middle of the night—but is it possible for God to give us visions, too?

Could it be there is something about the end of a life that helps us to hear God in ways that we otherwise don't?

105.7 IT'S GOING TO BE OKAY

Nicki was a typical kindergartner, except for one thing: She was obsessed with death. And not just the general concept of death, but with thoughts of her own death. Nicki was terrified that she was going to die soon.

Mrs. Knight, the headmistress of Nicki's school, had spent decades in education, but this was the first time she had seen a young child so troubled by thoughts of death. Nicki's brother, Cole, was in the second grade, and though he was shy, he never seemed to express any fear. As Nicki's anxiety increased in frequency and duration, Mrs. Knight didn't know what to do.

She spoke with Nicki's parents, and together they decided the best thing to do was remind Nicki that Jesus was looking out for her. So each time Nicki came to Mrs. Knight's office, Mrs. Knight hugged her and said, "Jesus is with you, honey. You're not going to die, I promise." Her words seemed to help. Nicki wore a special cross necklace given to her by her mother, and when she was really troubled, she would finger it. It seemed to help her gain control over her thoughts. Eventually, she returned to class, and Mrs. Knight returned to her paperwork.

With the responsibility of caring for hundreds of elementary students each day, Mrs. Knight was the model of self-control. But she lost her usual control the Saturday she learned that Cole and Nicki had been in a car accident. Their car was hit by a drunk driver. Cole survived, but Nicki died instantly.

After getting the tragic news alone in her kitchen, Mrs. Knight cried and screamed, and, from what she vaguely remembers, even threw something. What could she have done to prevent this? Did Nicki somehow know this would happen? Why hadn't she paid more attention to the girl's fears? Why didn't she protect her? Why didn't *Jesus* protect her?

She took a deep breath and tried to reassure herself that her thoughts were irrational. But what she couldn't be assured of was that Nicki was okay. Before she calmed down, she screamed one last prayer, "God, just let me know she's okay!"

Mrs. Knight pulled herself together before school on Monday. She had to break the news to the staff, the students in Nicki's class, and all the parents. Mrs. Knight's school was more than just an educational facility; it was a living, breathing family of connected people. She knew she had to choose her words carefully.

With her typical restraint, she was able to notify everyone and put a plan in place to allow teachers and others to attend the memorial service. But what she didn't plan on was the parade of parents who found their way into her office for the next few days. Was it her imagination, or were they all asking the same question? It seemed that each parent wanted to know if Nicki was okay.

Though Mrs. Knight intellectually accepted the tenets of her Christian faith that said Nicki was now in heaven, emotionally she was uncertain. While she tried to reassure parents and teachers that Nicki was in a better place, she found herself with more questions than answers.

The Catholic church was packed at the memorial service. Some quietly wiped their eyes, some sat stoically, others cried with heaving sobs. Mrs. Knight tried to get control of herself. After all, that was her responsibility. She had to be the leader that everyone had come to depend on. Maybe that's why she was so disturbed when she saw Nicki.

"Nicki was just hovering around the priest the whole time he spoke," said Mrs. Knight. "She floated over one shoulder and then the other. I thought I was crazy. No one else seemed to see her. But, I promise you, she was there."

Note that Mrs. Knight didn't say she saw a vision or an image. She saw *Nicki*.

Yes, she knew it was a strange thing to say. But she said she saw Nicki as clearly as she saw the people sitting next to her in the pew. Nicki stayed through the whole service. When it ended, Nicki was gone. Was this God's way of saying that Nicki was okay?

Mrs. Knight couldn't restrain herself. She wept.

A long line of people wanting to pay their respects to Nicki's parents had formed. Mrs. Knight got in line and knew she had to get ahold of herself before she got to the front. She blotted her eyes as the line snaked past a picture of Nicki. It was this year's school picture. Nicki's head was cocked to the side, and the cross at her neck was revealed.

Oh, God, is she okay? Mrs. Knight prayed silently through her tears.

As she made her way to the front, Mrs. Knight noticed how brave Nicki's parents were. They smiled and greeted everyone, thanking them for their sympathy. Cole, who was painfully shy, stood behind his mother, holding on to her leg, staring at the floor.

What could she say to bring this grieving family comfort?

Mrs. Knight wiped her eyes and took a deep breath as the person in front of her reached the front of the line and hugged Nicki's mom.

At that moment, Cole stepped out from behind his mother, looked up at Mrs. Knight, cocked his head just like

Nicki's picture, and said, "In case you want to know, I'm okay." Immediately, he went back to his former position behind his mother, put his arm around her leg, and looked back at the floor.

Mrs. Knight was so astonished she can't remember what she said to the parents. But she knew God had answered her question with a vision and then confirmed it.

Nicki was okay.

105.8 IT'S UP FOR INTERPRETATION

"God can speak in English, of course. But it doesn't seem to be his first choice," said Kristi Graner, a pastor at Hosanna!, an evangelical Lutheran church in Lakeville, Minnesota. "Most of the time his language seems to be pictorial, in dreams and visual impressions."

She should know.

Kristi's team hangs out at a Christian coffee shop in Dinkytown, near the University of Minnesota. Twice a month, somewhere between six to twelve trained people join together for the same mission.

Biblical dream interpretation.

"We come here and put up a sign offering to interpret dreams. People just come," said Kristi. "It's amazing what God does in the process. We just want to affirm that God has great plans for these young people. Occasionally, Christians think we're doing something New Age, and they have a problem with it. But the students down here also think it's New Age, so for them it's totally acceptable. When we tell them that God can give dreams and can speak through them, they are really open."

Several team members sit in the background and pray

through the evening while two or three actively engage students in biblical dream interpretation.

One night, Kristi met a frat student selling hot dogs as a fund-raiser. "We're learning to interpret dreams," Kristi said. "We'll buy a hot dog if you let us interpret a dream for you."

The young man shrugged. "Sure," he said.

He had a recurring dream that had been bothering him. In his dream, he was at a stadium for a big event. But he was always in the wrong seat. Because of this, everything went wrong.

"God has a perfect place for you," Kristi said. "And your life is intended to be significant. It's a big event." As she continued, she felt God prompting her to say, "But you are making choices that keep you from your destiny. As long as you continue to make these choices, you won't be in your sweet spot in life."

The young man turned pale. "It's true," he said.

The dream was God speaking, but Kristi's clarification gave the dream a meaningful translation. She simply confirmed what the guy already knew, the same thing God had prompted him on earlier.

Another night, a young man who was obviously drunk came to their table for a dream interpretation. Since childhood, he'd dreamed that he was driving his father's tractor very fast through a farm field. Up ahead was a big fence. As he approached it, he didn't know whether to plow through or to turn and avoid it. He was always aware that his father wasn't there to help him find the answer.

Kristi spoke, "The tractor is your life. It's powerful. Your destiny is powerful. But you don't know how to leverage your potential. You don't have direction. And you don't have anyone to help you know which way to turn. God wants you to know that he is your true Father, and he knows how to drive your tractor. He has a direction, and he's close enough to tell you, if you'll come close to him to listen."

The young man sat and listened. He was instantly sober and coherent. He took her counsel, considered it, and then sincerely thanked her before he walked away.

"We're just one link in a chain of what God is doing with these kids," Kristi said. "He's been working on them before we get here through their dreams. He's working while we talk with them. And he'll be working on them after they leave us. We won't always see the outcome, but we know we're helping the seeds to grow."

To many, this would seem weird or "out there." But it wouldn't to Joseph.

Like Kristi, Joseph had the gift of dream interpretation. In fact, his ability is what got him out of prison and landed him a cushy government job. But his gift also alienated him from his family and almost got him killed when his brothers didn't believe that God spoke through his dreams.

You can learn more about the fascinating details of Joseph's life in Andrew Lloyd Webber's musical about the boy and his outer garment, *Joseph and the Amazing Technicolor Dreamcoat.*[21] Or you can read directly from Webber's source material—the last chapters of Genesis.

If you're someone who knows the Bible so well you can quote it, you might be thinking of Genesis 40:8 right now. In this verse, two men have just said to Joseph that they had dreams but that no one seems to be able to help them figure out the meaning. "Interpreting dreams is God's business," Joseph replies.

This clearly seems to suggest that we should stay away from dream interpretation, but the next words out of Joseph's mouth are, "Go ahead and tell me your dreams." Then Joseph hears their dreams and provides them with the meaning.

Huh?

First, Joe says it's God's business. Then he makes it his business.

Confusing, isn't it?

Maybe it's cleared up in the next chapter. In Genesis 41:15, Joseph is asked if he will interpret Pharaoh's dreams, and Joseph replies in the next verse, "It is beyond my power to do this. But God can tell you what it means and set you at ease." And once again, Joseph interprets the dreams.

Isn't it odd that Joseph keeps contradicting himself? On the one hand, he keeps saying it's God's work. On the other hand, he does the work himself.

That doesn't make sense . . .

unless . . .

Joseph is doing God's work.

Maybe Joseph is saying that even though he appears to be the one interpreting dreams, he's not doing it in his own power. *God* is doing the work through him.

Joseph is admitting that when it comes to dream interpretation, he doesn't have superpowers; he has *supernatural* powers.

In an earlier chapter, we said it was not the speaker but the listener who chooses to believe that God is speaking. Likewise, the dreamer, not the interpreter, decides whether he or she believes a dream has real meaning.

"There are counterfeit spiritual uses of dreams, which

may incite fear in Christians about God's use of dreams," says Kristi, reminding us that Christians must make certain that dream interpretation is rooted in Scripture. Dream interpretation doesn't come with a degree from the psychic institute, but rather with guidance from the Holy Spirit.

"It is certainly true that Christians need to be careful to avoid ungodly uses of dreams," said Kristi, "but we also have to be careful not to ignore a clear method that our Creator God uses to communicate with the people he created."

105.9 FOOTNOTES

As responsible guides on your listening journey, it is only fair for us to admit that one of us had some doubts about all this. When we started writing this chapter, Jennifer wasn't convinced that God spoke through dreams. Sure, the Bible says he does, but that was to biblical characters. And yes, some of the stories in this chapter make you think. But because Jennifer hadn't experienced God speaking through her dreams, she wasn't sure she believed it was a way that God spoke *to her*.

Then one night she had a dream.

Jennifer has known the Sprague family since she moved into their neighborhood fifteen years ago. Erin and Lacey, now in college, babysat for Jennifer's son. Their mother, Mary Anne, had helped Jennifer lead extracurricular activities at school. The families often traded favors, bringing in mail while the other was on vacation or providing rides when a car was in the repair shop. Though they hadn't seen each other in months, Jennifer and Mary Anne had recently exchanged e-mails about getting together for lunch. But Mary Anne's days were filled with work and visiting her daughters at college, and Jennifer was busy writing this book.

Not long after finishing the initial draft of this chapter, Jennifer dreamed that something had happened to Mary Anne's daughter. In the dream, Jennifer was washing Mary Anne's feet because she felt so bad for what had happened.

The next morning, Jennifer recalled the dream and laughed it off. Next time she went to lunch with Mary Anne, she'd tell her about the dream, and they'd share a good laugh.

Then Jennifer thought of this chapter.

Could God be speaking through her dreams?

"Okay, God, if you're speaking to me through my dream, what are you trying to say?" asked Jennifer.

Immediately, Jennifer had the impression that she was to serve Mary Anne.

Serve Mary Anne?

What did that mean? Next time Mary Anne was on vacation, she should also mow the lawn? Jennifer quickly dismissed the thought.

A few days later, Jennifer received a call from Mary Anne, but it wasn't to make their lunch date. Mary Anne's husband, Tom, had been rushed to the hospital with symptoms of a stroke. Mary Anne called to tell Jennifer that Tom was in a coma, and the outcome was uncertain.

"Should I come to the hospital?" Jennifer asked.

"There's nothing you can do here. I'll call you if anything changes," said Mary Anne.

Jennifer agreed and hung up the phone.

She then recalled her dream, only this time the sorrow and sadness she felt in her dream was real. She pictured herself washing Mary Anne's feet, and once again God seemed to be saying, "Serve her."

So Jennifer went to the hospital. And over the next five or six days, Jennifer stayed with Mary Anne as they prayed for Tom to come out of his coma, for his brain function to return, for the surgery that would remove the life-threatening tumor that had caused the symptoms, and for test results that wouldn't include the word *cancer*. Jennifer recalls the time she spent with her friends:

> It was amazing to stand next to that family as they struggled through the ups and downs of Tom's cancer diagnosis. I was humbled and honored to see them work through that devastating blow, and yet they kept their faith and their sense of humor. It changed me. Yet, I almost didn't go to the hospital. Without the dream, I would have assumed the family wouldn't want me there, or that I'd be in the way. If I had not had the dream, and had not at least for a second believed that God could use it to speak to me, I would have missed out on being a part of this incredible faith-building experience.

God speaks through dreams and visions.

And now, even Jennifer is sure.

Dreams and visions are often hard to believe. Scary. Energizing. Confusing. Amazing. And sometimes downright freaky.

But regardless of how or why they come, they seem to suggest an action on our part.

Perhaps like Jill and her son Matthew who had the 9/11

dreams, God wants us to pray even though there isn't anything we can do about it.

Perhaps like Wade, we need to pray even if it seems crazy.

Maybe we're to pass a message on, like Kathy.

Could it be that we're to learn something new when our own ways don't work out—like Nan, whose life was saved by her dream?

Joseph said that dream interpretation was God's business.

Then Joseph interpreted dreams.

Could it be that this is what we're supposed to do also?

Maybe we're not called to interpret dreams like Kristi and her team, but we must be open to the idea that communicating through our dreams is something God can and does do.

Dreams aren't some optional accessory to our life experience. They are a natural part of who we are and who God created us to be. It seems clear that when God speaks through this channel, he doesn't want us to hit the snooze button. He wants us to get up.

Our dreams can be a call to action.

And when God calls, he awaits our response.

At those times, we must be like Joseph and make God's business *our* business.

CHANNEL 106.0
THE NATURE CHANNEL

IN 1869 JOHN MUIR, founder of the Sierra Club, and one of America's first conservationists, spent the summer traversing the rugged granite passes of California's Sierra Nevada mountains. In late August, Muir came to Upper Tuolumne basin, home to a cluster of majestic, heaven-reaching granite spires that form the great Cathedral Peak. A bit of a spiritual free spirit, Muir recorded the moment in his journal:

> It is a majestic temple of one stone, hewn from the living rock, and adorned with spires and pinnacles in regular cathedral style. The dwarf pines on the roof look like mosses. I hope some time to climb to it to say my prayers and hear the stone sermons.[1]

Most of us would just see rocks and trees, but John Muir saw a cathedral. He wanted to climb the mountain, but not for the physical challenge of conquering it and getting a T-shirt to prove he did. He wanted to climb it for spiritual reasons. His desire was to experience God through nature, to say his prayers, and to listen to God speak through the rocks.

That's remarkably similar to a verse in the Gospel of Luke. During the Triumphal Entry, the disciples are praising Jesus, bursting out in song, and dancing about. Then the Pharisees turn to Jesus and say, "Tell them to shut up!"

"I tell you," he replied, "if they keep quiet, the stones will cry out."[2]

If the disciples stopped praising Jesus, would the stones cry out?

Can stones speak?

Rocks reveal?

Boulders babble?

If so, what do they say? John Muir believed they were issuing an invitation to a holy church.

> No feature, however, of all the noble landscape as seen from here seems more wonderful than the Cathedral itself, a temple displaying Nature's best masonry and sermons in stones. How often I have gazed at it from the tops of hills and ridges, and through openings in the forests on my many short excursions, devoutly wondering, admiring, longing! This I may say is the first time I have been at church in California, led here at last, every door graciously opened for the poor lonely worshiper.[3]

Muir described this bulge on the earth's surface as a place that beckoned him—a place he pondered, admired, and longed for. He recognized it as a church—nature's church—a place for a lonely worshiper to enter.

Come in.

Sit down.

Pray and listen.

When he listened, did he hear rocks cry out with a language we can't speak but only hear? A language we can't study but only experience?

Perhaps in this natural church God's sermon is subtle.

106.1 BEING THERE

Though it may seem obvious that God speaks through grand vistas, there are other ways he speaks through nature. Rather than coming from the outside in, could it be God uses nature to call forth something from *inside of us*? Maybe he communicates not only through the actual physical environment, but also through the thoughts and feelings that bubble up as we try to make sense of all we see.

Maybe during creation,

our creation,

he planted seeds in our souls that suddenly, in response to nature's call, burst forth from their pods.

When we stand in a meadow exploding with wildflowers, before an endless ocean, or on top of a mountain, could this be God's reminder of *what* he's made and *that he made it for us*?

He could have placed us into a two-dimensional, black-and-white world. We could be living in pen-and-ink drawings. Instead, we live in three-dimensional oil paintings of color, light and dark, texture and brushstroke, lines and shading. In this multicolored, multitextured world, we're more than cardboard cutouts. We're made of flesh: worn, leathery skin hanging from an old man's face, tiny fingernails on a newborn baby's pudgy hands, and the wet tongue of a toddler tasting ice cream for the first time. When we look around, we do more than appreciate the view; we marvel that we're a part of it.

Nature expands our understanding of who God is and what he can do. But it can also expand our view of ourselves. Separate and set apart from the rest of creation, humans not only have the ability to *observe* God's creation; we have an ability to *appreciate* its beauty.

Ordinary people can have extraordinary religious experiences when God's creation calls to them. Curtis felt that sense of excitement and wonder in Vail, Colorado. After riding an enclosed tram to the top of Eagle's Nest, he stepped out and was awed by the panoramic view of the Rockies.

> Every time I see this magnificent view, I think, *Why does this impress me?* There is an awe about that perspective. I'm closer to the heavens than ever, and in a miniscule way, I get closer to what God's view looks like. I gain a sense of his majesty. I'm not sure what makes me appreciate this magnificence, but I can tell you I've never seen an elk standing up there saying, "How cool is *this*?" nor any other breathing mammal I know of that looks at the same view and says, "Wow!"

Not only do we have the ability to recognize the divine fingerprints in nature, but as Curtis described, we have a *need* to stop and appreciate it. From somewhere deep inside us, we are compelled to respond to nature, to pet the dog, to admire the view, or to taste the fruit from a tree.

Those expressions help us to know and hear God in different ways.

Irenaeus of Lyons said, "The initial step for a soul to come to knowledge of God is contemplation of nature."[4]

Contemplating butterflies, seaweed, and tree rot helps us to know God?

Can't that kind of knowledge be bought in a gift shop?

106.2 WHAT'S THE MESSAGE?

Have you ever seen the "Footprints in the Sand" plaque?

If you've ever visited a tacky gift shop, you have. The poem reveals the lament of the narrator that there was only one set of footprints on the beach during the most difficult time of his life—the implication being that God had left him alone. But God responds by saying, "That's when I carried you."

Hmm. Is that how God uses nature to communicate his message?

How about this one—after ruminating on the meaning behind a random seashell, an anonymous writer penned a poem that he or she thought summarized the religious meaning found in oceanside debris. There are three or four versions of "Legend of the Sand Dollar" floating around on the Internet. Here is the shortest one:

> Upon this odd-shaped seashell a legend grand
> is told,
>   about the life of Jesus, that wondrous tale of old.
>   At its center you will see, there seems to be a star,

> *like the one that led the shepherds and wise men*
> *from afar.*
> *Around its surface are the marks of nails and*
> *thorns and spear,*
> *suffered by Christ upon the cross; the wounds*
> *show plainly here.*
> *But there is also an Easter lily, clear for us to see,*
> *the symbol of Christ's resurrection for all eternity.*[5]

Is this how God uses nature?

Does he create seashells with the entire gospel message metaphorically imprinted and lying in wait for an inspired poet to share the tale of the shell?

Maybe the sand dollar is a backup plan for those who missed the meaning behind the footprints in the sand. If so, why didn't God make it easier for those of us who are a little dull, by just engraving on it the contents of John 3:16 in 12-point Times New Roman?

Though it appears that God *can* speak through nature in profound ways, are there times we just read too much into it?

106.3 CaLL TO OrDer

Like many other first-time expectant mothers, Heidi Murkoff picked up several books to learn about the changes her body and her baby would experience during the next nine months. But the books Heidi read raised more questions than they answered, so she decided to write her own.

Teaming up with medical writers Arlene Eisenberg and Sandee Hathaway, Heidi wrote *What to Expect When You're Expecting*. Today it is often referred to as the pregnancy bible, with almost fourteen million copies in print.

USA Today claims that 93 percent of all expectant mothers who read books on pregnancy read Heidi's book.[6]

What is it about Heidi's book that makes it so popular?

Heidi and her husband have only two kids, so it's not that she's had that much personal experience. She's not a medical expert. She's not even the first to write a book on pregnancy.

What makes Heidi's book so popular is that it chronicles in detail a series of events that happen in every pregnancy. Pregnancies are rather predictable. Other than conception, things happen in a structured and orderly way. Despite what we might say about it, nothing is an accident.

Women know about cycles. For the most part, every twenty-eight days the same thing happens to a woman's body. The cycle is knowable and repeatable.

Pregnancy is also a cycle. Specific things usually happen at specified milestones. Egg and sperm join. Cells divide. Organs are formed. Limbs grow. Hair and teeth appear. Contractions start. A baby squeezes through the birth canal. A mother smiles at the newborn's first cry.

Nature, it seems, comes in predictable cycles.

> tides
> days
> phases of the moon
> seasons
> pregnancy

They all follow a definable schedule. They are patterned. Ordered.

That's why Heidi's book is successful. Readers learn

they are not alone in their journeys. Identifying predictable cycles, definable schedules, and developmental milestones, Heidi helps pregnant women make sense of what is happening to their bodies. Readers realize they aren't alone in experiencing the kinds of changes that come with pregnancy. Heidi's book serves as a pregnancy road map.

. . .

As a pioneering geneticist and former leader of the Human Genome Project, Dr. Francis S. Collins was one of the first to see and understand the intricate physical blueprint of humanity. Collins calls the human genome "the language of God."[7] Could this be right? What if every human cell holds a kind of cosmic codebook reflecting the intentions of God? If this is true, then Collins and his team have accomplished not only a revolutionary scientific achievement, but also an expression of worship.

Hmm. Our genomes are God's language?

Perhaps a future literary translation of the Bible could replace "the rocks will cry out" with "your DNA will cry out."

. . .

Just as Heidi's book speaks to pregnant women and the genome text speaks to Francis Collins, so the orderly, predictable, and reliable cycles of nature speak to us. The repetition of the sun rising and setting, the changing of seasons, or the phases of the moon and tide all tell us we're not random creatures tossed about in a chaotic ocean. We are not without a map.

There is intentionality.

Constancy guides us.

Natural order is God's reminder that we're not random.

This isn't random. We aren't here by chance.

We're here by a series of ordered events.

Could it be that nature gives us another perspective on all the extraordinary signs and circumstances we discussed in the first chapter?

If we live in such an ordered universe . . .

If everything from our DNA to the movement of the planets is ordered . . .

perhaps the seemingly improbable coincidences aren't *chance* encounters.

Maybe they are as ordered and beautiful as nature itself.

Could these coincidences be considered divine appointments?

106.4 BALANCING THE EQUATION

Perhaps the closest an eighth-grade boy will get to a religious experience in algebra class is staring at the cute girl in the front row. Even a gawky teen knows beauty when he sees it. And when he does, his body responds by executing a series of finely tuned chemical reactions that connect his eyes to the sweat glands in his armpits and in the palms of his hands. Her presence distracts him from balancing the equations written on the board. If only he knew that his hormonal rush likely began with an equation—and a lesson in Euclidean geometry.

In 300 BC, Euclid recorded a simple but brilliant mathematical formula that was newly believed to link all things humans considered beautiful. It was called the divine proportion, or the golden ratio. Put simply, Euclid found things in the physical world whose proportions balanced with a ratio of 1 to 1.618 were universally recognized as beautiful.

The proportion is found naturally in the symmetry of flowers, the delicacy of snowflakes, and the fractal patterns of ferns. Successful architects balance their structures by this law. Modeling agencies use this formula to predict whether an aspiring model will make it on the runway. Consciously or innately, artists as diverse as Leonardo da Vinci and Salvador Dalí deliberately used this formula in their work.

Beautiful things in the natural world have a certain universal proportion to themselves and to other things. Those facial structures that conform most closely to the proportion of 1 to 1.618 are deemed aesthetically pleasing.

Like the girl in the front row, they are labeled beautiful.

Though none of the boys in the room will pull out his protractor to analyze the girl's facial structure, instinctively they each know she measures up. The result: their eyes stare and their palms sweat.

The old adage "Beauty is in the eyes of the beholder" should, according to Euclid, be rendered, "Beauty is in the ratio of the eyes to the chin and forehead of the beheld."

Pattern.

Symmetry.

Balance.

Beauty in the body of a woman; order in the DNA of her cells.

Beauty in the first flower that emerges after the spring thaw; order in the seasons.

Beauty in the tides of an endless ocean; order in the phases of the moon.

Beauty isn't the result of random chance. Beauty is the outcome of order. Though we think of order as being stiff and structured, order is more like a creative expression of beauty. Beauty and order are jazz musicians; one keeps the beat, freeing the other to improvise in the created space. Together they make music.

Abstract and concrete.

Loose and tight.

Literal and metaphorical.

Seemingly disparate pieces fit together in our natural world. Could it be that through nature God wants us to discover connections between seemingly disconnected things?

Could it be that *he* is the connection?

C. S. Lewis believed that nature represents an intentionality:

> It is not an accident that simple-minded people, however spiritual, should blend the ideas of God and Heaven and the blue sky. . . . The huge dome of the sky is of all things sensuously perceived the most like infinity. And when God made space and worlds that move in space, and clothed our world with air, and gave us such eyes and such imaginations as those we have, He knew what the sky would mean to us. And since nothing in His work is accidental, if He knew, He intended. We cannot be certain that this was not indeed one of the chief purposes of which Nature was created.[8]

Could that be true?

That when God made the sky, he knew, and therefore intended, that in our minds we would link the sky to him?

Could it be that the primary purpose of nature is to help us make these connections? If so, are there more connections lying around just waiting for us to discover?

Is God intentionally trying to tell us something through his creation?

106.5 Beer and Peanuts

St. Patrick's Day in America is merely an excuse for kids to pinch someone not wearing the right color and for adults to drink green beer. The shamrock is little more than an advertising icon for the seasonal green milkshakes McDonald's sells or the Muscular Dystrophy Association fund-raiser. But these holiday connections are a far cry from the things the real St. Patrick celebrated.

Patrick was a Brit, and as a young man, he had been taken as a slave to Ireland. After he escaped and returned home, he felt God directing him to return to Ireland as a missionary. Many amazing tales surround Patrick's adventures in Ireland, including his respect for the natural beauty of his adoptive land and his willingness to leverage it as a tool for the gospel. One of the most famous examples of this was St. Patrick's using the shamrock as an illustration of three in one.

The ancient Druids worshiped nature in general. They considered the trifoliate plant sacred. They associated it with the coming of spring and the rebirth of the world after the vernal equinox.

Instead of running from that pagan picture of nature, Patrick borrowed it, converted it, and revealed a new meaning within it. The clever saint used the three leaves of the clover to explain the counterintuitive doctrine of the

Holy Trinity. God is three persons yet one God. The concept is abstract. But a small piece of nature gave that idea a visible form.

Remember the C. S. Lewis quote about the association between sky and heaven—that God knew we'd make the association?

Did God also know what the shamrock would say to the Irish?

If he knew, perhaps he intended it from the moment he created it.

Perhaps God created the shamrock purposely to represent something more than green beer in March. If so, what other clues could we find in nature if we would only pay attention?

. . .

George Washington Carver also believed God spoke through nature. "I love to think of nature as an unlimited broadcasting station, through which God speaks to us every hour, if we will only tune in."[9]

Carver believed there was something special about experiencing God in nature. "Reading about nature is fine," said Carver, "but if a person walks in the woods and listens carefully, he can learn more than what is in books, for they speak with the voice of God."[10]

And Carver listened.

"When I was young, I said to God, 'God, tell me the mystery of the universe.' But God answered, 'That knowledge is for me alone.' So I said, 'God, tell me the mystery of the peanut.' Then God said, 'Well, George, that's more nearly your size.' And he told me."[11]

Apparently, George acted on what he learned.

Over the course of his life, Carver discovered hundreds of marketable products made from the peanut, including mayonnaise, cheese, shampoo, instant coffee, flour, soap, rubber, face powder, plastics, adhesives, axle grease, and pickles.[12]

For Carver, hearing God's voice went beyond immersing himself in nature. Carver learned to love what God loved.

"Anything will give up its secrets if you love it enough. Not only have I found that when I talk to the little flower or to the little peanut they will give up their secrets, but I have found that when I silently commune with people they give up their secrets also—if you love them enough."[13]

Carver learned to hear God's voice in nature, not by *listening* harder, but by *loving* more. That's what St. Patrick did; he loved the Irish people so much and so passionately that when he wanted to explain the difficult mysteries of God, the shamrocks cried out.

Next St. Patrick's Day, when you're drinking your favorite green beverage and eating a handful of nuts, tell your friends you hear God speak through shamrocks and peanuts. Maybe we could make this a worldwide witnessing strategy: invite people over for peanuts and drinks, and then hand out copies of "Footprints in the Sand" and gospel tracts in the shape of sand dollars.

Or, instead of hearing what God said to George Washington Carver or St. Patrick, we can sit still and listen to what God has to say to us.

As Carver said, "If you love it enough, anything will talk with you."[14]

106.6 TALK TO THE ANIMALS
Anything will talk?

It seems so.

Scripture is filled with parables of the ordinary communicating extraordinary truths. Often natural examples are used so we can relate to the abstract or eternal truth. God did this from his earliest communications in the Bible. Scripture tells us God is a shepherd, a father, fire, a solid rock, water, or a mother nursing her infant.

When God wants to talk about himself, he doesn't use abstract ideas. He uses concrete images, natural things to give us a hook on which to hang his words. Often the things he uses are unexpected. Occasionally, they are shocking.

Skeptical? Past examples include

> a burning bush,
> stone tablets,
> and a donkey.

Balaam had a reputation. The things he blessed stayed blessed. The things he cursed stayed cursed. So when the Moabites and Midianites were afraid of being wiped out by the Israelites, they sent emissaries to Balaam, asking if he would come and curse their enemies. They offered him the cursory cursing fee, but Balaam wanted to pray about it first.

God warned Balaam not to go, so Balaam declined their offer. However, the king was not an easy man to say no to. He sent higher-ranking officials to plead with Balaam.

Balaam prayed again, and this time God told Balaam he could go, but he warned him to do absolutely nothing unless

God said he could. In the morning, Balaam saddled up the donkey and headed out.

Oops!

God hadn't said, "Simon says saddle up the donkey and be gone." Balaam did it on his own.

That made God mad enough to send an angel to block the road. Balaam was probably texting while driving his donkey, and he didn't see the angel. Balaam's donkey, however, did see the angel. The angel was holding a sword, so the donkey veered off the road straight into a ditch.

Then Balaam was the one who was mad. He did what every God-loving, nature-respecting man would do when his donkey gets out of control: he beat the donkey. They continued and passed a vineyard. The donkey again saw the angel and tried to avoid the sword-wielding figure by walking so close to the fence it crushed Balaam's foot.

Balaam returned the favor with another whipping.

Finally, they headed down a narrow path, where once again the angel appeared in front of the donkey. The animal couldn't move. The donkey stopped where it was.

Balaam lost his cool (if he ever had it). He took a stick and beat the donkey.

He hadn't yet figured out God was trying to speak to him through the actions of his donkey. So God tried again in a slightly less subtle way. He gave the donkey the ability to talk: "What have I ever done to you that you have beat me these three times?"

Balaam said, "You've been playing games with me! If I had a sword I would have killed you by now."

The donkey said to Balaam, "Am I not your trusty donkey,

on whom you've ridden for years right up until now? Have I ever done anything like this to you before? Have I?"

He said, "No."

Then God helped Balaam see what was going on: he saw God's angel blocking the way, brandishing a sword. Balaam fell to the ground, his face in the dirt.

God's angel said to him: "Why have you beaten your poor donkey these three times? I have come here to block your way because you're getting way ahead of yourself. The donkey saw me and turned away from me these three times. If it hadn't, I would have killed you by this time, but not the donkey. I would have let it off."[15]

Pretty wild, huh?

On two occasions, Balaam spoke with God and received clear responses. But once Balaam was on the road, it appears he stopped listening. For whatever reason, Balaam wasn't hearing God on the usual channel, so God had to use a freakish asinine way of getting his attention.

That also explains how he can talk through us occasionally.

And why not?

There seems to be something deep within us that longs to befriend animals and make them our confidants. We teach birds to mimic our language. We laugh when they chatter at us, imagining they actually understand the random sounds we've trained them to make. We joke with our dogs, seek counsel from our cats, lecture our horses, and philosophize to our goldfish, half-believing they understand us. And that we understand them in return.

We love our animals.

Perhaps too much.

Richmondpetlovers.com has the following stats on their Web site:

Fifty-six percent of dog owners and 42 percent of cat owners bought holiday gifts for their pets last year.

Seventy percent of people sign their pet's name on greeting cards and 58 percent include their pets in family and holiday portraits.

Some 39 percent of pet owners say they have more photos of their pet than of their spouse or significant other. Only 21 percent say they have more photos of their spouse or significant other than of their pet.[16]

Could it be our desire to talk to the animals is really a misplaced desire to talk to God?

Do we have it backwards when we experience unconditional love from our d-o-g rather than our G-o-d?

Our response to animals teaches us something about ourselves. Could this be part of God's purpose for them? Is our desire to connect with an animal actually a desire to connect with God? We're awed by magnificent beasts: lions, tigers, and bears, oh my! But we take away their magnificence when we try to tame and domesticate these wild animals.

Are we also guilty of trying to tame and domesticate God?

God uses nature to transcend the gap between us and him. He makes the Word into natural flesh, and not just metaphorically. God showed us what that means when he himself came into our natural world. He became human, with hairy arms and fingernails needing to be trimmed. God is down to earth.

If God uses nature to connect with us, shouldn't we use nature to connect with him?

Jesus is the best example of this. He is a hook that pulls us from the natural world to the spiritual world. Are we allowing ourselves to be hooked?

Jesus continues this natural dialogue while on earth by using wheat seeds, grape vines, fig trees, mountains, water and wine, birds, and fish as earthly symbols of his heavenly message. In fact, Jesus was one with nature to the point that he let nature speak for him.

In the Gospel of Matthew, Jesus explains how much God loves us and that he will take care of us. Like Elizabeth Barrett Browning, he could have said, "Let me count the ways,"[17] followed by an eloquently stated list of how God loves us.

But Jesus doesn't do that.

Instead, Jesus points to a plant.

> Look at the lilies of the field and how they grow. They don't work or make their clothing, yet Solomon in all his glory was not dressed as beautifully as they are. And if God cares so wonderfully for wildflowers that are here today and thrown into the fire tomorrow, he will certainly care for you.[18]

Jesus aims his index finger at nature and says, "Here's your example of how he cares for you." The lilies of the field aren't used as Jesus' sermon anecdote; the lilies *are Jesus' sermon.* His three-point plan?

> See it.
> Believe it.
> Remember it.

106.7 HOOKED ON GOD

When Jesus wanted to teach his disciples to be fearless,
he used an opportunity they couldn't control. When a big
storm came up and the disciples were alone on the boat, he
walked toward them. *He walked on the water.* And he told
the disciples they could do the same thing.

Only Peter was brave enough to try. He got out of the
boat, walked a few steps on the water, but gave in to his fear
and ended up gargling lake water.

Jesus gave him a hand and said, "You have so little faith
. . . why did you doubt me?" Jesus could have given the disciples a PowerPoint presentation on what it means to be the
Son of God. Instead, Jesus let nature make his point.

He stopped the wind.[19]

To men who well knew when it was safe to take a boat
out, to men who had in the past found themselves in some
bad weather on the lake, to men who wished they could
make it stop raining when they wanted to fish—walking on
water and controlling the wind were proof Jesus was the
Son of God.

So they did what we do when we see God in nature.

They worshiped him.

There was deliberateness about those scenes. Jesus sent
the disciples out without him. He knew a storm was coming.
He knew walking on the water and calming the winds would
be a powerful example of God's sovereignty. He could do
what the disciples knew from a human standpoint was
impossible.

The ancient Hebrews listened for God's voice in storms.
They heard him. The psalmist wrote, "The voice of the LORD
strikes with bolts of lightning."[20]

Storms put them on alert. Instead of the National Weather Service warning them of an oncoming storm, perhaps the storm alerted them of an oncoming God. For the ancient Hebrews, perhaps it wasn't *how* God said it; maybe it wasn't even *what* God said.

It was enough that *God said*.

The theme is that *God speaks*. Jesus knew his natural demonstrations would be the faith hook to catch the fishermen. God knew St. Patrick would see the Trinity in a shamrock, Francis Collins would see God in our DNA, and all of us would see connections to heaven in the infinite blue sky.

God's nature is very deliberate in its conversation.

In fact, the Bible says not only that God deliberately speaks to us through nature, but also that we're stupid if we're not listening:

> For ever since the world was created, people have seen the earth and sky. Through everything God made, they can clearly see his invisible qualities—his eternal power and divine nature. So they have no excuse for not knowing God.[21]

Nature helps us not only to know *of* God,
  but to *know* God.

106.8 PERSONAL MESSAGES

Ever since he was born, Bryan has spent every summer at the beach, playing in the water, eating fresh seafood, and of course, collecting shells. Unlike the author of "Legend of the Sand Dollar," Bryan had never found a whole sand dollar; instead, all he found was sand change.

To Bryan, those moments of searching for shells on the beach made God seem closer. Maybe it was the early morning walks where he talked to God, or maybe it was the break from his everyday life that allowed him to hear God better. So it was only natural when Bryan began a ministry for Christian screenwriters that he decided to hold his writing retreats at beach locations. Bryan's prayer was that these two-week beach retreats would help writers hear God in new ways too.

On one such trip, Bryan did what he always did. He got up early in the morning to collect shells and talk to God. This particular beach was littered with broken sand dollars. It was the ultimate tease. As he sorted through broken seashells looking for a whole sand dollar, he noticed a pattern in his moods and in his connection with God.

If the day before had been productive, if he had accomplished something, Bryan felt closer to God—like he was making progress using his talents to encourage the writers he mentored. But if the day was unproductive, if the creative exercises hadn't worked or the writing conversations faltered, Bryan felt like a failure and far away from God. He wanted to accept God's grace and his love, but Bryan didn't feel he was worthy unless he had somehow earned it.

The next morning he was grappling with these ideas and arguing with himself when a man ahead of him on the beach suddenly stopped, bent over, and picked up a shell. As Bryan approached, the man turned with a big smile on his face and said, "Look at this!"

Bryan looked. It was a large and perfectly whole sand dollar.

"Oh, cool," Bryan said, trying not to betray his jealousy.

Now he was completely convinced that without achieving something great for God, not only did he not deserve God's love, but he didn't deserve a sand dollar, either.

That evening, in an attempt to help the writers to dig deeper, he had them discuss their greatest fears. As each one talked about what they feared most, Bryan realized he feared not accomplishing something big for God and spending the rest of his life feeling like a failure.

When it was Bryan's turn, he shared the story of Peter. Peter loved Jesus and wanted to do great things for him. He was the only one who got out of the boat to meet Jesus on the water; he was the one who cut off the ear of a guard who tried to take Jesus;[22] and when Jesus told his disciples he was about to die, warning they would all desert him, it was Peter who said, "Even if I have to die with you, I will never deny you!"[23]

Bryan understood Peter's zealousness and desire to serve his Lord. Bryan felt the same passion and desired to change the world for Christ. But Peter also screwed up a lot, and Bryan sometimes felt he could relate to that side of Peter as well.

For example, after Jesus was taken away by the Roman guard, Peter denied knowing his friend three times. The last time, he said, "A curse on me if I'm lying—I don't know the man!"[24] and a rooster crowed three times, reminding Peter that Jesus had warned this would happen.

Peter was crushed. Not only had he betrayed the best friend he'd ever had, but he had denied his Lord and Savior. In his grief, we're told, he wept bitterly.

Bryan discussed how worthless Peter must have felt— he had been the leader of the disciples. Christ had promised some amazing things would happen through Peter, whom he called "the rock"—the very foundation of the church that would carry Jesus' message into the future.

When he finally reconnected with the resurrected Jesus around the campfire, Peter must have doubted the things Jesus said: *I'm the wrong man, I'm not worthy, and the job should be given to someone more deserving.*

That's when Jesus did something astonishing. He asked Peter if he loved him.

Peter basically said, "Yeah, you know I'm *fond* of you."

But the word Jesus used for love in his question is the word *agape*. *Agape* doesn't mean the kind of I'm-fond-of-you love Peter responded with. Instead, it's the word used to describe God's overwhelmingly amazing love as demonstrated by Jesus' sacrifice.

Jesus asked the question again. "Peter, do you love me?"

"Of course, I do," Peter said, still not getting the difference.

One more time, Jesus asked the question. This time he stressed the word *love.*

The fullness of its meaning was felt by Peter and he got it. He told Jesus he *agaped* him back.

"I can see what Christ was doing," Bryan told the writers. "He was trying to wipe away Peter's fear that he wasn't good enough. Peter believed this huge lie that he wasn't worthy of the calling before him. He needed Jesus' affirmation to root out the lie that he wasn't worthy."

The moment was a breakthrough for the writers. They began to understand that, as with Peter, their greatest fears were all lies that stood in the way of their being fully used by God, and that the real, sacrificial love for Jesus is the only qualification God has for all of us.

When Bryan woke the next morning, his heart felt buoyant. He praised God for the spiritual breakthroughs of the previous day. Instead of walking on the beach, he *ran* on the beach, worshiping God. He had never felt closer to his Lord than he did right then.

But twenty-four hours later, once again on his early morning walk, Bryan crashed back to earth. The previous day had been terrible. The writers were struggling, the creative exercises weren't working, and the juices weren't flowing. The writers were frustrated with their projects and with Bryan.

Once again, Bryan felt like a failure. It was confirmation that he didn't have what it took to lead the group; he would never see his goal of bringing Christ's message to Hollywood, and he was foolish for trying.

As he walked along the beach, kicking sand, he spotted a large sand dollar. He picked it up and dusted it off.

It was perfect.

In almost forty years of looking, this was the first one he had ever found. He smiled and kept walking.

A few feet later he spotted a second one. He picked it up. Once again, it was perfect.

Glancing down, he found a third perfect sand dollar. He picked it up and looked to see if there were any more. There weren't.

Bryan knew what it meant. With each sand dollar, God was asking, "Do you love me?"

God had to ask it three times before Bryan got the message.

Forget the maudlin metaphorical legend of the sand dollar. God tossed Bryan personal, handwritten messages on shells. God's agape love wiped out Bryan's fear—with a sand dollar. Today, Bryan continues to feed his screenwriting sheep even when he doesn't feel qualified or accomplished.

God uses nature to broadcast a mountaintop message of his majesty and glory. He reveals the infinitely complicated order and design behind the simplest forms of life. He uses nature to arouse our desire to worship and connect. He speaks through the ordinary to teach us the extraordinary. Sometimes he even writes notes and leaves them on the beach.

Whether it happens without warning, suddenly and surprisingly, or we spend our whole lives searching for it, God uses nature to nurture our relationships with him.

We can't stop the stones from crying out.

But . . .

we can pause . . .

to listen to what they say,

considering it an invitation to converse with the One who placed them in our path.

When it comes to hearing God speak through nature, reading a chapter about it will provide clues to the journey, but it's not the journey. To really hear God on this channel, we must experience him through his creation by spending time in nature worshiping him.

Once we're there, even the sand dollars will cry out.

106.9 Experiential Knowledge

John looks like a run-of-the-mill calculus teacher. And from 8:00 a.m. to 3:15 p.m. Monday through Friday, that's exactly what he is. But when he closes the math book, John cinches up his hiking boots, grabs his Bible, and heads to one of the many nature trails around St. Paul, Minnesota. Often he'll have ten to fifteen students following him. "I'm the rabbi," John says, chuckling. "These are my *talmidim*, my students." John believes nature can teach us about God.

John teaches math by profession, but he teaches the Bible by passion. He prefers to do so on the run, outside of the classroom.

"Jesus was a rabbi. He had no classroom," said John. "He called his students to follow him, and he started walking. They either followed or they didn't."

John has made many trips to Israel to walk the path of his rabbi, Jesus. But a few years ago, he had an idea. Many of the students in his Christian high school were curious to learn more about the origins of their faith. John knew he couldn't take them all to Israel, so he decided to give them a living lesson where they were.

Does it bother John that the flora and fauna—not to mention the climate and terrain—of the upper Midwest is unlike the Middle East?

Not much.

"We study the Bible in a natural environment similar to the biblical story we are trying to illustrate. There is something really powerful about sitting beside a lake—even a lake in Minnesota—and talking about Jesus feeding five thousand people with a few loaves and two fish."

One Saturday, John and his students hiked down a steep path to the St. Croix River that divides Wisconsin and Minnesota. They stopped near Taylors Falls on a vertical slope about twenty feet above the water. John gathered the gang of kids around him and read chapters two and three from the book of Joshua. Then he explained the relevance of their location.

Israel was at the edge of the River Jordan. They were also at the edge of their destiny. They had wandered in the desert for forty years. Now, across that river they could see their new home, the land God had promised them. All that stood between them and their future was that river. But it was at flood stage, and dangerous. There were a million Hebrews with children and livestock. Fear swept over them. How would they get down the steep slope and cross the wild waters?

His students looked down the muddy bank.

"Only one way: they had to believe God's promise, go down, and get their feet wet," said John. He pulled out a map of the Jordan Valley and a picture he'd printed of the area where most scholars believed the Israelites crossed. He showed them the steep slopes and had them imagine what the river at flood stage might have looked like.

"The key verse is Joshua 3:8," said John. "Joshua told the priests to take the ark, the symbol of God's presence, and stand in the river. To do this, they had to step off the ledge, like this one, and slide down the bank. Once they descend, there is no turning back. They didn't just dip their toes into the edge. They went all in, and that's when the miracle occurred. The text said when the priests carrying the ark got into the water, the flow stopped. And Israel was able to cross."

John turned and stepped off the edge of the bank. He slid down the mud slope and landed feetfirst in the water below. His students knew the drill—follow the rabbi. They all stepped off and skidded their way down.

"What does this say to us today?" John asked, once the kids joined him.

"We have to get our feet wet," said one student, standing ankle deep in the water of the St. Croix.

"Okay . . ." said John, waiting for more.

"When God sends us to do something, we have to jump in before the water will part."

"Miracles come only when we have over-the-edge faith," said another.

"Good. Are we ready to jump in?" asked John. "Are we ready to live in faith? To trust the Lord controls the flood and will honor the fact we got our feet wet?"

The lesson became real for the students when they experienced God in context. John has it right: Not only is it the grand things, like magnificent views, that instruct us about God's nature, but it's also the ordinary things—lakes and riverbanks—that give us insight and understanding into God's words. In fact, John has recently decided to go into full-time ministry. The name of his organization? The Rocks Cry Out.

And as the other John, John Muir, showed us, they cry out whether they are in California's Sierra Nevada, in Minnesota's lake beds, or rolled in front of a tomb near Calvary.

Perhaps it's not the *trees or flowers* of Israel that impart specific knowledge of God, but the trees and flowers everywhere that help us to better understand the *God* of Israel.

And maybe to experience that, it's as simple as looking up.

> The heavens proclaim the glory of God.
> The skies display his craftsmanship.
> Day after day they continue to speak;

night after night they make him known.
They speak without a sound or word;
their voice is never heard.
Yet their message has gone throughout the earth,
and their words to all the world.[25]

Jeremiah wrote:

> When he speaks in the thunder, the heavens roar with
> rain. He causes the clouds to rise over the earth. He
> sends the lightning with the rain and releases the wind
> from his storehouses.[26]

No innuendo there.

No double-talk.

No subtle whispers behind closed doors.

Nature bellows its beautiful message to the whole world.

Martin Luther said, "God writes the gospel, not in the
Bible alone, but also on trees, and in the flowers and clouds
and stars."[27]

Knowledge of God isn't hidden. But neither is it handed
out on a plaque. The act of stopping to observe, to appreciate, and to acknowledge is as important as the focus of our
observations.

Through creation, God speaks to us physically and
emotionally, which makes contemplating nature a moving
religious experience.

There isn't static on the nature channel.

CHANNEL 107.0
INFECTIOUS

LOTS OF WOMEN HAVE UNPLANNED PREGNANCIES.

Few have an unplanned adoption.

Cheryl and Erik Peterson are working on three.

The Petersons already have a house full of kids: teenagers Nicole and Scott still live at home, and three older children and their kids live nearby. The Peterson house is full on holidays and many days in between. As much as they love their children, Cheryl and Erik didn't want another one.

The Petersons' church has a relationship with Emmanuel Children's Home in Juarez, Mexico, just across the border from El Paso, Texas. Emmanuel provides a home for families who can't raise their own children due to addiction, poverty, or death. At Emmanuel, they feed, clothe, and educate these kids. Several times a year, the Petersons' church sends teams to Juarez to do manual labor. In June 2006, Cheryl and her daughter, Nicole, volunteered to join one of those trips.

"I was going to mop floors, peel potatoes, and clean toilets. That was my plan," said Cheryl.

But it wasn't God's.

"Before we left, I decided I wouldn't let myself fall in love with any of the children," said Cheryl. "Through the first part of the week, I stood resolved. I did chores and hid behind busyness. I wouldn't let myself get drawn to the children, but strangely, that didn't keep them from being drawn to me."

From the beginning, a young boy named Samuel took a liking to Cheryl. He followed her everywhere and wouldn't leave her alone. "He hovered around me. He took my hand, teased me, and tried to speak English with me. I could see he was starved for a mother's attention. As hard as I tried to hold back, I couldn't."

A few days into the trip, Cheryl found herself in conversation with the director of Emmanuel Ministries.

"Out of the blue," said Cheryl, "I heard myself ask, 'How much does adoption cost?' When the director told me, I gulped but felt relieved. We could never afford the thousands of dollars the process demanded." Cheryl planned to return to her scrubbing, but instead, the woman in the office showed her the files of three children in the home who were open for adoption.

"I was in shock. It was Samuel and his two sisters, Lucia and Eide," said Cheryl. She knew then that even if she *wanted* to, she couldn't adopt Samuel—it would mean breaking apart his family. No sooner had the thought passed than Cheryl began to feel her mothering instincts kick in.

"The haunting desire to mother all three overwhelmed me. I fought it. I rationalized. I thought about the cost and the size of our house. I thought about how hard Erik works to feed the family we have. But no matter how stalwart I stood, the compassion grew."

While Cheryl was torn between her thoughts and her feelings, the next few days passed quickly. On the day of their departure, Samuel presented Cheryl with a tissue flower he had made in one of the craft sessions she had led. In English he said, "See you soon?"

On the flight home, Cheryl *just happened* to sit next to a counselor for an adoption agency. They talked all the way home. Back in Minneapolis, Cheryl spent Saturday filling Erik in on all that had happened. She knew he would be the voice of reason, but when she finished, he smiled and said, "Maybe we're supposed to do this."

The next morning the Petersons attended church. The theme of the service was the need for Christians to reach outside of their comfort zones and let Jesus extend his love to the world. The irony wasn't lost on Cheryl. "All through the hour, I couldn't stop thinking of those three kids."

Her emotions were in overdrive.

"At the end of the pastor's message," said Cheryl, "the pastor paused and said something totally out of character: 'Someone needs to ask God about adopting a child from Mexico.' There were five hundred people in the room, and he certainly had no idea what was happening to me. I just lost it. I broke down and wept. My heart was broken with compassion. I knew God was talking to us."

Though it hadn't been *their* plan, they were sure it was *God's* plan. Love and compassion for the three children forced their rational thinking to take a backseat. For the past three years, the Petersons have pursued adoption of Samuel and his sisters. They've made numerous visits to

Mexico and faced unforeseeable trials, each time falling more deeply in love with the three kids.

Had they known three years ago what they would have to endure in financial and legal struggles, and still not have the kids as part of their family, they might have made a different choice. But the Petersons, as rational as they may be, weren't guided by their thoughts. They were guided by their feelings.

God used their emotions to move them to action.

And it's likely he wants to do the same with you and your emotions.

107.1 THINKING AND FEELING
Are you a feeler or a thinker?

When making a decision, do you go with your gut instinct, or do you carefully investigate all the data before you make a decision?

Most of us have a preference. Either we have a sensation that compels us in a direction—a compulsion we can't quite explain to others—or we can clearly articulate the criteria we use when we make a choice. We label those who sense their way through a decision *feelers* and those who examine the information *thinkers*.

But whether we're thinkers or feelers, it seems that sometimes God uses our emotions to speak to us—as he did with the Petersons. No intellectual argument would have convinced Cheryl and Erik to fight for years to bring three more kids into their full home. But when God used their emotions to speak his will, no other choice remained.

Sometimes feelers wish they had the ability to analyze data like their thinking friends, but when data and their feelings conflict, feelers can no more go against their instincts than a thinker can rely on his or hers. Perhaps that is why feelers are often at a disadvantage. Their data-based, decision-making friends can provide irrefutable, hard-core proof to support their decisions, but feelings-based decision makers can only reply with, "It felt right."

Experts are typically thinking people—scientists and academics. We rarely follow the advice of people who "just have a feeling" about what we should do. There's a perception that those who use intellect rather than emotions to make decisions are superior, that feelings-based decision makers are weak. People tend to be distrustful of all that touchy-feely stuff.

The opposite is true when it comes to faith. Perhaps faith is difficult for thinkers. Though apologists articulate amazing and intricate constructs describing God and eternity, they always fall short of absolute proof. For thinkers to become believers, they have to trust in things they can't see or prove.

They have to feel it.

Whether or not they have the data.

But for feelers, faith in the unseen is easier. To them, faith isn't much different from following their feelings.

They can't explain it.

But it *feels* right.

Jesus told the apostles to be like children, and there's no better example of going through life based on how you feel than that of a child. Children rarely think through the data— they just do what feels right in the moment. Part of what it means to come to Jesus as a child is to not overthink things, but to just feel them.

Maybe that's also why so many people stumble upon Christ with an emotional rather than an intellectual encounter.

107.2 TOUCHY-FEELY CHRISTIANITY

Robyn is a thinker. She carefully considers the evidence in front of her, weighs the alternatives, and makes a thoughtful decision.

She was fourteen when her parents divorced, and a family friend took an interest in her spiritual life. The older woman shared Scriptures with the teen. But frankly, not much of it made sense to Robyn.

"I kept reading the passages in John that she gave me and called her with questions, but it was all words to me," said Robyn. "I didn't understand what it meant to know Jesus."

Then one Sunday, the friend invited Robyn to attend church with her. "Halfway through the sermon a supernatural presence came over me," said Robyn. "I was overwhelmed with the feeling of God. It was like he was swimming in and out of every part of my body, and I was overcome with emotion. I had no control over it."

Imagine how upsetting it would be for a thinker to find herself immersed in such emotion. Robyn said at first she was scared. "I am a person who is always in control of my emotions and actions, and here was this presence, God, telling me he was in control."

Robyn's friend recognized what was happening and prayed with Robyn.

"Suddenly, I understood the words I had been reading," said Robyn. "They were no longer simply words in the Bible, but they were in my being, put there by God. I met God that day."

Though Robyn would still describe herself as a thinker, the first time she encountered God was in an emotional way.

A logical, thinking person gets the warm fuzzies—and her life is transformed.

No headlines here. This happens all the time.

Most Christians recognize these emotional encounters as manifestations of God. We can also agree that emotional encounters seem to be associated with the presence of God.

But what happens when the emotions hit extremes?

Is God there, too?

Or is something else going on?

Some churches encourage a holy laughter, dancing in the Spirit, or uncontrollable weeping. Does more emotion equal more of God?

Are these people somehow *holier*?

At times, emotional reactions are followed by division. People question whether an outburst of emotion is appropriate. Others question whether the reaction is real or manufactured. Churches divide into separate congregations and even separate denominations, based on their judgment of the appropriateness of such emotional displays.

Seems that a little bit of emotion is a good thing.

But too much apparently isn't.

If churches can't agree on the role of emotion in faith, think of the static and noise that is present when we try as individuals to tune in to God through our feelings. In fact, as you read this, it's likely you've already formed an opinion as to whether or not God can speak through your emotion.

Isn't it odd how we're quick to condemn what we consider over-emotionalism, yet we rarely condemn over-rationalization?

We often distrust our emotional responses. We consider them less worthy and certainly less trustworthy than our intellectual responses. We often treat our feelings the same way we treat a hormonal teenager—with eye rolling and a this-too-shall-pass kind of hope.

But if we believe the basic premise of our faith—that we were created in God's image—yet we've fallen out of relationship with him, don't we have to assume that our intellect is as fallen and corrupted as our emotions?[1]

If God can speak through our intellect,
help us recognize his voice in circumstances
and through the words and actions of others;
and if he can also use other internal channels, such as dreams and visions,
is it too difficult to believe he can also use our emotions?
It is if you believe God doesn't have feelings.

107.3 DIFFerent emotions

Imagine a theological conference where, after a day of presentations, the old guys in beards gather at their favorite watering hole to debate unanswerable questions.

At the first table sits a group of rowdy academics discussing whether or not God could make a boulder bigger than he could lift. The conversation from the second table sounds like pre-Trib and post-Trib rapture debates. At the third table there are two distinct groups, and written on the cocktail napkin is a single word: *immutable*.

On one side of that table is a boisterous and animated group arguing that God is passionate, emotionally responsive, and subject to mood swings based on the actions of his creation.

Sitting across from them are men and women with their backs turned to the first group. Their arms are folded across their chests. Instead of a heated debate, they would have neatly typed their responses onto paper, which would be precisely laid out on the table. Their argument would be that God has no emotions, that he is unchangeable, and that he is above something so base as feelings.

The doctrine of immutability was first articulated by early Christian theologians. They adopted the Greek idea called "divine impassibility"—a sophisticated phrase for the notion that God never changes and that he stands above and outside the realm of pain and sorrow, happiness and pleasure. Early church fathers took this for granted. The Council of Chalcedon in AD 451 made it official by condemning anyone who believed that God could be subject to feelings. During the Reformation, Calvin adopted the same idea. The Westminster Confession of Faith, built on Calvin's ideas, said that God is "without body, parts, or passions, immutable."[2]

The explanation, of course, really gets the first side of the table fired up. They argue that the Bible is full of examples of God demonstrating emotions. God is grieved by the wickedness of man in Genesis,[3] he is angry when he hears complaining,[4] and he is pleased when Solomon asks for wisdom.[5] In one passage in the book of Zephaniah, God speaks of his fierce anger, fury, and jealousy,[6] yet nine verses later he delights, loves, rejoices, and feels glad.[7]

Talk about mood swings.

The backs-turned side of the table retorts with the counterpoint that these are figurative descriptions of God. Despite the Bible's description, these things didn't really happen—God doesn't really feel. Their argument is the equivalent of describing animals using anthropomorphic terms, such as when we say a dog is thinking if he cocks his head. They believe that the Bible occasionally uses anthropomorphisms to ascribe human passions to God, just as the writers of Psalms talk of God's human body parts: hands, feet, and arms.[8]

At this point, most of us would close the door and let the theologians and academics continue the argument without us. It's hard to imagine, let alone convincingly prove, that God is either as cold and removed as an iceberg or has more mood swings than your mother-in-law.

But there is middle ground.

Or at least another way to think about it.

The way God experiences emotion isn't the same way we experience emotion. When God gets angry, it isn't a transformation worthy of The Hulk—responding to circumstances with bulging eyes, muscles popping from his T-shirt, and a sudden unibrow—instead, perhaps his anger is always there.

God—always angry?

That's how some people see him.

How can it be that anger, like the other emotions, is a part of his *unchanging* character?

In an article titled "God without Mood Swings," author Phillip R. Johnson quotes a famous theologian, J. I. Packer:

> [Impassibility is] not impassivity, unconcern, and
> impersonal detachment in face of the creation;
> not insensitivity and indifference to the distresses
> of a fallen world; not inability or unwillingness to
> empathize with human pain and grief; but simply that
> God's experiences do not come upon him as ours

come upon us, for his are foreknown, willed and chosen by himself, and are not involuntary surprises forced on him from outside, apart from his own decision, in the way that ours regularly are.[9]

What Packer seems to be saying is that God's emotions don't overwhelm him in response to a stimulus in the same way that ours do. If we yell at God, he doesn't react by yelling back. Rather, if God has the emotion of anger, it is because he chooses to reveal that part of himself to us at that point in time. He does the same when he chooses to reveal his love or sadness. It is an *intentional emotionalism* rather than our responsive emotionalism.

In other words, God has feelings, but they are unlike ours. It is unfair to compare them to what we know.

This isn't so hard to understand.

When we love, we often do it conditionally—

I love you because I have to; you're my brother—

not unconditionally.

I love you even though you've killed my son.

Face it.

God loves differently than we do.

He seems to be able to love us even when we can't love ourselves.

Considering this, it's not surprising that God might feel other emotions differently from the way we feel them.

For example, we all know what jealousy feels like. Shakespeare describes it as the "green-eyed monster." We know it as a knot in the bottom of our stomach when our less-deserving coworker not only gets our promotion, but then uses her raise to buy a Lexus while we drive a ten-year-old

Honda. Jealousy is the feeling we have when good things happen to *other* people—things that should have happened to us.

Yet Scripture is filled with examples of God being jealous. At one point, God is quoted as saying he is a jealous God.

Does that mean if you get a Lexus, God is going to *get you*?

That doesn't make any sense. If God wants a Lexus, he can have one—he's God. All he has to do is wiggle his nose, cross his arms, and blink or something, right? To wipe out the object of his jealousy, it only takes one tornado or tsunami for him to eliminate it.

God doesn't feel jealousy like we feel jealousy. We don't fully understand what it means when the Bible says he is a jealous God. At best we can only guess at how he experiences these feelings.

But we do know that we have emotions.

And that God uses our emotions to speak to us.

Though our emotions can sometimes be swayed or manipulated, God's can't.

Perhaps God is like a brilliant diamond.

Hard.

Impenetrable.

Unfathomable in his beauty.

And maybe God's emotions are like the various facets of a diamond.

When looking from other vantage points, we see different sides of the same stone—each facet representing another side or emotion of God. As the light moves around the diamond, different facets are reflected, but the whole thing is still rock hard.

This is unlike our emotions, which don't reflect the same steadfastness, to say the least. We're more like Jell-O

Jigglers, wiggling with every emotion that trembles us. Instead of becoming solid, we melt when heat is applied.

So what if our emotions are more easily persuaded than our thinking? Perhaps that's exactly why God uses emotions to speak to us.

We're more likely to hear him if we first feel him.

Like Robyn, who felt God swimming inside her before she intellectually understood, or the Petersons, who made a decision with their hearts that they never would have made with their heads, our emotions seem to be able to break down barriers we otherwise can't get around.

107.4 KING OF PEACE

Carmen didn't want a dog. But her two sons did. And when the boys learned that Carmen's fiancé, David, was also a dog lover, they united with him in a full-on puppy plea.

Outnumbered and glad for some unity among her men, Carmen relented.

Half standard poodle and half golden retriever, the puppy was, as Carmen described him, "100 percent adorable." He had dark brown eyes, silky, light brown fur, and a name that seemed too big for him: Brutus.

His first night in his new home was peaceful. He slept without waking, giving no hint of what was to come. The next day there was a minor disturbance when Brutus confused a pair of brand-new white shoes with a chew toy. Soon the minor infractions grew to major damage.

After the wedding, to tame the puppy and encourage the developing dog, Carmen sent Brutus to obedience school. Though David and both boys attended training with Brutus, it wasn't immediately clear who was schooling whom.

At home, they began calling the dog King Brutus because he acted as if he owned the house, running through the rooms, chewing on shoes, handbags, and other stray accessories. Any food left in sight became a Brutus snack. He grew fond of sunning himself on the glass-topped coffee table near the window until the day the glass shattered. As Brutus grew, he did more than increase in size; he also grew into his name.

When the wind slammed a door shut, trapping Brutus in the master bedroom, he clawed his way out of the hollow-core door, leaving behind a two-foot, jagged hole.

A smart dog, Brutus learned that he didn't have to wait for leftovers; instead he learned to open the refrigerator door and help himself to the bounty inside. When Brutus came across a special treasure, he would bring it to Carmen's side of the bed. In the morning, she would wake to chunks of food and half-chewed objects drenched in doggy slobber. Each time Carmen considered getting rid of Brutus, the pressure from the boys to keep him increased. But so did the damage to her home.

Brutus escaped through a broken door. They fixed the door to prevent him from escaping again. But he made it out again, only this time it was through the window. Screen and glass were mere nuisances to Brutus.

Finally, the day came when Carmen had to do something to protect her house—and her peace.

"The lines had been drawn, and Brutus had crossed them," said Carmen. "The damage, the dirt, the incessant barking contributed to the ultimatum. The dog had to go. My sons wailed in protest. I was the worst mother in the world. As the battle raged, my husband sat silently with an accusing stare. Finally, exhausted, I promised I'd sleep on it and have a decision by morning."

That night Carmen prayed to God to help her with her decision. She pleaded her cause, justified her actions, and was sure that God would see the error of Brutus's ways as evidence that he must go. "But the peace I expected to have once I'd made a decision simply would not come," said Carmen, who tossed and turned, unable to sleep. She got up and went to the living room. She saw the sofa where over time, eighty pounds of dog had demolished the cushions. She tried not to cry as she entered the kitchen and looked under the table where Brutus lay snoring.

That moment triggered something inside of Carmen. She suddenly recognized the unconditional love the boys had for that stupid dog. They sacrificed much to clean up Brutus's messes. They endured complaints from the neighbors. They even offered their allowances for the damage Brutus caused. Carmen saw something—the sacrificial love her sons had for Brutus was the same patient love God had for her, despite the messes she had created in her own life.

Instead of the anger and resentment she had been feeling toward the dog moments earlier, she felt love and thankfulness toward God. Carmen decided to keep Brutus. It was an emotional decision. One she believes God used to speak to her.

Rationally, it probably wasn't a good decision, though Brutus did seem to settle down as he matured. But Carmen kept him because she didn't feel a sense of peace about giving him away. She kept him because of the love she had for her children, the love they had for the dog, and most of all, because she was able to experience and understand the love of her Father in a practical way.

107.5 MOVED

The ancient Israelites were to follow God to the Promised Land. By day, he led them with a pillar of cloud. By night, he led them with a pillar of fire.

Imagine the sweltering one hundred-plus degree temperatures of the Sahara Desert. The sun so hot, your skin blistered. Thousands of wanderers around you, all moving en masse. Stinking animals. Sweaty people. Wouldn't it be nice to have a little shade? Just a bit of break from the sun's rays? If you could only get under the cloud ahead of you, it would offer a much-needed respite. It's doubtful that those in the back of the pack knew exactly where they were going or why, but they did know that the extreme heat was lessened by the shade of the cloud. There wasn't much to *think* about. They simply *felt* more comfortable when they followed God. But they were also taking those steps by faith. In other words, if you were an Israelite in the desert, following God made you feel better.

Imagine being on the move at night. An enormous desert as far as the eye could see (which at night isn't far at all). No light spilling from houses and streetlamps, no skyscrapers or lighted billboards to illuminate the darkness. Even the Energizer Bunny flashlight batteries have died. It's as dark as it gets. So the Israelites feel better if they can keep their eyes on the light. Following a pillar of fire—the only light source other than the distant moon and stars—makes them *feel* safe.

God literally moved the Israelites through their feelings of comfort and discomfort.

We experience the same thing.

But our deserts may be more metaphorical.

For example, you probably had a time in your life when you were disturbed about something you'd done. Maybe it was something you said to a friend or how you treated a loved one. That uncomfortable feeling eventually unsettled you enough to do something about it, perhaps to apologize or make amends. That's not so different from moving closer to the streetlight on a dark night or a pillar of fire in a dark desert.

In the same way, God can use emotions to move us.

If you attended church when you were little, it's likely you remember a Sunday school teacher who used to sing, "I've got the joy, joy, joy, joy down in my heart."

Where?

Down in her heart.

And she wanted it to be down in your heart too.

Can you picture the goofy smile she had on her face as she coordinated the words with the hand motions? She was like a Christian cheerleader trying to cheer you into making a touchdown in your soul.

Is it possible that the joy she so boldly sang about wasn't as deeply felt as it was sung?

We probably all know people who seem to have happiness permanently painted on their outsides. But do they have real joy on the inside, too?

Suzy Sunshine Christians may be well and good, or . . .

. . . maybe they are neither *well* nor *good*.

Sometimes the most boisterous people have inch-deep faith. Plastic faith. Trials melt their smiles.

Real joy isn't some kind of überhappiness molded onto

a plastic doll face. Instead, there is something warm, responsive, and attractive about authentic joy. Joyfulness isn't worn like clothes. It radiates out from the inside.

Like the kind Emily found at her first ballet lesson.

Though she had always been a happy child, something new came over Emily when she started dancing. Even the video camera captured the radiance of the four-year-old at her ballet recital. Emily's face shone when she danced. As she grew in age and ability, her face shone brighter.

Emily was happiest when she was on the dance floor, which is why she devoted much of her free time to lessons and performances. Her work culminated in a college scholarship to the school of her choice, where she would be a part of their illustrious ballet company. Though it was hard work and hard on her body, her passion couldn't be contained. Emily had a God-given talent, and when she used it, she displayed a holy euphoria.

Remember the 1981 film *Chariots of Fire*? It's the true story of two Olympic sprinters competing in the 1924 Olympics. In the film, Scottish missionary Eric Liddell said, "I believe God made me for a purpose, but he also made me fast. And when I run I feel His pleasure."[10]

To paraphrase Liddell, God gave Emily the ability to dance, and when she danced she felt his pleasure.

His pleasure equaled her joy.

That's why the doctor's diagnosis was so devastating. Though she had been having lower back trouble, she never expected him to say that she couldn't dance like she always had. His medical opinion was that she should stop dancing five days a week. This meant she could no longer be in the ballet company.

Or keep her scholarship.

At the end of the year, Emily was forced to leave school and move home.

As much as these changes hurt Emily, what hurt the most was giving up that which brought her joy; the very thing that brought her closer to God and that she felt brought God pleasure.

Would God still be pleased with her even though she could no longer feel it?

Since then, Emily has found a new school, where she is studying musical theater. She's also taking art classes. And with her doctor's consent, she's exploring modern dance. Emily is trying to experience God's pleasure again.

She is chasing joy.

Each pursuit takes her either closer to or farther from the joy she experienced on the dance floor. And through that process, she is finding God's new plan for her life.

Emily seeks joy, but many people simply seek peace. They're upset, confused, or hurt, and they want to make it stop. Their decisions are based on a desire to rid themselves of negative emotions and replace them with a sense of calm. You hear people say things like, "I just had a sense of peace about that decision," or "I had a sense of peace about taking that job."

Can feeling peace about a situation be used as a sort of divination stick for God's will?

If you lack peace, is the discomfort you feel God's prodding to move, change, or seek something different?

Does God speak through your discomfort?

Does that mean he is also behind the peace you feel after taking action?

When the cloud and the fire moved forward, the people followed.

When joy leaves, we chase it.

When uncomfortable, we seek peace.

Is this how God speaks through our emotions?

Seeking God's peace is actually a reasonable way for God to speak to us. He is a God of peace. He's even called *peace* in the Old Testament: Yahweh Shalom. We often translate the word *shalom* to "peace." But *shalom* means more than a lack of conflict. Shalom means a state of perfect order and balance.

In shalom, nothing is out of sorts.

Everything is complete.

God himself is shalom.

When God is present, shalom is established. To feel true peace is to feel God's presence. Likewise, he communicates his presence by radiating this sense of peace.

When we seek peace, we seek God.

And when we find shalom, we find God.

107.6 UGLY Emotional Stepsisters

It is no accident that the first three mentions of the fruit of the Spirit—the by-products of living under his guidance—are all emotions.

> Love.
> Joy.
> Peace.

It's easy to see how God uses our desire for these feelings to speak to us. But if God speaks through our emotions, shouldn't he also be able to speak through the uglier, more negative emotions, such as jealousy and anger?

. . .

"I am a Christian, and I try to serve God. But when I first met Andrew, he irritated the snot out of me," confessed Nathan. "I had always thought I was a decent guy, but when I had lunch with Andrew and listened to his stories, I suddenly felt like a fraud. He talked about carrying on an actual conversation with God. I knew I wasn't at that level, and the competitive side of me felt envious."

The more time Nathan spent with his new friend, the more jealous Nathan grew of Andrew's relationship with God.

"Andrew once said he felt he was supposed to give away a particular amount of money to someone he knew was in need. Andrew *needed* that money for a bill, but he still gave it away. A week later he got an unexpected check in the mail for the same amount. My first thought was, *Yeah, right.* But deep down I knew it was just sour grapes."

Nathan wanted to belittle Andrew's story, not because he didn't think it was real, but because he knew he himself didn't have that kind of faith. Seeing it in Andrew made him want it too.

"Honestly? I felt inferior, like I was missing something. But that irritation—jealousy, I guess it was—drove me to look into myself and to look harder for God. I had been coasting. But to see the fire and joy and adventure that Andrew experienced. . . . I coveted what he had."

Romans 11:11 would have given Nathan some comfort. In it Paul writes

> Did God's people stumble and fall beyond recovery?
> Of course not! They were disobedient, so God made
> salvation available to the Gentiles. But he wanted
> his own people to become jealous and claim it for
> themselves.

In essence, Nathan was experiencing exactly what God had hoped for—a jealousy that caused his people to seek more of him.

"Meeting Andrew set me on a quest," said Nathan. "It prodded me to explore some mystical spiritual disciplines that would normally have freaked me out. God teased me, and it worked."

Did God plant Andrew in Nathan's life to agitate him out of lethargy?

Did Nathan's jealousy make him hungry for something truly spiritual?

Perhaps God allowed Nathan to feel a bit of what God feels—jealous that Nathan had passions for things other than God?

Nathan thinks so. He believes God spoke through his jealousy.

• • •

Karen left her first Bible study embarrassed that everyone seemed to know things that she didn't. She wanted what they had. That feeling drove her to read her Bible, ask questions, and eventually become a Christian—just because she was envious.

Seems like a rather petty rationale for becoming a Christian, doesn't it?

But it seems to be okay with God.

After all, the verse above from Romans 11 tells us he started it.

And if God started it, Jesus certainly continued the example. Jesus had a full range of feelings. Though we already discussed the fact that we don't know how God experiences emotions, we do know how Jesus experienced them—like us. And his emotions were real. This was no plastic joy, because he knew the source of his joy. But he also wept. The Bible doesn't spell it out, but we know Jesus had to laugh. He told too many funny stories not to.

But Jesus also experienced the uglier emotions.

He got mad.

Boiling mad.

From the descriptions we have of his outbursts, it wouldn't be a pretty scene to be on the sharp end of his verbal blade. For example, look at what he once said:

> What sorrow awaits you teachers of religious law
> and you Pharisees. Hypocrites! For you are like
> whitewashed tombs—beautiful on the outside but
> filled on the inside with dead people's bones and all
> sorts of impurity. Outwardly you look like righteous
> people, but inwardly your hearts are filled with
> hypocrisy and lawlessness.[11]

He called them hypocrites and said that, though they looked good on the outside, on the inside they were cadavers.

Eww! But that's still not as pointed as what he said a few verses earlier:

> Woe to you, teachers of the law and Pharisees, you hypocrites! You travel over land and sea to win a single convert, and when he becomes one, you make him twice as much a son of hell as you are.[12]

Jesus called them "sons of hell"?

That's pretty direct, isn't it?

Can you imagine telling your local preacher that not only is he bad, but the people he converts become sons of hell, just like him?

How about telling the IRS agent conducting your audit that he's corrupt?

Or maybe you'd like to shout at the trooper that pulled you over that, though he looks righteous, he's really lawless.

It's hard to imagine doing this, right?

But . . .

Jesus

did.

It's easy to see his emotion stirred something inside those he spoke to.

On at least one occasion, Jesus was so angry, he got violent.

Near the time of the Passover feast, thousands of visitors flooded Jerusalem to worship. When Jesus arrived at the Temple, he was disgusted to see a marketplace. Merchants had set up shop in the Temple and were selling, for a hefty profit, religious items required by Old Testament law to be used for sacrifices. The pilgrims had to have them in order to worship. They had traveled a great distance; they had little choice but to pay the inflated prices. So in the name of religion, the local entrepreneurs got filthy rich.

When Jesus saw what was happening, he turned all Chuck Norris on them. He grabbed a rope and wove it into a whip, which was another way of saying that his action was deliberate and somewhat premeditated. Then he charged into the crowds, drove out the sheep and cattle, and kicked over the tables.

"This is my Father's house," he yelled.

His friends saw a different side of him. At that moment, they were reminded of something from the Scriptures, written hundreds of years earlier, "Passion for God's house will consume me."[13] The disciples realized the moment had been perfectly predicted—prophesied about since the days of King David. God knew *then* that Jesus would be angry *now*.

An intentional expression of emotion.

In his passion, Jesus spoke *through* his anger. But the text shows us that God also spoke *to* the disciples—they recalled his words from Scripture—the same prophetic words they now saw being fulfilled.

It's also likely that God spoke to the merchants through their individual feelings of fear and anger. When they left the Temple, they had to be uncomfortable—and reevaluating their careers.

Jesus used his anger for good.

Not all anger is good anger. God doesn't speak through every instance of anger.

However, like Jesus in the Temple, sometimes our anger can be justified.

And, perhaps, even godly.

On April 12, 1963, an African-American pastor sat in a musty jail cell in Birmingham, Alabama. He was angry. Hours before, eight white Alabama clergymen had signed and released a statement titled "A Call for Unity." Those ministers acknowledged that racial segregation had perpetrated social injustice, but they urged patience. They argued that the battle should be fought in the courts, not in the streets. "Wait," they said.

The imprisoned man knew that his Christian brothers had aimed their words at him. Their cowardice riled his indignation. But in jail, there was little he could do. As his anger grew, so did his resolve. Eventually he responded by turning his emotion into 6,921 elegant and forceful words.

Words that changed America.

On April 16, 1963, Martin Luther King Jr., in jail for leading a peaceful protest against segregation, released an open letter to the citizens of the United States of America. It has come to be called "Letter from Birmingham Jail." In his statement, King argues that without premeditated, defiant—but peaceful—action against unjust laws, civil rights could never be achieved. Time alone does not heal. Justice demanded action, and as he said in his letter, "faith without works is dead."

Reading Dr. King's words decades after the moment, you can still feel the penetrating pathos. "'Wait' has almost always meant 'Never,'" he wrote. Borrowing the words of Thurgood Marshall, who four years later would become the first African-American appointed to the U.S. Supreme Court, King said, "Justice too long delayed is justice denied."

Dr. King felt anger.

His own.

And Another's—God's driving anger.

Dr. King's words forced America to feel that anger along with him. Some feared, and others turned away. Some let it infect their own hearts.

His anger was like that of the prophets of the Old Testament. They, too, railed against unjust rulers who knew better than to rob widows and orphans of their just due. Dr. King, like the biblical prophets before him, embodied God's fury in the language of human emotion.

107.7 CATCHING IT

We think of emotional experiences as something deeply personal and private. Sometimes we hide—or at least attempt to hide—our emotions from others. Recent research has shed new light. It turns out that emotional experiences are not so personal after all. Though they are indeed a chemical storm inside of us, like a virus they can be caught and, in turn, spread to others.

Carl Jung was the first psychologist to suggest that emotions are contagious. It wasn't until Daniel Goleman and others did extensive research into how emotions work that Jung's hunch could be confirmed. Goleman himself has done a lot of work on something called Emotional Intelligence (EI). EI is the theory that some people are more nimble at deciphering others' emotions and managing and projecting their own. EI research also shows that emotions move socially through groups of people.[14]

We *know* this is true.

We've all had an experience where we were having a good day, and then someone in a bad mood enters the room and changes everything.

It's the old story about the dad who comes home from the office and yells at the mom, who in turn yells at the boy, who kicks the dog. Dad's mood has now moved through the house.

To be gender fair, the bumper sticker/T-shirt slogan "If Momma ain't happy, ain't nobody happy" articulates the same principle.

Sometimes this phenomenon is innocuous—upon seeing The Beatles, one teenage girl starts crying, and soon they're all crying.

Sometimes it is deadly—fear spreading through the community of Salem, Massachusetts, and resulting in the witch trials.

Regardless, moods are infectious.

They can be caught, like colds.

What's interesting about the new research is that it shows some people are better at transmitting moods, whereas others are more likely to catch them. The transmittal device is mimicry. Dr. John Cacciopo, a psychologist at The University of Chicago, is quoted in the *New York Times*:

> The more emotionally expressive people are, the more apt they are to transmit their moods to someone they talk with. People who are easily affected by the moods of others, on the other hand, have especially forceful autonomic reactions when they unconsciously mimic someone who is highly expressive.[15]

The autonomic nervous system, which controls certain involuntary physical behaviors, can be affected by someone else's physical behavior. And the more expressive a person is, the more likely we are to catch that behavior. Dr. Cacciopo and Dr. Hatfield theorize:

> It is through such unconscious mimicry of another person's facial expression, gestures and movements, tone of voice and the like that people create in themselves the mood of the person they are imitating.[16]

In other words, the more a person is able to convey his or her mood, the more likely we are to imitate it and therefore ultimately share it.

Hmm. Gives increased importance to the title of the book *Imitation of Christ*, doesn't it?

So here's the question: If God *feels* certain emotions, is it safe to assume his emotions are *contagious*?

If we get close enough to mimic him, would we be "infected" with those emotions?

There is some biblical evidence for this.

The prophets in the Bible seemed to be particularly attuned to God's presence and therefore to his moods. They felt the heart of God.

Jeremiah became a prophet in the southern kingdom of Judah in 627 BC. Times were tough. It wasn't a role Jeremiah aspired to. When he got his draft notice, he tried to refuse. The prospects for prophets weren't promising. But God insisted and finally Jeremiah conceded.

His assignment was not pleasant. He was sent to tell his fellow Israelites bad news. Babylon, the rising empire to the east, would soon conquer them and drag everyone into exile. This would happen because Israel had chosen to leave God's protection. There was no changing the inevitable.

Naturally Jeremiah, being the deliverer of bad news, wasn't popular. Patriotic Israelites hated his gloom and doom. No one believed him. No one changed their ways as a result of his message. That made Jeremiah weep, and the responses grew colder and colder.

They called him the weeping prophet.

The title was fitting. He cried for forty years. It seemed the closer he got to God, the more desperate his heartbreak. Jeremiah felt God's deep sorrow over Israel's rebellion—and it was compounded when his people rejected him, as they rejected God.

Getting close enough to become infected by God's emotion cost Jeremiah deeply. He had no personal life to speak of. He had no joy. He spent his days lamenting what should have been. Jeremiah caught God's contagions of sadness and sorrow. And his love for God meant he could never shake them off.[17]

Being infected by God's emotions isn't always Emily chasing joy. Sometimes it's keeping Brutus after he's destroyed your house, being jealous that you don't have a relationship like Andrew has with God, or spending years cutting through international red tape to bring your kids home, like the Petersons.

Are you jealous about what he is jealous about?

Do you get angry at the injustice in our world?

Do sickness, poverty, and lack of clean water in nations ten thousand miles away make you cry yourself to sleep at night?

Are you passionate about pleasing him?

Getting close to God and being infected by his emotion ruin many people for ordinary life. But it prepares them for an extraordinary one. The apostle Paul said in his letter to the Christians at Philippi, "I want to know Christ and experience the mighty power that raised him from the dead. I want to suffer with him, sharing in his death, so that one way or another I will experience the resurrection from the dead!"[18]

How well do you want to know Christ?

How much do you want to feel what he feels?

How much do you want him to speak to you?

Emotions are easily transmitted from one person to another, yet many of us don't share God's. By the sheer force of his presence, there is nothing to stop him from taking over the mood of a room, no matter whether Momma's happy. Yet it seems God doesn't take over our emotions by force, or by the force of his personality.

For God's emotions to become dominant in a room, we have to get close to him, to mimic him, to experience emotions as he feels them. This is a cognizant act. An act of thinking, of choosing to be infected, that only then leads to feeling.

You've probably experienced a time when you consciously turned your thoughts over to God—in an extraordinary moment of worship, at the deathbed of a loved one, or at the birth of a baby. At that moment, everyone in the room seemed to sacrifice their own thoughts to catch the feelings of those around them. For a moment, they chose to be infected with God's emotion.

If we want to hear God speak through our emotions . . .

we must choose to mimic him.

When we mimic him . . .

his emotions become our emotions.

When we imitate him . . .

we take on his feelings.

We began this chapter by acknowledging that many people think our intellect is less corrupted than our emotional side. But we end a chapter on emotions with the need to make a conscious choice to feel what God feels. It is a *thinking* act of our free will to be infected *emotionally* by God.

Get close to him and feel what he feels.

Stand back and you will miss his emotions.

It is a thinking choice that decides what you'll feel.

CHANNEL 108.0
PUSHY LITTLE WEENIE

IF YOU CAN FEEL SENSATION IN YOUR FOOT, thank your nervous system. When functioning correctly, your nervous system tells the brain your bare foot is being tickled, you just stepped on a LEGO, or the bath water is too hot. You laugh when you're tickled, get mad at the kid who left out his toys, and jerk your foot out of the hot bath. You don't think about it; you just do it. Those are signs that your nervous system works.

Due to injury or disease, sometimes a nervous system may not function properly. When that happens, the signals may not be as reliable. For example, diabetics have to take special care of their feet. Poorly controlled or long-term diabetes can cause peripheral neuropathy—nerve damage to the patient's foot. The first sign of peripheral neuropathy may be tingling or numbness, perhaps an inability to feel a light tickle. Coming into contact with a minor irritant—

sandals that rub or a rock in the shoe—the diabetic may not feel the irritation and subsequent pain. That could lead to serious injury or infection.

If the neuropathy progresses, lack of feeling in a foot can affect balance or even the ability to walk. In extreme cases, a diabetic patient could step on, say, a rusty nail and not realize it. Then, when the infection becomes serious, the only option is to amputate the foot and possibly part of the leg.

Even then, the nervous system continues to play a role. Amputees report a kind of misfiring of the nervous system— phantom pains. Their toes will hurt, or their calf will itch even though it is no longer there.

Joe was a diabetic. In his seventies, he had his leg amputated below the knee. He complained of itching and burning in a foot he no longer had. He could feel his toes move, but without a foot, there were no toes.

What if our conscience is like a nervous system for moral behavior? When functioning properly, it acts as a reflex, sending messages to avoid things that would injure or cause pain. But when it malfunctions, it misfires, and we experience phantom pangs of guilt,

or worse,

we can't feel it at all.

108.1 WHAT IS CONSCIENCE?

When we think about having a conscience, the immediate association is usually "guilty conscience." So if we ask *how* God uses our conscience to *speak* to us, most of us think he does it by making us feel bad, heaping on the guilt for our indiscretions.

There is some truth in that response.

But what if God uses our conscience in more subtle ways?

Just as a nervous system can bring us different sensations and messages, could God use the conscience as a delivery system to communicate something other than guilt?

Can our conscience nudge us—or *shove* us—into actions we might not otherwise take?

We're familiar with that voice inside encouraging us to call a friend or warning us not to speed. Sometimes, we call that inner sense of right and wrong the conscience. In movies and television, conscience is often personified as an angel on the right shoulder and a devil on the left. Those talking representations of the psyche then argue in an attempt to influence the decision of the person.

Does that mean God is sitting on your collarbone, yelling in your right ear while a guy in a skintight red suit with horns is yelling in the other?

Does God speak to us through that inner voice?

Or is that voice an irritating echo of someone else? Perhaps a nagging mother or a meddlesome teacher from childhood?

What exactly is a conscience, and who speaks through it?

If you really want to know . . .

Google it.

There you will find a mess of competing theories. Some say we're born with a conscience, some say we develop it, and some say it develops us. There are philosophical, social, and religious explanations of conscience (which don't all agree, by the way), and some guy with a blog who has an opinion. It's all quite confusing.

In Walt Disney's *Pinocchio*, the 1940 cartoon adaptation of the children's book by C. Collodi (1883), the Blue Fairy tries to simplify life by telling Pinocchio to "let your conscience be your guide." That seems like sound advice. We've all experienced a time when our conscience prevented us from doing something wrong. Or scolded us after we misbehaved.

But unlike the nervous system, which is easily identified in an autopsy, there is no conscience organ, gland, or muscular tissue. We know it's real only because we interact with it in the same way we interact with thoughts or ideas. Though we can prick it, we can't poke it.

Does that mean our conscience is some weird amalgamation of our thoughts?

How do we distinguish *our* thoughts from thoughts *God* places in our minds?

Is there a difference?

108.2 TELLING RIGHT FROM WRONG

In his book *Mere Christianity*, C. S. Lewis discusses what he calls "the Law of Human Nature." It is a sense of right and wrong that Lewis believes we are each born with. According to Lewis, we hear examples of it every day: "Hey, that's my seat," "I got here first," "You need to share your orange with me; I shared mine with you," or "You promised!" Lewis writes,

> Now what interests me about all these remarks is that the man who makes them is not merely saying that the other man's behaviour does not happen to please him. He is appealing to some kind of standard of behaviour

which he expects the other man to know about. And the other man very seldom replies: "To hell with your standard." Nearly always he tries to make out that what he has been doing does not really go against the standard, or that if it does there is some special excuse. He pretends there is some special reason in this particular case why the person who took the seat first should not keep it, or that things were quite different when he was given the bit of orange, or that something has turned up which lets him off keeping his promise. It looks, in fact, very much as if both parties had in mind some kind of Law or Rule of fair play or decent behaviour or morality or whatever you like to call it, about which they really agreed. And they have.[1]

Lewis refers to this rule of right and wrong as the Law of Human Nature, because it doesn't have to be taught. Everyone knows it. Though there may be an aberrant soul or two—just as there is someone who is color-blind or can't carry a tune—overall, Lewis believes that humans understand and agree on the Law of Human Nature. If the standard weren't true for all humans, we couldn't say that the Nazis were wrong and should have acted differently. Lewis argues that if the Nazis truly didn't know what was right, "we could no more have blamed them for that than for the colour of their hair."[2]

Lewis's critics claim that morality differs by time and location. But that simply isn't true, Lewis argues:

I need only ask the reader to think what a totally different morality would mean. Think of a country

223

> where people were admired for running away in battle,
> or where a man felt proud of double-crossing all the
> people who had been kindest to him. . . . Selfishness
> has never been admired. Men have differed as to
> whether you should have one wife or four. But they
> have always agreed that you must not simply have
> any woman you liked.[3]

In other words, Lewis says there seems to be some sort
of general morality all humans subscribe to. We can agree
murder is wrong, yet argue that self-defense, abortion, or
the death penalty isn't murder. We agree there is a standard; we just disagree about when and where the standard
applies.

Could it be that your conscience is somehow an internal
broadcast system for the Law of Human Nature? If we were
born with that law inside of us, there must be some mechanism by which we interact with it. There must be a way for
the angel of right living to sit on one shoulder and argue
with the devil of what-we-want-to-do on the other.

Perhaps our conscience is the *hardwiring*, the moral nervous systems that react to stimuli by jerking us back from
what hurts us. If so, one way God speaks to us is through
our conscience, advising us when we are breeching the Law
of Human Nature. We don't have to understand the law for it
to work: "Even Gentiles, who do not have God's written law,
show that they know his law when they instinctively obey it,
even without having heard it."[4]

Inside each of us is a seed of belief that it is wrong to
steal, murder, abuse little children, and so on. That idea is
broadcast through the conscience, which takes the seed and

puts it into full bloom at the moment we most need to be reminded of it.

The fact that the instructions are common to all of us is what allows us to live together in organized societies. We can agree on a common set of behaviors. We can also agree that people who go against those norms should be punished. Though we may not acknowledge them as such, our internal promptings about the Law of Human Nature are as natural and as much a part of God's creation as the sunset.

Maybe that's what the Blue Fairy meant when she told Pinocchio to let his conscience be his guide. She wanted him to follow that God-given sense of inner morality that every human (and at least one wooden puppet) has.

108.3 LET YOUR CONSCIENCE BE YOUR GUIDE?

Abraham's wife was hot. She was the kind of woman other men ogle and wish they had married. In fact, Sarah was so good looking, Abraham was terrified that King Abimelech, the godless ruler of the territory in which Abraham was temporarily living, would take his life in order to take his wife. So Abraham came up with a plan. Instead of telling everyone Sarah was his wife, he introduced her as his sister. Of course, that raised some interesting consequences for Sarah, but Abraham figured at least he'd be alive to worry about them.

As expected, King Abimelech sent for Sarah and took her into his house. But before he could sleep with her, the king had a dream. In the dream, God told him he was as good as dead, because Sarah was a married woman.

Abimelech then reminded God that he was innocent. Speaking of Abraham, he said, "Did he not say to me, 'She is my sister,' and didn't she also say, 'He is my brother'? I have done this with a clear conscience and clean hands."[5]

In other words, Abimelech used the Blue Fairy defense. He understood there was a standard, and when he took Sarah into his house, he didn't believe he was breaking it. He let his conscience be his guide.

His argument worked.

> Then God said to him in the dream, "Yes, I know you did this with a clear conscience, and so I have kept you from sinning against me. That is why I did not let you touch her. Now return the man's wife, for he is a prophet, and he will pray for you and you will live. But if you do not return her, you may be sure that you and all yours will die."[6]

Abimelech believed he had done the right thing by being true to his conscience. God agreed and accepted the argument.

How cool is that?

We can all stay out of trouble by following our conscience. No more guilt. Let's party! (Well, at least to the point it doesn't encroach on our internal standards.)

If we don't go against our conscience, God won't find us guilty.

Seems like an open-and-shut case, doesn't it?

Guilt is not God's way of imposing shame; rather, it is a signal from our moral nervous system that our shoe is rubbing against our foot, and if we don't do something about it, we'll get an infection. It's almost as reflexive as yanking a foot out of a tub of steaming water. Feeling a little guilty is equal to feeling an irritation in our shoe. If we persist in disobeying the early signs, we could end up with a full-blown guilt infection.

Donna Jordan teaches and writes on the subject of listening to God's voice, and she believes a guilty conscience is one way God speaks to us about specific problem areas in our lives. Until we remedy them, she believes guilt is a hindrance from hearing anything more God wants to share.[7]

If she's right, guilt isn't just about what happened in the past; it's also about what will happen in the future.

Visit a concentration camp memorial, and you will notice that a holy, horrific hush falls over the crowd as they enter the gate. Lost in their own thoughts, each person silently reflects on the lives lost there. Some may feel guilt for things they, or their ancestors, did. Without an absolute morality given to us by God, we would have no basis for saying the Holocaust was evil.

The Nazis didn't wake up one day and begin throwing Jews into crematoriums. There was a progression of smaller wrongs that grew into major atrocities. For those who participated in those evil acts, their consciences provided initial warning signs.

But after being ignored long enough, like atrophied muscles, their consciences stopped broadcasting the Law of Human Nature. And that's when they stopped hearing God's voice.

Yet God continues to use our inner senses of right and wrong. The abhorrence we feel when visiting the place of such atrocities suggests God continues to speak to collective consciences through the guilt we feel.

Guilt is a peculiar kind of pain, isn't it?

And confession seems to be our first antidote for guilt. Talk shows such as *The Jerry Springer Show* have become a cultural confessional, with no contrition necessary. And Web sites like dailyconfession.com and ivescrewedup.com give people an online place to purge their shame.

A recent *Wall Street Journal* article titled "Confession Makes a Comeback" describes how "aggressive marketing by churches has helped reinvent confession as a form of self-improvement rather than a punitive rite."[8] The article quoted several people who acknowledged that confession brought them peace and restored things to where they were before.

But sometimes confession isn't enough.

In those cases where our guilt isn't eased by confession, it seems our conscience compels us to *do* something about it.

> Apologize.
> Return the money.
> Change our behavior.
> Forgive.

It makes sense.

Admitting you have a rock in your shoe might help you understand what causes your foot pain, but to relieve the pain, you have to remove the rock.

The intense and communal feelings we have at a place like Auschwitz or the United States Holocaust Memorial Museum should be all the encouragement and reminder we need to act differently. It's not just an intellectual understanding of a standard broken, trampled upon, and burned in the fire; it's also an emotional weight visitors carry with them when they leave.

Those feelings compel us to *do* something.

> Donate money.
> Say a prayer.
> Tell a friend.

Conscience changes our behavior—in dozens of little and big ways.

That seems like a godly thing, doesn't it? That he would spur us on to do better when we've broken his universal rules of right and wrong.

But if that is how our conscience works, setting off alarm bells when we or others close to us have breached the Law of Human Nature, why do we feel guilty even when we haven't?

In other words, why do we feel guilty when we play tennis?

108.4 RELATIVE CONSCIENCE

When Jennifer was trying to figure out what it meant to be a follower of Jesus, she overheard Linda, a friend whom she admired for her spiritual maturity, tell a mutual friend that playing tennis was a sin. That confused Jennifer because she had never heard that.

Jennifer went home and used her pocket concordance to look up *tennis* to see what commandment it fell under. But the word wasn't even in the Bible. Jennifer puzzled over the meaning of Linda's words.

Were the short skirts the girls wore on the courts too revealing? Was that the sin?

Was there some satanic origin to the game Jennifer didn't know about?

Did Linda curse when she lost a game?

At the next youth group meeting, Jennifer cornered Linda and asked why tennis was a sin.

"It's not a sin for *you*," said Linda, who knew Jennifer rarely played.

"Then why is it for you?"

Linda explained that when she played tennis, she didn't just *play* the game; she *obsessed* over it. She would spend every waking moment thinking about her next match. When she was on the court, winning was more important than anything else. She made tennis a god, and if she continued playing tennis at the same level of intensity, it would be sinful. Things were out of balance. Tennis had become more important than God, and her shorthand way of describing it to her friend was, "Tennis was a sin" *for her*.

Can something be a sin for one person and not for another?

Jennifer intellectually understood what Linda was saying, but it wasn't until fifteen years later that she experienced something similar. She saw a new musical and was impressed with the creativity of the team who wrote the show. She wanted to hear more. During intermission, she bought the double-CD set. For the next week, Jennifer listened to the CD nonstop.

One day, she went to turn on the CD player, and she heard something else. Perhaps *felt something* is a better way to describe it, because it wasn't audible. The voice or feeling seemed to suggest she should break the CD in half. That was a ridiculous thought and one Jennifer would never have suggested. At that time in her life, the CD purchase had been an expensive splurge.

No need to break it, she thought; she could give it away. In those pre-iPod days, giving it away was the equivalent of breaking it—she would never hear it again. Plus, she had friends who were musical enthusiasts, and most of them were broke. They'd love the CD.

But the voice/feeling persisted.

"Break it."

The more she argued, the stronger the voice grew until she felt compelled to do it. She broke the first CD and thought that would be it. But it wasn't; she heard that inner voice again.

"Break it."

She broke the second one, too.

Then she felt a weird release of tension—as if it were a confirmation she had done the right thing. She took both CDs and buried them in the trash. She didn't want to explain to her husband what she had done to her brand-new CDs.

Over the next few weeks, Jennifer realized some of the lyrics on those CDs had dark themes and promoted ideals she wasn't comfortable with. Because she had played the CDs repetitively, the lyrics had become part of her thinking. Over time, that held the potential to erode her values.

Though Jennifer's conscience caused her to do something drastic, she never believed it was wrong for anyone else. Her friends could still listen to the same CD without it being wrong or sinful for them. But Jennifer believed that, at that time and place, God was telling her something.

He wanted to protect her thoughts, get her attention, or increase her awareness. Whatever it was, it was specific to *her* conscience.

Breaking the CD was not Lewis's Law of Human Nature. It was Linda playing tennis. It was God using an individual's conscience to communicate a specific message.

Some conscience triggers are, or should be, universal. But just as some people have sensitive feet and prefer not to have them tickled, or hate wearing pointed shoes because they pinch their toes, so there are specific things that can irritate an individual conscience.

The apostle Paul understood that our conscience responds to a specific morality that is unique for each person. Paul addresses the matter in-depth in his letters.[9] He argues that he is free to do anything his conscience does not condemn. And so is everyone else. For example, Paul doesn't feel guilty about eating meat offered to idols.[10]

Yet Paul goes on to say that for the *sake of love*, when he's in the presence of people who feel eating idol meat is wrong, he will *yield his right*. In other words, not only is Paul paying attention to his own moral nervous system, but he takes into account the sensitivity of others, too.

That's similar to the stance some churches have taken on drinking alcohol. They encourage members to make their own decisions as to whether to drink or not, but suggest they not do it when socializing with others—so it won't tempt someone who may be struggling with the issue or who has an addiction.

Is that hypocritical?

Or is that sensitivity and kindness?

108.5 GETTING THE MESSAGE

All parents feel anxiety when their child gets his or her driver's license . . . and promptly asks to borrow the car. So when Emily passed her driver's test and asked if she could celebrate her new freedom by driving her sister to the mall, Jill cringed. But reluctantly, she agreed.

The sisters were gone about twenty minutes when it occurred to Jill that Emily might not be on the insurance policy. Though she was busy, Jill became obsessed with the thought—to the point that she stopped what she was doing and picked up the phone.

"I called our insurance agent, though I didn't exactly mention Emily was at that very moment already tooling around the city," said Jill.

"No, Emily's not listed," the agent told Jill.

"Can we add her right now?"

"Sure," the agent said. "What's her driver's license number?"

Jill had no idea. "I don't know. But I'll find out and call you back."

Jill tried Emily's cell phone, but there was no answer. She called the DMV directly. Unfortunately, the DMV refused to give that information over the phone. Next, she called her husband to see if he could get to the DMV and get the information personally. But he was across town and couldn't get home for an hour or more. Something told Jill this couldn't wait. For whatever reason, she was compelled to get this taken care of now.

"I hung up and panicked. I felt genuine terror. I knew this was an urgent crisis. I simply had to talk to Emily," said Jill. "I fell down on my knees and cried out, literally—'God, help me find her. Help me find her!'" Jill was desperate.

A bit melodramatic?

Perhaps.

Most people would chalk Jill's reaction up to an overly nervous mom of a first-time driver. Jill would probably describe it the same way. But she couldn't stop. Something inside was screaming for her to take care of this *now*.

"Then I remembered something," said Jill. "I remembered one of the stores where the girls were going to shop. I called, described the girls to the employee, and left a message for Emily to call home immediately. Then I hung up."

Fifteen minutes later, Emily called.

"She was a bit irritated, thinking I didn't trust her. But I got her license number and called the agent back. She assured me that yes, Emily was now, as of 3:15 p.m., officially on our insurance." Jill's panic lifted. She returned to what she was doing.

Did Jill make too much out of the anxiety any parent might feel?

Or was something more going on?

Thirty minutes later, Jill got another phone call from Emily. This time Emily was crying. Three hours after passing her driving test and a mere half hour after she had been added to the family insurance policy, Emily turned left at a busy intersection in front of an oncoming car. She couldn't stop in time and hit the other car. Both vehicles were totaled. Neither sister was hurt.

The policy was in effect at the time of the accident.

Overreacting mom?

Or a mom who heard God's voice through her conscience and listened to it?

Jill doesn't care what other people think. She believes God spoke to her, gave her the initial nudge, and kept up the pressure even when it wasn't easily resolved. "I cringe to think what might have happened if I hadn't panicked, if I hadn't felt I had to do that paperwork right then," said Jill.

Many people describe an inner voice or feeling that nudges them to do something they otherwise wouldn't do. Yet, most of us haven't ever felt as compelled as Jill did to follow the inner voice. Then again, most of us haven't had the kind of dramatic experience she did.

Does that mean God isn't speaking to us?

If we don't hear him like Jill did, does that mean we're not good enough?

For a minute, let's assume God sends us the same kinds of messages he sent Jill. That changes our question then, doesn't it? The question is no longer, Why isn't God speaking? It's, Why aren't we hearing?

Could it be we're not *open* to receiving God's messages?

Or that when we do receive one, we ignore it because we don't recognize God's voice?

Earlier in this chapter we talked about the ways our nervous systems could fail us. Is it possible that our conscience could fail us too?

Could they mislead us?

108.6 MALFUNCTIONING CONSCIENCE

King Saul doesn't know where David is, but he's hunting him down, and when he finds him, he'll kill him.

But before Saul can locate David, the king stops in a cave

to . . . uh, relieve himself. Unfortunately for Saul, David happens to be hiding farther back in the cave. As Saul gets busy doing his business, David sneaks up on him. Considering Saul's delicate position, it would be easy for David to kill him, but instead David cuts off a piece of the king's robe and returns to his hiding place. Presumably, Saul is too busy reading the royal newspaper to notice.

Immediately, David knows he's done wrong:

> David's conscience began bothering him because he had cut Saul's robe. "The LORD knows I shouldn't have done that to my lord the king," he said to his men. "The LORD forbid that I should do this to my lord the king and attack the LORD's anointed one, for the LORD himself has chosen him."[11]

But here's what's interesting. David's conscience wasn't a part of the equation until *after* the incident. What good is a conscience that doesn't show up until it's too late? Sure, David feels guilty—*now*. And when he connects the dots, he knows his conscience is bothering him because he did what God told him not to. But he was *already* guilty when his inner voice began to throb. David's conscience was apparently *dormant* at the time he made the decision to go forth and cut.

Or . . .

was it?

Had David negotiated some kind of truce with his conscience?

If you're familiar with the story of David, you know how he's considered a role model of the faith. Yet, David apparently struggles with his conscience.

A lot.

And unfortunately, it seems David wins.

A lot.

Could it be that pushing aside his inner voice in the little things makes it harder for him to hear God in the big things?

Previously in the Old Testament, we heard the story of Joseph, who was disliked by his brothers so much they decided to kill him and blame it on wild animals. But when Reuben heard of the scheme, his conscience got the better of him, and he suggested they toss Joseph in an empty well.

Everything went as planned. They lowered Joe in the hole and sat down for sandwiches. As they got ready to eat, they saw traders headed to Egypt. By now, some of the brothers were starting to feel guilty.

Perhaps the traders offered a way to ease their guilt?

Judah spoke up. "What will we gain by killing our brother? We'd have to cover up the crime. Instead of hurting him, let's sell him to those Ishmaelite traders. After all, he is our brother—our own flesh and blood!"[12] Instead of killing him, they sold Joseph and split the profits.

Joe's life was saved first by Reuben's conscience, then Judah's, and finally by the collective conscience of his brothers.

. . .

King Abimelech was saved by following his conscience.

David felt guilty because his conscience didn't speak up until it was too late.

The brothers' consciences flashed on and off like a strobe

light at a rock-and-roll concert, yet they still sold Joseph into slavery.

Three stories, three different results of letting your conscience be your guide. What's the point of all those crazy stories?

Only God knows.

But we can draw a few conclusions.

The Bible seems to confirm we each have a conscience— an inner voice that guides and directs us—and that God will find us innocent if we don't go against that voice. However, it appears that voice is also capable of failing. Sometimes, it doesn't speak up until it's too late.

If God speaks through our conscience, it appears sometimes he doesn't do a good job of it.

Great.

What do we do with that?

It's difficult to build your entire moral development around letting your conscience be your guide if it doesn't speak up until it's too late.

Or . . .

could part of the job belong to us?

For example, David heard from his conscience. He knew not to *kill* King Saul. He knew God told him that. Then why didn't he get the part about not cutting the robe?

The brothers had pangs of conscience about killing Joseph or leaving him in a well, but apparently not enough to change their minds and take him home.

Could it be God always speaks through our conscience . . .

but sometimes we refuse to listen to the *whole* message?

Instead, we pick and choose the parts we want to hear.

108.7 NOT SEEING THE ELEPHANT

In an episode of *The Simpsons*, Lisa tells Homer her conscience is bothering her. Homer replies, "Your conscience? Lisa, don't let that pushy little weenie tell you what to do."

Then a tiny Homer angel appears and speaks:

Homer's conscience: Homer, that's a terrible thing to say.

Homer: Aw, shut up!

Homer's conscience: *[meekly]* Yes, sir.[13]

Poof! The angel is gone.

If there are situations in which our conscience is a good guide, we also have times when that inner voice fails us. We tell it to shut up, and away it goes. It seems that inner sense of right and wrong can be controlled by something other than God. Like Homer Simpson, it seems we can make our conscience disappear.

Christian illusionist Brock Gill is very good at his job. Using sleight of hand, props, and other tools of the trade, he helps people see things that aren't really there—or blinds them to things that are. But the tricks are just part of his routine. He knows how to convince people to see things the way he wants them to, and he does it by manipulating their entire experience.

From the posters that advertise the show, to the lighting and staging of the performance, Brock creates an environment where people respond to his suggestions. Everything about the performance is designed to get the audience to see things the way Brock wants them to see it—not necessarily the way things really are.

"I lead an audience to where I want them to go," says Brock. "I make them believe certain things I want them to believe even before the show starts."

In other words, not only does Brock mind the tricks; he also tricks the mind.

"Everything that is presented as magic works in the mind," he says. "Tricking the eyes is nearly impossible because the eyes see so much more than the mind does."

If an illusionist makes an elephant disappear, the elephant doesn't just disappear. Poof! Elephant gone. No, the elephant is still there. The audience doesn't *see* the elephant, but the elephant is present. The magician has concealed it from the audience's minds.

"What the audience *sees* and what they *think they see* are two different things. After my show, you can go up and ask someone what they saw, and their version is very different than what actually happened."

Brock gives an example. In some of his shows, he announces he is going to make three Ping-Pong balls disappear. It's a silly joke: While facing the audience, he does the trick by putting three balls in his mouth one at a time. Then with a mouthful of balls in his chipmunk cheeks, he announces they've disappeared before spitting them out in front of the audience.

Yet, months later, the host of the event will invite him back and tell him to make sure he does the trick where he makes the Ping-Pong balls disappear into thin air.

Could it be that our conscience is susceptible to the same gag?

When we do something against our inner voice, can we convince ourselves the Law of Human Nature isn't there?

Like Homer Simpson, can we just tell it to shut up?

And if we do, will it go away?

Could it be that our conscience is like the magician's elephant—concealed from our minds?

There is historical evidence that people have ignored their conscience.

> The Holocaust.
> Genocide in Rwanda.
> Slavery.
> Child sex-trafficking.
> The injustices that were done to *you*.

In each of those cases, people disobeyed the rule of right and wrong, went against human nature, rejected their conscience, and pushed aside the pushy little weenie.

And, in doing so, they stopped hearing God's voice.

108.8 CLEANING OUT THE PIPES

Michelangelo Merisi da Caravaggio came to Rome and settled in with the underbelly of the city. The rogues he lived among became models for the stories of grace he told in his paintings. He often cast religious narratives in his own contemporary context. Frequently his own face played the role of wayward sinner or defiant antihero.

By the time he was thirty years old, Caravaggio had a price on his head. He had rocked the art world with his revolutionary, earthy portraits of biblical stories. No one before him dared portray such realistic baseness in religious art. In *The Calling of Saint Matthew* and *The Martyrdom of Saint Matthew* (ca.1598–99; San Luigi dei Francesi, Rome), he depicted saints as flawed humans marred by the profane world around them. Caravaggio seemed to hear God best when he painted grace within the darkest scenes. In doing so, he put a price on his own head long before the officials in Rome did.

Caravaggio's art imitated his life. He had a fierce temper and was prone to brooding seasons of almost animal-like rage. In 1606, after taking offense at a spurious remark hurled toward him in a dark street outside a tavern, Caravaggio demanded a duel. During the swordplay, he killed his opponent.

He fled Rome. Wandering from city to city, he painted prodigiously and yearned for some sort of genuine atonement. Eventually, he collected many of those later paintings and sent them to Rome as a gift to church officials, hoping to win their pardon.

One of those paintings, completed not long after the murder, was his famous *David with the Head of Goliath*. Caravaggio's own likeness is etched in the face of not only the somberly triumphant boy, David, but also the gory, severed head of the fallen giant. Bearing his guilt in full, Caravaggio delivers his own head in a quest for atonement.

His paintings arrived in Rome, but tragically, Caravaggio died before he could return to claim his pardon.[14]

How does one find atonement and pardon?

How does one cleanse a stained conscience?

Like Caravaggio, do we find it in church officials?

Is saying confession either in person or on a Web site *enough*?

• • •

Before Paul was the man of wisdom and letters, he was Saul, a Christian-killer. Probably one of the best. But something happened to Saul. He met Jesus in a profound encounter and was temporarily blinded by the experience. In the process of his miraculous recovery, he became a believer.

Over the next few years, as he grew in his personal understanding of Jesus, Saul (who was also known as Paul) came face to face with his own moral weakness. As a Pharisee, he had focused on behaviors as a moral barometer. But the closer he came to Jesus, the more aware he grew of his own inner failure to stand up to the moral demands of God's standard of perfection. He might be able to act like he was good, but inside he remained chained to his immoral inclinations. He could never be good enough.

Meeting Jesus awakened his conscience. He came to understand that regardless of how hard he worked, he felt more and more helpless. He was too deeply compromised.

In his famous letter to the church in Rome, Paul pours out his own helplessness to resist the judgment of his conscience.

> I have discovered this principle of life—that when I want to do what is right, I inevitably do what is wrong. I love God's law with all my heart. But there is another power within me that is at war with my mind. This power makes me a slave to the sin that is still within me. Oh, what a miserable person I am! Who will free me from this life that is dominated by sin and death?[15]

Is Paul describing the angel and the devil on the shoulder? Paul said he loves the law of God but something inside of him struggles against it.

Could it be that even the best-intentioned conscience can become hijacked by something other than what God put there?

If so, is there a way to shut our conscience off?

Or can we select the message our conscience broadcasts?

Everybody has a conscience, said Paul.[16] And that conscience is given to them by God. God speaks through our conscience about what he does and doesn't want us to do. But no one in the world, no matter how hard they try, can fulfill all the demands of their conscience. Neither the general nor the specific.

Paul should know. He tried harder than anyone. In the end, he was left feeling futile and helpless. Paul himself seems to have lived out the parable Jesus told during his earthly ministry.

> Two men went to the Temple to pray. One was a
> Pharisee, and the other was a despised tax collector.
> The Pharisee stood by himself and prayed this
> prayer: "I thank you, God, that I am not a sinner
> like everyone else. For I don't cheat, I don't sin, and
> I don't commit adultery. I'm certainly not like that
> tax collector! I fast twice a week, and I give you a
> tenth of my income." But the tax collector stood at
> a distance and dared not even lift his eyes to heaven
> as he prayed. Instead, he beat his chest in sorrow,
> saying, "O God, be merciful to me, for I am a sinner."
> I tell you, this sinner, not the Pharisee, returned home
> justified before God. For those who exalt themselves
> will be humbled, and those who humble themselves
> will be exalted.[17]

The Pharisee, the agitator of the consciences of others, seemed to have no conscience. In contrast, the tax collector (in that culture, the worst kind of sinner—a traitor *and* a thief) felt the personal weight of his own sinfulness. He heard God speak through his own shame and was therefore able to come close to God. Paul's spiritual journey seems to metaphorically have moved from Pharisee to tax collector. That brought Paul into a position to hear God's words of love and mercy.

Paul understood the power and wonder of God's gift of goodness offered freely to anyone who believes in Jesus. He put it this way at the end of the conscience-stricken confession in Romans 7: "Who will free me from this life that is dominated by sin and death? Thank God! The answer is in Jesus Christ our Lord."[18]

How exactly does that work?

It's like any electronic signal. Wiring that is crossed, receiving multiple signals, or in the process of transmitting something doesn't work as effectively as a delivery system that is waiting to be used.

Pipes that are dirty and clogged won't allow much through.

A nervous system that is disconnected from the foot misfires and sends false signals, or none at all.

When our conscience is freed, when we're not burdened by pain signals—guilt, sleeplessness, questioning, doubt— we are receptive to new messages. By turning to God through confession, contrition, and faith that his grace is big enough, we clean up our wiring. Instead of being burdened by the pangs of our conscience, we're open to receive other messages. We can hear God in the smallest nudges of an inner voice or a feeling.

108.9 open ears

On Friday afternoon, Howard had a strange impulse to return to the nursing home he had visited earlier that morning. He knew the inner prompting; he had felt it before. But he didn't know why he needed to go back.

He felt a bit foolish walking through the door and signing his name at the registry again. He felt more so as he walked back toward the room of the elderly woman he'd visited earlier. On his way, he passed a nurse in the hall. She stopped him and asked, "You're a pastor, aren't you?"

"Yes," said Howard.

"Good. There's a man down the hall. He's not well. And he's been calling for a pastor for two days. We haven't been able to get anyone here."

He followed the nurse to a room that smelled of death. Vern, the old man in the bed, had been drifting in and out of a coma for days.

"I understand you've been calling for a pastor," Howard said.

"Are you a pastor? You look too young," the man muttered.

"I'm a pastor. I wasn't planning to come here, but I felt God speak to me. I think he sent me to you."

"I've hated the thought of God," said Vern. "Truthfully, I've hated most people, too. I've been evil. I've done terrible things, evil things. I'm an atheist."

"Then why did you want a pastor?"

"Because I'm dying. And underneath, I guess I'm not an atheist; not anymore, at least."

"Then you want to get right with God?" asked Howard, pulling a chair next to the bed. Vern turned his head and looked Howard in the eye.

"Is it too late for me?" Vern asked.

"It's never too late," said Howard. "The guilt you're feeling is God calling you. You didn't initiate this. He did." Howard began a story from the Bible: "Two criminals hung on the cross next to Jesus. One mocked him. One asked for pardon. As Jesus and that criminal hung there dying, Jesus promised the criminal he would be in heaven because of his faith. He didn't have time to do anything but believe."

Vern started praying, "God, I'm sorry for being such a jerk," Vern said. "I'm sorry for mocking you and mocking others who believed in you. If there's any chance, please forgive me." He paused and then said, "I wish now I'd done that sooner."

Howard said nothing. He just patted Vern's hand.

"That good enough?" asked Vern.

"Yep," said Howard. He pulled out his pocket New Testament and opened to 1 John 1:9. He read in the old King James, "If we confess our sins, he is faithful and just to forgive us our sins, and to cleanse us from all unrighteousness."

Howard paused. "Vern, I'm here as your witness. You've confessed, just like the Bible says. Jesus forgives you. Your sin is gone."

He showed Vern several examples in the Bible of people who had been forgiven. David's Psalm 51, written after he'd stolen a man's wife and killed him to cover it up. Zacchaeus the tax collector, who invited Jesus to his house for a meal and confessed that he'd stolen money.

After a time, Vern grew weary. Howard stood and walked toward the door. Vern rolled over and faced the wall. As Howard paused by the door, he heard the old man say, "Oh, thank you, God; thank you for cleaning me up and lifting all that garbage away. I don't deserve it, but I feel free. I know it's true. I know you."

Howard drove home. Later that day, he received a phone call from Vern's son. "I don't know what you did with my father, but thank you. He's a changed man. He's called the whole family to come and see him. One by one he told us what happened when you came. He asked all of us to forgive him. Pastor, my father was not a pleasant man. Honestly, he was miserable and selfish. He made our lives hell. But he asked us to forgive him. He said he knew for the first time that there is a God and that he's good, because he knew God forgave him. He asked if we would do the same."

Over the next two days, Vern was alert and out of his coma. He spoke with each of the doctors and nurses in the convalescent home, all of whom had dreaded serving him because he'd been so troublesome. He asked their pardon. He called friends and people he'd worked with, and when they came to his bedside, he wept and asked forgiveness.

On Monday, Vern died a free man.

Vern's conscience burned with a message of what a miserable man he was. After he *cleared* his conscience, he heard more subtle messages.

> To apologize.
> To ask for forgiveness.
> To clear up bad feelings with friends and family.

Vern was like a diabetic who treats the foot problem before it spreads. He freed his moral nervous system to receive other sensations—the feel of sand on the toes, the tickle of a loved one, the warmth of soft socks.

If you think our point is that you should confess to clear your conscience like Vern did, you missed the more important issue. Yes, Vern's story is life-changing, not only for him, but for each person he made amends with before his death.

Yes, this is dramatic.

Yes, this is moving.

But no, that's not the *most* important point.

The real point is much subtler. None of that would have happened for Vern if Howard had ignored the voice inside of him, the little nudge that said, "I know that isn't what you planned. It's inconvenient, and you've already been there once today. But go back to the nursing home, anyway."

Howard felt the nudge.

He listened to the message his conscience quietly spoke to him.

He heard an inner voice.

He had a feeling.

And he did something about it.

What he did changed the life of Vern and all those who knew him. But it also changed Howard. It reaffirmed how important it was for him to pay attention to the tiniest of urges from his conscience.

108.10 WHOSE VOICE?

If the Law of Human Nature is what God placed inside of us at Creation, perhaps he quickly saw it wasn't enough. Like Homer Simpson said, our conscience is a pushy little weenie. Yet we're pretty good at pushing back.

Not all internal events originate with God. Our conscience is used to communicate his message. But consciences can be manipulated and "bent" away from God's absolute standard to communicate other messages. We allow others to hijack our sense of right and wrong and make us feel guilty for things we shouldn't.

Sometimes we even learn to feel guilty about the wrong things.

In Mario Puzo's *The Godfather* and Francis Ford Coppola's film adaptation, Michael Corleone, the son of mob boss Don Vito Corleone, is resolved to resist the family pressure to enter the Mafia. But that decision is not without guilt. Michael feels shame for choosing an honest lifestyle. That resistance collapses when his father becomes the target of an assassination attempt. Michael yields to the family pressure for revenge and is pulled into the spiral of violence, eventually becoming a villain.

The conscience is not absolute.

It has to be trained to hear the voice of God, whether in an absolute standard of morality like Lewis's Law of Human Nature or in a specific set of moral behaviors like Linda not playing tennis and Jennifer breaking CDs.

Knowing our conscience can be used and misused, sometimes we're just not sure.

Whose voice is it, anyway?

With so much confusion, not only about the message but also the source of the message, perhaps that's why God sent Jesus.

For three years he traveled with the disciples. He was their guide to truth and wisdom. When the disciples heard a voice, it was his audible one. Jesus spoke the words of

God. He served as their living standard. Then he said he was going away. The end had come, and he was the only person in the room who knew what it meant.

Jesus tried to explain things to his students as plainly as he could. They heard what he said, and they knew something was up, but the magnitude of the moment escaped them. That night, Jesus would be arrested, taken away, and executed. Jesus comforted them by saying that once he left, he would send another helper in his place. He called the helper the Holy Spirit and described how it was best that he leave so the helper would always be with them.

> But in fact, it is best for you that I go away, because if I don't, the Advocate won't come. If I do go away, then I will send him to you. And when he comes, he will convict the world of its sin, and of God's righteousness, and of the coming judgment.[19]

As Jesus had done while he lived with them physically, this new Advocate would work within their consciences to bring knowledge and clarity of what was true and right. He would also help them to discern what was evil and wrong. The Holy Spirit would be their guide. He would work through the mechanism of their consciences to speak God's practical, specific moral direction.

It was the promise God had made centuries before to a troubled and beat-up old prophet named Jeremiah:

> "But this is the new covenant I will make with the people of Israel on that day," says the LORD. "I will put my instructions deep within them, and I will write

them on their hearts. I will be their God, and they will
be my people."[20]

The "law on our hearts" that he speaks of is put there by the
Holy Spirit. His presence, working through our conscience,
means not only can we *know* what is right and wrong, but
we can also begin to *want* what is *right* more than what is
wrong. As that takes place, we will find new abilities to *do*
what is right. His presence in us is like our conscience on
steroids. Like an actual nervous system, it moves us from
warning to action.

When developed under the leading of the Holy Spirit,
our conscience can be our guide. The problem is, our
conscience doesn't develop that way. Sometimes parents
hijack a child's conscience with other messages. The culture
manipulates the conscience. Like Brock Gill, who creates an
environment to trick the minds of his audience, our environ-
ments can drown out the voice of the Holy Spirit.

Is your environment set up to hear God's voice?

Or do you drown it out through the noise of this world,
the busyness of your life, and your skepticism about how
you think God speaks here and now?

If you can't hear God speak, is it because he isn't speaking to you?

Or is it because everything about the ambience of your
environment has set you up to believe the elephant isn't
there?

If your conscience isn't saying anything at all, if you don't
hear God speak through it, ask yourself what you're saying
to shove the pushy little weenie away.

Do the following statements sound familiar?

"God doesn't talk to people like that."

"That's not God talking—that's indigestion."

"God doesn't talk to *me*."

If your conscience is clogged by guilt, take a look to see if the feeling is real pain—a message that you have a rock in your shoe and you need to do something. Or consider whether it might be a phantom pain, placed there by a misguided parent, friend, or life experience, and now it's blocking receptors so you can't feel anything else.

Your conscience is a tool used to communicate sensation. Working properly, it is a friend that nudges, guides, and directs you through the codes and standards God put inside you.

When you're unsure how to navigate, let your conscience be your guide.

And let the Holy Spirit guide your conscience.

CHANNEL 109.0
INHALING THE BIBLE

LET'S SAY YOU'RE LOOKING for some direction in your life. Can you randomly flip open the Bible, point your finger at a verse, and expect it to contain divine counsel customized for your specific needs?

What if we try it right now?

We'll go first. As authors of a book on the ways that God speaks to us, we'd like to hear from God on how he speaks through the Bible. We want to know how we can best hear his voice through this channel. This will serve as our Bible-as-Ouija-board experiment.

Using Excel's random-number generator, we randomly generate the forty-ninth book, the first chapter, and the twenty-second verse, which turns out to be Ephesians 1:22, "God has put all things under the authority of Christ and has made him head over all things for the benefit of the church."

Everything is under the authority of Christ.

Does that also mean random Scripture generation is too?

Is this verse *the answer*?

Perhaps.

Is God trying to tell us that even random readings of his Word are worthwhile?

When most of us need instant wisdom from the Book of Wisdom, it's likely we won't use random-number generators. So now we'll do what you do. We'll use our finger.

Ladies and gentlemen, hold your breath as we randomly flip the Bible open, twirl a finger in the air over the Bible, and allow it to drop onto the page. We read in 1 Corinthians 15:40, "There are also bodies in the heavens and bodies on the earth. The glory of the heavenly bodies is different from the glory of the earthly bodies."

Huh?

What's the relevance of this verse to our needs?

How does it answer our questions?

We would have preferred a more definitive verse like, "Ye go forth and flip through the Bible pointing thy finger at my words for your answer."

Does that mean we shouldn't point our finger and expect results?

Should we have stopped this experiment with the more relevant verse above?

Maybe you'd argue that neither verse we selected answered our question on how God speaks through Scripture. Perhaps you'd even say that if there *were* links between the verses and our situation, *we* created them, not God. It was our creativity rather than God's divinity.

But what if random finger-pointing only works when you look through a spiritual lens?

What if your result is specific and direct communication from God *only if you believe it to be*?

You believe it's from God, and it is.

You don't believe it's from him, so it's not.

Seems kind of like believing in the Ouija board.

Or not.

But there's spiritual precedent for this. When Jesus walked on earth, some believed the things he did were divine miracles. Others believed they weren't. Those who believed, those who saw his works through a spiritual lens, were changed. Their lives were transformed not only by what they saw, but what they *believed* about what they saw.

In other words, faith matters.

109.1 LIFE-CHANGING MESSAGES?

When the preacher's car broke down on an old country road, he walked to a nearby roadhouse tavern to use the phone. After calling for a tow truck, he noticed his old friend Frank, shabbily dressed, drunk, and drooling at the bar.

"What happened to you, Frank?" asked the good minister. "You used to be rich."

Frank told a sad tale of bad investments that led to his downfall. "Go home," the preacher said. "Open your Bible at random, stick your finger on the page, and there will be God's answer."

Some time later, the preacher bumped into Frank, who had just stepped out of a Mercedes. He was wearing a Gucci suit and sporting a Rolex watch.

"Frank," said the preacher, "I am glad to see things really turned around for you."

"Yes, preacher, and I owe it all to you," said Frank. "I opened my Bible, put my finger down on the page, and there was the answer—Chapter 11."[1]

Seems Frank got the answer he was looking for. This obviously fictional story from *Reader's Digest* illustrates an important lesson.

We're willing to believe the Bible is speaking to us when it's something we want to hear. At those moments, we're not worried about context or meaning. But this can get us in trouble. For example, what if you happened to read Matthew 27:5 and combined it with another random verse, say Luke 10:37?

You would get, "Then Judas threw the silver coins down in the Temple and went out and hanged himself.[2] Then Jesus said, 'Yes, now go and do the same.'"[3]

Frank filed for Chapter 11 based on what he read in the Bible. If he had kept reading, would he have hanged himself too?

Random verses do have meaning for some. In certain situations, a random verse can have transformational power.

• • •

Elliot's life was a mess. He was more than addicted; he was in bondage to drugs and alcohol. In a hotel room on Christmas Eve, Elliot decided the only way to end his pain was to take his own life. He looked at the Bible sitting on the dresser beside his bed and, in anger, flung it to the floor. It fell open at his feet. For some reason, he reached down and picked it up. As he did, he read Jesus' words in John 14:27, "I am leaving you with a gift—peace of mind and heart. And the peace I give is a gift the world cannot give. So don't be troubled or afraid."

Elliot took these words as a sacred message for his life. Instead of killing himself, he turned to God. Eventually, he broke through his addictions and started fresh. Today, Elliot has a family and serves as a pastor of a local church.[4]

With a random Bible verse, Elliot seems to have gotten a specific message from God. He heard life-changing directions and acted on them.

This true story makes the same point as Fictional Frank's—the Bible has the power to transform lives.

. . .

In Noyabrisk, Siberia, a hungry Nenets fisherman left his town on the Yamal Peninsula, Ceaca, in search of food. Desperate, he prayed to any god who might hear him and give him a sign.

After he finished his prayer, a Bible fell from the sky. He understood this to be the sign he asked for, so he picked up the book and carried it back to his little town, where he told everyone what happened.

From a Bible that fell from the sky and the faith of one man in God's Word, that tiny fishing village now has a church with thirty Nemets Christians.

What the fisherman didn't know was that on the day the Bible fell out of the sky, a helicopter had flown from Salekhard with two government officials bringing aid to nearby locations. Sorting through the cargo in the air, one man turned to the other and said, "The cans of food are good, but what do we need with these books?" With that, they threw the Gideon Bibles out the window, and one apparently random seed produced a crop in Ceaca.[5]

Does being literally hit over the head with the Word somehow make it more sacred?

· · ·

A successful pickpocket from Brazil lifted what appeared to be a wallet full of money off an unknowing tourist. After he got away and was able to examine his treasure, he discovered it wasn't a wallet after all. He had stolen a copy of the New Testament. He tossed it aside.

That night when he couldn't sleep, he picked it up and read it. It changed his life. Eventually, he recovered from his addictions and surrendered his will to Christ. Later in life, he dedicated himself to distributing Bibles. [6]

· · ·

A pickpocket who believes God spoke to him through a stolen Bible.

Bibles falling on the floor
and falling from the sky.

It seems even the most random readings of the Bible have transformative powers.

But interestingly,
only for those who put some sort of belief into it.

It seems those who want spiritual answers find them.

And no matter how convincing the answer, for those who refuse to believe, no amount of evidence will be enough.

Do we all get exactly what we're looking for?

109.2 FINDING WHAT YOU'RE LOOKING FOR

Jana had always been a good student, an obedient daughter, and a faithful Christian, but her conservative, homeschooling parents questioned her decisions when she started rebelling.

Jana didn't rebel in traditional ways: mouthing off to her parents, running away, or turning to sex, drugs, and rock and roll. No, Jana rebelled by having quiet discussions with her parents about where she would attend college.

In an effort to protect her from the evils they perceived in large state schools, Jana's parents decided she should continue her higher education at a small, safe, conservative Christian college. But Jana had other plans. She wanted to attend a state university where she felt that she could be a powerful witness for Christ. As noble as that sounded, her parents didn't agree.

Jana wasn't sure what to do.

Should she listen to her parents or do what she thought God was calling her to do?

How would she know the difference between her own wishes and God's real desire for her life?

It was confusing. Jana spent time praying about it. One day while reading her Bible, she came across Acts 17. In this passage, Paul was preaching in Athens, a fact that was mentioned several times. He even directly addressed the crowd, saying, "Men of Athens."

In Jana's mind, this was the confirmation she needed. God was calling her to be a Georgia Bulldog and attend the University of Georgia, located in Athens.

Isn't that a wonderful example of God giving Jana a perfectly timed, personal, and customized message specific to her needs?

We should all be so lucky to receive such an unambiguous answer, right?

But wait . . .

What if Jana had randomly read a different section of the Bible, say, Exodus 20:12? "Honor your father and mother. Then you will live a long, full life in the land the LORD your God is giving you."

Or what about its variation in Deuteronomy 5:16? "Honor your father and mother, as the LORD your God commanded you. Then you will live a long, full life in the land the LORD your God is giving you."

What if she had inadvertently tripped across similar verses in Matthew, Mark, Luke, or Ephesians?

Would she have been equally convinced that her parents were right and that she should go to a small Christian college?

If not, why does one verse work and not the other?

If she had been convinced by *either* verse, is her answer found in the fact that she found the Athens verses *before* she found the honor-thy-parents verses?

Did she cheat and use a concordance?

Jana stumbled across a verse that loosely fit her circumstances and also her desires, so we have to ask, Who was speaking through her reading: God or Jana?

But Jana's not alone. We've all tried to make our case with biblical evidence. Heroes of the faith and some of the most respected Christian scholars have at times used the Bible in this way to hear directly from God regarding specific questions in their own lives. And their methods were not all that different from those of Chapter 11 Frank and Athens Jana.

For example, Augustine was thirty-two years old and

enjoying a prestigious career as a teacher of rhetoric in the city of Milan. Yet for all his success, Augustine struggled to know the purpose of his life. His mother, Monica, was a devout Christian and had prayed relentlessly for his conversion. Augustine himself had tried everything, exploring the furthest reaches of exotic Greek philosophy and religion. He also took every opportunity to indulge his ravenous desires. But nothing filled the emptiness he felt.

Out of curiosity, Augustine visited the church to listen to the famed preaching of Ambrose, the bishop of Milan. He also read the Bible. Then, some time in the year 386, while Augustine was spending time in Cassiciacum, a small village near Milan, he finally had the epiphany he longed for.

He was walking outdoors, feeling guilty about how he had spent his life. He wondered if, and when, he would yield his life to God; he heard a child in the garden near him say, "Take up and read; take up and read." He describes what happened next:

> I rose up, interpreting it no other way than as a command to me from Heaven to open the book, and to read the first chapter I should light upon. . . . I grasped, opened, and in silence read that paragraph on which my eyes first fell—"Not in rioting and drunkenness, not in chambering and wantonness, not in strife and envying; but put ye on the Lord Jesus Christ, and make not provision for the flesh, to fulfill the lusts thereof." No further would I read, nor did I need; for instantly, as the sentence ended—by a light, as it were, of security infused into my heart—all the gloom of doubt vanished away.[7]

Augustine wasn't the only one to use random verses to direct his life.

John Wesley, the great English revivalist, readily admitted—and even advocated to others—the practice of looking to the Bible for personal messages. When faced with a perplexing question, he prayed and asked God to guide him through the Scriptures. Wesley would then open his Bible and randomly point his finger at the page. He took direction from the words where his finger landed, without regard to their context.[8]

As eccentric as that might seem, it also seems to have worked for Wesley. He not only developed one of the most astounding personal ministries in the history of the Western church, but Methodism, the movement that grew from his teaching, had a defining influence upon evangelical and charismatic Christianity for nearly three hundred years.

Blaise Pascal, the French mathematician and philosopher who lived in the seventeenth century, wrote in *Pensées*, "The Old Testament is a cipher."[9] He seems to have believed that the Bible held layers of truth and meaning. Though the words can be understood on a cursory level and mean exactly what they say, Pascal believed the words could be read on a deeper level that peels away new layers of meaning through careful analysis and study.[10] He discusses this in the "Typography" section of *Pensées*.

Even Isaac Newton saw the Bible as a kind of secret language to be solved. Early in his career, Newton saw the order in the universe as reflective of God's nature. He studied it like a puzzle that held answers. Later in life, he developed a ravenous curiosity for biblical prophecy. He seemed to have turned his analytical genius on the Bible, seeing it, as he had seen nature itself, as a cryptogram.[11]

The conviction that the Bible not only holds God's truth but, in fact, speaks for God about specific matters is a conviction as old as ancient Jewish tradition. During the exile in Babylon, the Jews came to see the Torah—the first five books of Scripture—as having a particularly miraculous power. Not only did they believe those words told the literal story of God's activity in saving Israel, but they also carried the power to speak *directly* to individuals and groups.[12]

Could it be true?

The ancient Jewish people.

Smart, learned men like Newton, Pascal, and Augustine.

The Nenets fisherman and Athens Jana.

Each life was *transformed* by their reading.

Each believed God *spoke* to them through the Bible.

Why?

109.3 THE BIBLE AS ORACLE

For those who believe God speaks through the Bible, studying it like a historical text is certainly one way (even the primary way) we can train our ears toward him. But as far back as the Old Testament, worshipers took a much wider (we might say wilder) approach to hearing God from the words of Scripture.

Studying biblical facts was important to them, but they also believed God was bigger than the Bible itself—he wasn't bound by any predictable discipline of study. They believed the meaning went beyond the context of the printed words. For them, it wasn't beyond their faith to actually see the Bible as an oracle.

Even Paul and the writer of the book of Hebrews use Old Testament passages in creative ways.

In Paul's letter to the Galatians, he takes the freedom to make a metaphorical interpretation out of Sarah and Hagar, comparing them as representatives of the law and the gospel.

In the first chapter of his letter to the Hebrews, the anonymous writer bends some standard hermeneutical rules to make his point: Jesus is superior to angels. He attributes lines originally written about one of Israel's kings to Jesus himself. The writer at the time clearly didn't intend this, but Hebrews' author sees no contradiction in suggesting that this original writer meant much more than he ever knew himself.

The passages were originally intended to communicate one message. But under the inspiration of the Spirit of God, the words took on new meaning.

If that was true for them, can it be true for us?

Is it possible words written many years ago, directed at a different audience with particular needs, can be written in such a way as to hold a double meaning—one universal, the other specifically personal to us?

For the first time in her life, Kathy had career choices to make. In the past, her employment was based on what would work best for the family. Over the years, that typically meant a job doing work that was unsatisfactory to her, rather than the career in the arts she dreamed of when she was younger.

One day while driving to work, she was burdened by thoughts of a profession. "I was crying and asking God what I should do," said Kathy. The traffic ahead of her came to an abrupt stop. She pulled off the freeway to take a different route so she wouldn't be late for work.

"Through tear-blurred vision, I could see the traffic was bad on the new route as well," said Kathy. "Resigning myself that despite the detoured course, the ride to work would drag, I slowed my car to a stop behind a black SUV with heavily tinted windows. The white lettering in the back window caught my attention before I was close enough to read the inscription. I assumed it was an advertisement, possibly for the vehicle owner's business. Already bored at the thought of the long commute, I waited for the lettering to come into focus and read, 'In his heart a man plans his course, but the Lord determines his steps'" (Proverbs 16:9, NIV).

Kathy felt the message was intended for her.

"I marveled that God used typical Atlanta traffic to pry me from my familiar route to make my car end up behind that SUV. I'm amazed at the lengths to which God will go to speak to his children."

Kathy felt those ancient words held particular and personalized meaning for her at that place and time in her life. Though she recognized the words as Scripture written thousands of years ago, at that moment they felt fresh, new, and original to her.

Cynthia had a similar experience. One of her children was going through a particularly difficult time. As a result, Cynthia felt a lot of emotional pain—like a massive earthquake that wouldn't let her sleep. "I sat upright in bed, a pillow clutched to me as I rocked back and forth in what was probably as close to despair as I've ever been. I cried out into the night, 'Lord, I need something from your Word!'"

Hearing her own words, she reached for the Bible on her

nightstand and opened it to start reading where she had left off the day before.

2 Chronicles 6:1.

She remembers thinking, *Great! Lots of comforting passages in Chronicles.* But as she read the words of the passage, she felt as if they had been chosen for her.

> O LORD, you have said that you would live in a thick
> cloud of darkness.

"I couldn't imagine a darkness any thicker than what surrounded us. And the Lord promised to live in the middle of it. He was there. Aware. And caring. I closed my Bible and laid my head on my pillow. That was all I needed to know."

Years later when Cynthia recalls that passage, it brings her hope.

Did God hand-select a verse for Kathy?

What about for Cynthia?

What about for *you*?

Dick thinks God might have selected a specific verse for you.

A number of years ago, God gave Dick an assignment. He believed God wanted him to memorize individual verses from the Bible. Memorizing didn't come easily, so he knew it would be a challenge, but nagged by a conviction that this was something God wanted, he did it.

Verse by verse, Dick committed significant portions of Scripture to memory. Ultimately, he memorized several thousand verses.

Then weird things happened.

Dick would meet someone, and a verse would pop into

his mind. Dick realized God was placing specific verses there as a message for the person whose path he crossed. Out of obedience, Dick began to say risky things like, "Excuse me, but I think God has a promise for you . . ." and then he'd follow up with the verse God gave him.

Inevitably, the person would tell Dick this was the promise, advice, or direction he or she needed to hear. Emboldened by the reaction, Dick has now traveled across the planet listening and repeating the things God has said. Sometimes he gives encouragement, other times it is a Scripture that challenges or corrects the listener. But each message contains a personalized verse for the recipient. Dick believes it is chosen by God himself.[13]

What if our random readings weren't really so *random*?

109.4 SAVED BY THE BOOK

During the Civil War, Sam Houston Jr. fought for the Confederates, despite his father's opposition to secession. During the war, Houston was shot in the back. The bullet pierced his knapsack and ripped into the pages of his mother's King James Bible. The ball lodged inside the book at the end of Psalm 70: "O God: Thou art my help and my deliverer."

The Word of God saved Sam's life. The Bible is now on display at the Texas State History Museum.[14]

Julius Glover Elmore of Arkansas had a similar experience during the same war. A Federal bullet hit him in the chest, and he fell. His captain, James Franklin, thought he was dead and ordered nearby troops to pull him out of the way. But they quickly discovered Julius was unconscious—not dead. He carried the New Testament in his breast pocket. It was found with a mini ball almost completely through it. After the war, he brought home the Bible with the evidence still in it.[15]

These stories aren't unique.

> Frank Richards was shot in World War I, and the bullet passed straight through the Bible, deflecting it from his heart. He escaped with nothing more than bruised ribs and a Bible with a hole.[16]
>
> When Patrick Caruso was evacuated from Iwo Jima during World War II, he found his steel shaving mirror (which he had been using as a bookmark in his Bible) had been hit by a bullet. The mirror inside his Bible saved his life.[17]
>
> PFC Brendan Schweigart was sent to retrieve a tank in Iraq when he was hit by enemy sniper fire. Schweigart carried the Bible he was given at boot camp in a pocket over his heart. The Bible acted as a shield, trapping the bullet and sparing his organs from a hit.[18]

And there aren't just war stories. Apparently, the Bible can protect outside of the battle zone as well.

> In 2001, Kenny Wallace stood near the entrance to his Ft. Meyers, Florida, storefront church when his mother drove up and shot him. Police report the bullet hit Wallace, but the Bible the teen carried took the brunt of the gunshot.[19]
>
> A 54-year-old man in Florida was taking out the trash when he was attacked by two men and shot with a rifle. Police investigations revealed the man had

a red mark and pain in his chest, but the bullet was stopped by two small Bibles he carried in his shirt pocket. Police took them as evidence.[20]

Evidence of what?

Of the crime?

Or of the power of the Bible to save lives?

Should we invest in New Testaments rather than Kevlar vests to keep our troops safe?

In courtrooms all over our nation, we put our hands on the Bible and swear to tell the truth, the whole truth, and nothing but the truth—as if God himself will come track us down and haunt us if we perjure ourselves. It's a good way to intimidate a believer who plans to lie after being sworn in, but what good does it do for those who don't believe?

Perhaps it doesn't matter.

Even those who don't appear to believe in God find the Bible unique. They are superstitious about its use, even if they don't believe the content. An online message by a person calling himself Squalor says,

"I carry around a pocket-size stoner's Bible. Bible paper is thin enough that it rolls easy, and the Bible has many pages with very little or no ink. Some people think they will go to hell if they smoke the Bible. I make sure to *read the page before I smoke it.*"[21]

When it comes to warding off hell, even a stoner acts as if there's some kind of power in the Bible.

Was it God's intention that the power of his words be demonstrated by their ability to stop bullets?

Did he plan for the sacred text to be read before rolled?

What does God think about such superstitious uses of his Holy Word?

109.5 CRACKING THE CODE

Recently the idea that the Bible can serve as a mystical mouthpiece capable of delivering detailed, historical, and personal messages has found controversial new life in something called the "Bible Code." With the emergence of new technology, mathematicians and scientists have begun to examine whether there are codes somehow encrypted in the letters that make up the text from the Hebrew Bible.

Mathematician William Dembski describes how researchers use computer-generated sequences of letters, string all them together, delete spaces between words, and then do the following:

> Instead of running through the text letter by adjacent letter (as we do in ordinary reading), they run through the text by skipping a fixed number of letters. The resulting sequences, known as equidistant letter sequences (or ELSs), are then inspected for patterns that cannot reasonably be attributed to chance. The Bible Code comprises such equidistant letter sequences.[22]

Supposedly, this Bible Code has revealed some remarkable messages buried in the Hebraic texts of the Torah. Researchers claim to have found references to Hitler and the Holocaust, Israel's peace treaty with Egypt, the fall of the Berlin Wall, the terrorist attack of September 11, 2001, and many more specific events in history.

They claim the formula even works for individuals. Several software programs allow anyone to search for their own names and important personal events in the Torah texts.

Hugh Ross is skeptical. A Christian cosmologist—someone who engages in a philosophical study of the nature of the universe—Ross questions the statistical methodologies on which the whole Bible Code premise is built:

> I oppose the search for hidden codes both on a mathematical basis and on a biblical basis. The book of Colossians condemns the pursuit of secret mysteries and esoteric messages. Paul exhorts Timothy to devote himself to reading, preaching, and teaching from Scripture. He warns Timothy and us that "the time will come when men will not put up with sound doctrine. . . . Instead, they will turn their ears away from the truth and turn aside to myths." With so much still to learn and understand and apply in the words of the Bible, who can afford to waste time and effort looking past those words? [23]

But several credible Christian scholars take the Bible Code quite seriously and are willing to cautiously consider the matter. Researcher Jeffrey Satinover's book *Cracking the Bible Code* takes a sober, but generally open-minded approach to the idea of a Bible Code. Dembski (quoted above) is one of the chief advocates of the so-called intelligent design theory, yet he cautions Christians against either ridiculing the notion of a buried code in the text or blindly accepting it.[24]

Is it possible that under the words lie layers of personal messages waiting to be discovered?

Or is it a matter of interpretation?

Sometimes that's the problem, isn't it? We use our interpretations of the words to draw distinctions between us and other believers rather than to draw us closer to the One who created them.

Despite our sacred sabotaging, the Bible continues to powerfully affect lives. The Bible has been banned and burned by tyrants, chopped to pieces by "open-minded" scholars, lampooned by poets, demythologized by academics, and bludgeoned by pop-thriller novelists. Voltaire once mocked, "Another century and there will not be a Bible on earth!"[25]

Yet the Bible endures.

Most Americans possess a scant knowledge of the stories and messages contained in the Bible. When pressed, only a select few have considered how it should be studied, know where it came from, or understand why it is considered holy.

We debate words like *inerrant*, *inspired*, and *infallible*, but every year more Bibles are sold around the world than any other book in print—Harry Potter notwithstanding.[26]

Weird theories aside, people believe the Bible is special. Though the percentage of those who say the Bible is the "actual Word of God and is to be taken literally" has declined in the last decade, nearly 50 percent of Americans still call it the "inspired Word of God" and believe it is worthy of due respect and consideration.[27]

It can't be extinguished.

In fact, it seems to take on a life of its own.

Still, we can't always easily explain why we revere the Bible.

Dottie understands the unique attraction the Bible holds because she has experienced it in her life. Though she made a commitment to God as a child, Dottie wandered away during her college years. However, the desire to return to church resurfaced when she became a mother.

"I remember discussing this with my next-door neighbor," says Dottie. "We had never discussed spiritual things, but she gave me a book she thought I would enjoy. It was a book on prophecy."

Dottie remembers that, while reading that book on prophecy, she had a compulsion to find her old Bible.

Interesting.

She was reading a book on prophecy, and yet she had a compulsion to pull out a *different* book. Though she can't remember the title of the first book, she remembers the second book was the Bible.

Can you imagine that happening with any other book? You're in the middle of reading Stephen King when you suddenly have a compulsion to pull out a Jodi Picoult book?

It's weird, huh?

Dottie got out her Bible, dusted it off, and remembers holding it in her hands, thinking it was a treasure. For some reason, the thought occurred to her that if she opened the Bible, her life would never be the same.

She opened it anyway.

> Though I didn't hear an audible voice, I knew the
> Lord was speaking to me, and I sensed his love and
> presence like never before. I later told my friend who

had given me that little book that I had an encounter with the Lord Jesus and a desire for Scripture that surprised me. She cried and told me she had been praying for me for several weeks.

For Dottie, that wasn't a onetime reading of the Bible. Instead she describes it as a transformation, "a lifelong journey to know God through his Word," a compulsion that has lasted for years. "The Lord speaks to me most directly through his Word," says Dottie.

Even when God speaks to her in other ways, she says, "It always lines up with his written Word, and since I'm such a slow learner, when he wants me to learn something, he tends to say it several times, in several ways."

In other words, Dottie believes God speaks to her through the Bible in multiple ways. First, he does it through her reading of the words and learning more about him. Second, he speaks to her personally about her concerns or life circumstances. But interestingly, he also seems to use the Bible to speak confirmation to her of things he is saying through other ways. God may speak through multiple channels, but at least for Dottie, he confirms what he is saying through the Bible.

That's an interesting concept.

What if God did that for everyone?

Can the Bible help us make sense of what God is doing in other areas of our lives?

Perhaps there are also cryptic messages hidden in our lives. What if the Bible—instead of being a hidden code—is instead a decoder?

Could it be that by bringing our questions and problems to the sacred text, we can actually get real answers?

When we have trouble discerning what God is saying through circumstances, other people, dreams and visions, and nature, can the Bible help us make sense of it all?

109.6 TAKING IT TO THE STREETS

God doesn't play games.

He is committed to keeping his message accessible.

When there is confusion, he doesn't wait for us to come to him, he comes to us.

He translates.

One way he did this was by making the Word flesh through Jesus:

> In the beginning the Word already existed.
> The Word was with God, and the Word was God.
> He existed in the beginning with God.
> God created everything through him, and nothing was created except through him.
> The Word gave life to everything that was created, and his life brought light to everyone.
> The light shines in the darkness, and the darkness can never extinguish it. . . .
> So the Word became human and made his home among us. He was full of unfailing love and faithfulness. And we have seen his glory, the glory of the Father's one and only Son.[28]

Jesus is the Word come alive.

With the birth of Christ, the Word is no longer text; it is *texture*. Whatever power is in the book is multiplied in the person. That's why religious leaders of his day were so alarmed by Jesus' talk about a personal relationship with God. They accused Jesus of attempting to abolish the Torah and set up a direct line to God. This frightened them, for the law of Moses was their only anchor.

The religious leaders of that day memorized the first five books of the Bible.

Word

for

word.

Why? Because by knowing the Scriptures word for word they could better live out the Scriptures action by action. For them, the Bible was the very Word of God. They feared that Jesus was minimizing the importance of the Bible.

Jesus' response was, "Don't misunderstand why I have come. I did not come to abolish the law of Moses or the writings of the prophets. No, I came to accomplish their purpose."[29]

He answered that he never intended to supersede the Scriptures, but to fulfill them.

Scripture doesn't disappear with Jesus; but it does move—from outside to inside, from words written on stone to truth written on the heart. Jesus takes the scriptural message—what God wants to say to us—and moves it from something that *restrains* our behavior to something that *compels* our behavior.

In the verse above, Jesus says that he comes to accomplish the purpose of the Scriptures. When we have the commands inside of us, we can also be used to accomplish that goal.

We *become* the Torah . . .

Ashley was twenty-three, fresh out of graduate school, and stuck between her old college life and the life that was yet to come. For months she prayed she would get a job—and not just any job, but the job God wanted her to have.

She was first turned down for, and then later offered, a job as a social worker in a hospital in Monroe, Louisiana. The new job was nearly two hundred miles away from her family, but without hesitation she prepared to move. She believed God was in control.

Her parents drove her to Monroe, and in one day they found the perfect apartment. It was exactly within Ashley's budget and in a great location. It felt like a sign from God, but on the way home, doubts crept in. "I began thinking about the new job, moving away from all of my family and friends, questioning if I had really heard God. Is this really what he wanted? Could I do this?" asked Ashley.

She looked out the car window and saw a rainbow. To many, a rainbow is a sign of hope; the rain has ended. But to Ashley, it was more than that. "I was reminded of God's promise to Noah that he would be faithful. Then God gently reminded me he was going to be faithful to *me*, too. He would never leave me, even when things were hard."

Ashley has been in Monroe since 2004, and though she will tell you it hasn't been easy, she will also tell you God has been faithful.

In a very personal way, Ashley has ingested God's Word. When she saw a rainbow, it didn't give her warm fuzzies or remind her of leprechauns. Instead, Ashley immediately saw the natural phenomenon of the rainbow as an image that pointed back to Scripture.

Scripture that she knew.

Scripture that told a story of God asking Noah to step out of his comfort zone.

Scripture that spoke to Ashley personally that day in the car.

When she acted on what she heard, Ashley became a living Torah, a walking Bible.

Occasionally, you will see a bumper sticker or T-shirt that says, "Your life may be the only Bible some people read." In ultra-evangelistic communities, the implied message is, "You better not screw up, 'cause it's your fault if those around you burn."

Perhaps there is a subtler interpretation. You can become the Bible that many people read if you intentionally make Scripture the root from which all your actions grow. It sounds difficult, and it can be. But maybe it isn't about doing everything right as much as it's about allowing things to happen organically.

Earlier in the book, we told you Jennifer dreamed about washing Mary Anne's feet and the strong association in her mind with serving.

Her thought may have been a random coincidence, or perhaps God was helping her make that association by directly influencing her thoughts. But the most likely explanation is that Jennifer has heard the story countless times.

On the night before Jesus died, he and his apostles gathered in an upper room to celebrate Passover. During this celebration, Jesus washed the apostles' feet. That was considered a lowly job. Someone of Jesus' status would never be asked to do such a thing, which is likely why the apostles took such notice of it.

Jennifer has read the story in the Bible, heard pastors preach on it, and even written about it. That portion of Scripture has become so ingrained in her life that when she thinks of foot-washing, she can't help but think of the concept of service. In her mind, foot-washing is a metaphor for serving others.

It's not surprising that when Jennifer asked God what the dream meant, she instinctively knew she was to serve Mary Anne.

Days later, when Mary Anne called with the terrible news of her husband's brain tumor and insisted that Jennifer didn't need to come to the hospital, her dream gave her the courage to defy Mary Anne's words and go anyway. She didn't arrive at the hospital with a pan of water and a towel and ask Mary Anne to take off her shoes. Instead, she found unobtrusive ways to comfort and serve the family. Jennifer became a living Torah. She became the words of the Bible as she attempted to carry out Jesus' purpose of fulfilling Scripture.

In fact, weeks later when Mary Anne wrote a thank-you note she said, "I asked God for help, and he sent you."

The association between foot-washing and service came through Jennifer's knowledge of Scripture. She heard God speak through her dream because the Bible gave her a foundation to understand her dream. If her dream had been about washing Mary Anne's dog, the association would have been meaningless.

What's remarkable about both Ashley's and Jennifer's stories is that we don't need the Bible open in front of us for it to have meaning in a specific circumstance. We don't need a seminary degree to understand the confusing parts. God speaks through what we know of Scripture and uses it even when we're not thinking about it.

Scripture *lives* and breathes outside of the pages it is written on.

109.7 BECOMING THE BIBLE

More than just a bullet-stopping piece of Scripture, the Twenty-third Psalm has layers of meaning that reveal God's mind and heart. Familiar to many, this poem was written about four thousand years ago by David, king of Israel. But before he was a king, David was a shepherd, and he used his experience working with sheep to poetically represent his relationship with God. It is one of the most enduring and tender forms of worship ever expressed in human words.

> The LORD is my shepherd; I shall not want.
> He maketh me to lie down in green pastures:
> he leadeth me beside the still waters.
> He restoreth my soul: he leadeth me in the paths
> of righteousness for his name's sake.
> Yea, though I walk through the valley of the shadow
> of death, I will fear no evil: for thou art with me;
> thy rod and thy staff they comfort me.
> Thou preparest a table before me in the presence
> of mine enemies: thou anointest my head with oil;
> my cup runneth over.
> Surely goodness and mercy shall follow me all the
> days of my life: and I will dwell in the house of the
> LORD for ever. (KJV)

This poem has been a source of comfort to those facing trials. The soothing images, the idea of God always being with us, caring for and protecting us, have provided solace to those who grieve. God speaks comfort and hope through even a cursory reading of the words.

However, from a historical context, the poem can also be understood for what it is—an ancient worshiper's expression of dependence on God. If we explore the context of the environment in which it is written and learn more about the role of a shepherd in that time and place, about his tools—the rod and staff—we'd have a more detailed understanding of the relationship between sheep and shepherd.

And therefore, between ourselves and God.

If we understood the geography of the region and how important (and how difficult) it was for shepherds to protect their sheep from wild animals and flash floods, we would gain additional insight into the protection God provides us.

Knowledge of the role of hospitality in that culture helps us to make sense of the relationship between shepherd and stranger and to appreciate the kindness of our Shepherd God.

Each new piece of information we learn about a passage of Scripture helps us hear and apply God's truth to our lives. God speaks not only from these ancient words, but through our understanding of them.

We can go further.

Going beyond the historical context, we can use our imagination to picture ourselves *in* these words. After reading the poem and understanding some of the background, we can place ourselves in the scene, seeing God protecting us as a good shepherd would. We can visualize walking through a dark valley and imagine God by our side.

What does a cup overflowing with blessings *look* like?

What does goodness and unfailing love pursuing us all the days of our lives *feel* like?

God's words can become personal in these moments. We can hear him speak into our lives in ways that random finger-pointing at Bible pages cannot.

Indeed, one entrepreneur has taken this personalization idea to the extreme and created a Personal Promises Bible. For $65 to $110 you can purchase a Bible personalized with your first name in more than five thousand verses, saving you the trouble of visualizing it yourself.[30]

But no matter how you do it, the point is the same. You need to insert yourself into the text to gain another level of meaning.

Finally, we can wait and allow God's Spirit to meld with ours and to take us further into the text itself. We can let *his Word* work on us, growing and shaping our thoughts and our character.

If we do, maybe this is how we, like Jesus, can make the words come alive.

This is also how we remember certain images, stories, or passages and use them to decode the things God is saying to us in other ways.

The prophet Ezekiel had visions, most of them bizarre experiences he had to describe in human words. The Old Testament book that bears his name is a strange compilation of weird apocalyptic images. Readers are left scratching their heads trying to imagine what's really going on behind his words. One of his first visions was also one of his most personal. It sets the stage for all that follows.

God comes to Ezekiel and hands him a scroll.[31] The

scroll, he understands, is covered with God's words. God tells him to eat the scroll. He does. He puts God's words in his mouth and swallows them. He describes the effect: the scroll tastes as sweet as honey.

The Word of God is often associated with food; particularly, with bread. Jesus answers Satan's temptation to turn stones into bread by reminding him humans can't survive on bread alone. Humans also need every word that comes from God.

Of course the image of eating the words of God implies more.

What we consume, we become.

What we eat becomes us.

When we consume the Bible as God's Word, God's Word becomes absorbed within. Over time, our souls conform to the truths and messages of God.

Eugene Peterson, the poet behind *The Message*, wrote a book called *Eat This Book: A Conversation in the Art of Spiritual Reading*. In it he says,

> What I want to say, countering the devil, is that in order to read the Scriptures adequately and accurately, it is necessary at the same time to live them. Not to live them as a prerequisite to reading them, and not to live them in consequence of reading them, but to live them *as* we read them, the living and the reading reciprocal, body language and spoken words, the back-and-forthness assimilating the reading to the living, the living to the reading. Reading Scriptures is not an activity discrete from living the gospel but one integral to it. It means letting Another have a say

in everything we are saying and doing. It is as easy as that. And as hard.[32]

To fully hear from him.

To know him.

We must ingest his Word to the point that it mixes fully with who we are.

Yet this is God's great risk.

He dares to put his real self inside of tarnished human souls. His words get mixed up with human words and intent. Even when we read the Bible, it's not hard to see the traces of human personality.

Muslims and Mormons both have texts that anchor their faith—the Koran and the Book of Mormon. Both of these scriptures are purportedly dictated words from God. And they claim to be free from human writers' *personalities*.

But the books of the Bible claim nothing of the sort. Every word of the Bible is the Word of God *in the words of humans*. Isaiah and Jeremiah both spoke God's Word, but they also spoke their own. We can spot differences between Matthew's and Luke's personalities. The Bible—and God himself—seems quite content with this messy complexity.

He made the Word flesh.

Perhaps our job is to make the flesh Word.

109.8 INGESTING AND INHALING

Sometimes when we leave the Bible and carry the words with us, we disassociate them from their context. We remove them from the whole, and we take the meaning of the words we carry with us out of context. The end result? Rather than being the Word, we misrepresent the Word.

A carpenter carefully measured each two-by-four to ensure it was cut to the exact size. For each board, he pulled out a measuring tape, laid it alongside the board, and carefully counted off inches before marking the exact spot he wanted. Only then would he make the cut.

The young assistant who observed all of this had a better plan. "If you just use the last board you cut to size the next one, you'd save a lot of time."

To which the experienced carpenter replied, "But by the eighth board, I'll also be a quarter of an inch off."

The carpenter knew he needed an exact standard by which to compare each board. Without that exacting standard, the problem would then grow. Not only would the boards drift in size, but eventually the house would too. The reason a house fits together is that the builder, and each of his suppliers, agree on a standard unit of measurement.

• • •

San Francisco's famous Boudin Bakery has been baking the same sourdough bread every day for one hundred and fifty years. Not only the same recipe, but *the same bread*.

The secret is the Boudin mother dough. Every day since 1849, Boudin bakers have held back a portion of their batch to use as a starter for the next day's bread. They let the dough ferment slowly and naturally for up to seventy-two hours. The mother dough retains the bread's original sour flavor and rich texture. It seeds the new batch with the precedent of the old.

In other words, San Franciscans and visitors flock to Boudin Bakery and Cafes for a taste of the same bread eaten by California Gold Rush miners. The tradition holds because the precedent holds.[33] Though the ovens have changed, ingredient suppliers have come and gone, and generations of employees have been born and died, today's fresh loaf is yesterday's old bread.

The words of the Bible are like the mother dough.

They are the daily bread that Jesus talked about centuries ago, yet those same words are fresh each day. Perhaps that is what makes the Bible unique. Not only does it live and breathe, but it lives through us. Through our interactions. Through our wrestling with the text,

or with our lives—

and using the text to decode our lives.

Random finger-pointing works when we have faith that it works and when we've ingested enough of the mother dough to know that what we're swallowing is the same as the original standard.

Doing this, we can become one with the text to the point we live out the *ancient* content in our *contemporary* lives.

We can *be* the Torah.

We can *be* the Bible.

We do it by becoming the words we read, by *acting* on what we've learned.

. . .

Remember Squalor?

He's the guy who read the pages of Genesis before he smoked them to ward off hell. He is not the kind of example we're using as a role model when we describe being one with Scripture. Yet we have hope for Squalor. We believe

God is big enough to use even a druggie's paraphernalia to speak personally and specifically to him. And it was easier to believe after we learned of this guy:

> A much-feared man—a known killer—in the village of Virirba, Russia, obtained some pages torn from a Gideon New Testament. In the process of rolling cigarettes with them, he read on one of the pages that God loved him. He wept all night because no one had ever loved him before. The very next day, he went to a neighboring town, found a pastor and was led to the Lord. Four years later, 150 people—nearly his entire village—had accepted Christ thanks to his testimony and the evidence of his changed life.[34]

This guy went from inhaling the Bible to completely ingesting it.

Apparently, there's still hope for Squalor.

And for all of us.

God speaks to us through circumstances, through encounters with history and nature, in dreams and visions, and through other people, yet his words still hold to an established precedent.

The Bible.

God speaks new things into our lives, and they always taste like things he has said in the past. Like the dough, what God says now is linked to what he has said before. And though his words may be specific to you, they will always carry the same flavor and texture of things he said long ago.

Regardless of which channel you tune in to, you can

know it is God speaking by using Scripture as your tape measure. His Word provides the standard by which all of his words are measured.

The author of *Pride and Prejudice* may speak to you through her book.

A hardbound copy of the same tome held in front of your chest may even stop a bullet.

But you can't smoke *Pride and Prejudice* and become more like Jane Austen.

Our job is not to wear the Bible like a Kevlar vest that wards off evil.

Our challenge is to fully consume it in our lives to the point that it becomes the measure of everything we hear and do.

CHANNEL 110.0
YOU MIGHT THINK I'M CRAZY, BUT . . .

JAN WAS TWENTY-TWO when she got married. And after that, she wanted nothing more than to get pregnant. But her plans were interrupted when, a month after her wedding, she needed open-heart surgery for a congenital heart defect.

She underwent the surgery and spent the next year recuperating. "At the end of the year, I was told I could conceive if I chose to," said Jan.

But a year later, Jan still wasn't pregnant. Each month she was reminded of her failure to conceive, and her bitterness grew. "Why wouldn't God allow me this joy?"

One night, Jan was awakened from her sleep by a voice. The voice said, "I *love* you enough to let you hate me."

Jan was sure the message was from God.

And the words changed her.

Getting pregnant was no longer the most important thing in her life—God was. "I changed my focus from trying to conceive to a better plan God had for me," said Jan. That plan led Jan and her husband to adopting four children, two from Korea and two from China.

After adopting the children, Jan learned that the doctors had made a serious, life-threatening mistake in her heart surgery. If she had gotten pregnant, both she *and* her baby would have died. Jan had a second open-heart surgery to correct the problem. That's when those words, "I love you enough to let you hate me," finally made sense. God was willing to go any length to protect her, even if it meant that she hated him.

Though she never became pregnant, becoming a mother brought Jan the joy she hoped for; in fact, it brought her double joy. One of her girls is named Joy, and another is named JoyJoy. "How's that for getting double joy?" Jan said, laughing.

It's quite a story.

But not every story ends so joyfully.

Not long after hearing Jan's story, Jennifer received an e-mail from a friend. Lyn, a bouncy redhead, was newly married, and the last time Jennifer had spoken to her, she was extremely happy. However, the mood of this e-mail was much different. Lyn and Larry were in a state of shock. Larry had fought testicular cancer ten years ago, and though he was doing fine, they had just learned the surgery had made him sterile.

Lyn knew Jennifer was writing this book, and she had been thinking a lot about how God spoke to her. "I think we are on the devastating end of NOT hearing God speak right now," wrote Lyn.

Similar situations.

One has heard from God.

One hasn't.

Why does it seem as if God lavishes his words on some, and yet others—maybe those who need it most—don't seem to hear him at all?

110.1 WHEN YOU DON'T HEAR

By now, you've probably made up your mind about whether the people in the stories we've included in this book are just a bunch of wackos, or whether they're people who have really heard from God.

Perhaps you've also experienced something similar to one or more of these stories. As a result, you're more trusting, believing God can and does speak through various channels.

Or . . .

. . . you *want* to believe,

but you don't.

You don't believe because you haven't experienced anything like this. And you're skeptical that anyone else could, either.

Maybe you're like Lyn, and God isn't speaking to you *right now*.

Or ever.

And yet . . .

you *long* for him to speak to you.

It's okay.

Whatever you're thinking or feeling,

it's *okay*.

Some people immediately assume if they haven't heard God speak, it's because they're not worthy of being spoken to. *God speaks only to holy people*, they think. *Or only to people who are holier than I am.*

If that's what you're thinking, too, we want to caution you—don't jump to conclusions. No one is *holier* simply because they hear God communicate. You're not less of anything because you're not hearing his voice. If you're not hearing God speak, that can change.

God speaks through an infinite number of ways. He speaks to and through all types of people. The Bible is filled with examples. In this book alone, we've shared the stories of God speaking to drug dealers, mean-spirited gossips, thieves, tax collectors, and oh yeah, . . .

. . . the authors.

If you take anything away from what you've read, we hope you'll understand that God doesn't play favorites. He doesn't speak only to the good and holy.

His words aren't for the righteous *or* the unrighteous.

They're for the righteous *and* the unrighteous.

Whether you believe it or not,

whether you've experienced it or not,

God is speaking to you.

Maybe even right now.

110.2 TEACH ME TO LISTEN

"The first time I heard God talk was when I was nine years old," said Lisa. It happened while she was living in Sonora, California, and singing in her elementary school choir.

> We had gone to the high school to rehearse with other local choirs for an upcoming county-wide concert. While we were there, a choir director from another school stood up to direct us in a song.
>
> As soon as she stood in front of us, I got a strange

sense about her. It was an overwhelming impression. It wasn't a thought, or a vision; it was more of a feeling. I felt that director was going to be in a serious accident with teenagers involved. I felt somebody was going to die—not necessarily her—but someone. And I felt it was going to be horrific. I didn't tell anyone about it because at the time, I couldn't put it into words.

The sensation was so vivid to Lisa that it affected her physically. "It made me sick to my stomach every time I looked at her. I couldn't shake the grief I felt."

Like a bad dream that lingers after you're awake, Lisa's bad feeling clung to her for days before it melted away.

"Several weeks later, I heard about a devastating car accident where some teenagers were killed—one was decapitated," said Lisa. "Like everyone else in our community, I was shaken by the news, but there was something more for me. Our director told us the other car was driven by a choir director from another school—the same one I had a feeling about."

Okay.

What's this all about?

A nine-year-old girl has a startling thought—

no, a vision—

no, really more of a *feeling*.

And it turns out to be prophetic.

"At the time, I never thought it was God speaking, but now I know it was," said Lisa. "I believe that by letting me first feel this terribly troubling agitation, and then following it with this specific sense of clarity and a kind of wild foresight, God taught me, even as a child, to hear his voice."

Could God use the sensations of a nine-year-old and a horrific car accident to teach a little girl how to hear his voice?

Does God do that?

Is this some kind of sick apprenticeship for hearing the Master's words?

If so, who would want to serve a God like that?

Lisa doesn't feel that way. She believes the drama of the event cemented the incident in her mind, as an experience so powerful that it would years later remind her of the power of God to speak to her—even with what at the time seemed to be a crazy message that she couldn't do anything about. It didn't scar her; it taught her a lesson she never forgot.

. . .

While writing this chapter, Jennifer had a speaking engagement for which she was asked to talk on a topic that she hadn't addressed in years. One of the examples she used in her speech was when she knew God was calling her to be a writer, and she was refusing to obey. She told it like this:

> I was driving downtown with my friend Terri, who is a real free spirit, laid back, and not at all intense. She turned to me and asked if I ever wanted to write. At that time, I had no desire to write, although others had been encouraging me to do so for years. So I responded by telling Terri all the reasons I wouldn't or couldn't and concluded by saying, "If God wants

me to write, he'll send an editor to my front door with a contract."

Then Terri said something so weird, it startled me: "I had a word from God."

A word from God? What did that mean?

"He told me you should write," said Terri.

Terri isn't the kind of person to get words from God. She is crazy fun but not the least bit Pentecostal or mystical. Terri doesn't get words from God, and neither do I. So when Terri said she had a word from God, I burst into tears because I knew God was telling me to be a writer.

Prior to that car trip, Jennifer will tell you she didn't believe God talked to Terri *or* that God talked to her. But somehow she took what Terri said as a message from God. Then she promptly did what most well-meaning Christians do: she ignored it. It wasn't until years later that she relented to the call, and a few more years before she found joy in the calling.

As Jennifer continued with her talk that day, she told several other stories and illustrations from her life as a writer. It was an informal session, so when a woman raised her hand, Jennifer stopped for her question.

"What's interesting to me is that you just said you *never* got a word from God. But then, suddenly, you started to hear from him a lot. What changed?"

And then in front of that woman, the audience, God, and everybody, for the first time, it occurred to Jennifer that she really started hearing God when she started *obeying* God. When Jennifer quit fighting God and his plan for her to be a writer, she began to hear him in new ways. Her ability to hear—to see him working in her life—began shortly after she decided to be obedient and follow his call for her life.

Obeying leads to hearing?

Or perhaps obeying leads to hearing *more*. Or more clearly.

Now, years later, with a history of hearing God, Jennifer has high expectations for hearing him. As discussed in the *his*-tory chapter (104), one of her expectations is that she will hear from God at conferences, and usually she does. In fact, Jennifer met Mark at a writers' conference not long after she prayed for God to arrange one of what she calls divine appointments—seemingly coincidental conversations with people God wants her to meet.

In the Bible, there's a story of the disciples asking Jesus to teach them to pray. But what's missing from the Bible is a story of the disciples asking Jesus to teach them to listen. Apparently, they learned to listen by being with him.

Maybe that's how he teaches us to listen too.

God taught Lisa to hear him through one unbelievable, dramatic vision when she was a young child.

Jennifer learned to hear him gradually after she stopped running from him and embraced his plan for her life.

God not only speaks to us,

but apparently,

he also *teaches* us to *listen*.

110.3 Ears of Faith

What's the difference between those who hear him and those who don't?

It's as simple as *how* they listen.

We know what you're thinking. *I listen, but I never hear him.*

Okay, we hear you.

But frankly, how hard, how intentionally do you listen?

> When you read the Bible, do you assume what you're reading applies to you and try to figure out what God is saying to you *personally*?
>
> When you have a stray thought, do you explore it to see if God somehow put it there for a reason?
>
> When you wake up after a particularly vivid dream, do you pray, asking God what he was trying to tell you?
>
> When a friend says something more direct and personal than usual, do you wonder if God could be behind his or her words?
>
> When an unlikely series of events happens, do you assume God arranged them for a reason and try to discover his purpose?
>
> Do you examine your history, your environment, and your emotions to see what you can learn from them?

That is listening.

Listening is an active awareness of what is happening around you and an intentional pursuit of God's voice. Many of us wrongly assume we haven't heard God unless we've heard a James Earl Jones–type voice amplified through the clouds. If you think that's the only way you will hear him, it is the only way you will hear him. But here's a hint—it's not one of the ways he always speaks; it's likely one of the ways he rarely speaks.

To hear God, we have to believe he wants to communicate

with us. That doesn't take a huge amount of faith, but it takes at least a drop. The people who hear from God all have a drop of that faith.

While gathering stories for this book, we noticed that almost everyone who had a story of God speaking started it the same way: "I know you're going to think I'm crazy, but . . ." Before they even explained their stories, they knew how unbelievable they would sound. They recognized that not everyone would believe them. But here's what's interesting—*each of them believed his or her story*.

As authors, we've been asked how well we know the people we wrote about in this book.

Did we check them out?

Did we investigate each of their stories?

The truth is, even if we wanted to investigate them or check them out, it would be nearly impossible to do so. Many of the stories took place inside of people's minds, when they were home alone, or in situations we can't re-create. When God speaks, it happens in a black box—outside of our view.

We can see what went in

and what came out,

but we have no way of verifying what happened inside.

Remember Brock Gill, the illusionist we mentioned in the chapter on conscience (108)? Brock is so good at what he does that the Discovery Channel hired him to do an investigation for them. Brock was given the task of re-creating the miracles of Jesus to see if they were truly miracles or mere illusions. In essence, the Discovery Channel asked the same thing about Jesus' miracles that friends asked us about the stories in this book.

Can you prove they're real and true?

After months of research, on-site investigation, and attempts to re-create the miracles of Jesus, Brock was able to conclusively prove that each miracle could be duplicated as an illusion. Feeding five thousand? No problem. Water into wine? Easy. Even walking on water could be replicated as an illusion.

But to create those illusions, Brock required millions of dollars worth of high-tech equipment, brought in and out by multiple semitrucks on specific cues communicated through extensive communication networks. In other words, stuff Jesus didn't have. Stuff that wouldn't even be invented for centuries.

Jesus performed miracles. . . .

We just don't know for sure *how* he did them.

That's what we've told our friends who've asked about the book. These stories *are* hard to believe. We could enlist someone like Brock to re-create these moments of God speaking to show they aren't just auditory illusions. But you know what? The people who experienced God speaking to them already know they aren't.

They heard from God.

And, seeing their belief, we also have faith that God spoke to them.

Frankly, it's always hard to believe the Creator of the universe takes a personal interest in us. That he speaks directly to us.

But maybe borrowing a drop of their faith—believing that God speaks personally to them—can help us believe he also speaks personally to us.

110.4 Teasing out the message

You don't have to have mountain-size faith; Jesus said even mustard-seed-size faith is enough to do anything, even *hear* God. But faith is also required to understand what God says to us. It seems God often sends us incomplete messages.

Teasers, really.

He sends us the back cover rather than the whole book, and it's up to us to discover what it means. We'd like God to toss a neatly typed manuscript into our lap, wrapped in a bow, with a card that says,

> Here's your answer in glorious detail.
> Love,
> God.

But he doesn't work that way. It seems he wants us to invest in what he's saying before we get the complete communication.

Perhaps when God speaks, it's like those souvenir washcloths that come in a quarter-size tin. When you drop one in water, it expands to become a full-size washcloth.

Could it be when we add a drop of faith, the whole message takes form?

When asked how she heard God, Sara said she's never heard him audibly speak: "I guess I would say I hear him speak to me in my mind and in my heart."

So how does she discern his presence?

"One way I know it's him, and not the spaghetti lunch I had that day, is that he's usually asking me to do something I would never do myself."

For Sara, one way to know it is God is by knowing it's *not herself*. Answers or instructions that lie outside of our own expectations can be a tip-off that God is at work.

Even the ancients who heard God speak were often surprised by what they heard. According to Job's friend, God is "famous for great and unexpected acts; there's no end to his surprises,"[1] and later in the same book he says, "We'll never comprehend all the great things he does; his miracle-surprises can't be counted."[2] In the book that bears his name, Zechariah has some far-out visions of colored horses, a man measuring Jerusalem, scrolls flying through the air, and women with wings like storks airlifting a basket.[3]

God is so much bigger and more amazing than we can comprehend; therefore, it's no wonder his messages to us would also be more amazing than we can comprehend. That's why his messages feel like teasers, like puzzles missing a few hundred pieces. At the time we receive his message, it seems as if we can't quite wrap our brain around the whole picture. God's messages might initially seem confusing, but it's not his intention to simply keep us in the dark.

Maybe the messages seem incomplete so that we'll invest ourselves in understanding them.

To ponder their meaning.

To reflect.

To learn more about their source.

Maybe God uses incomplete communication to "tease" us into a relationship in which he can reveal even more.

When we have sincere doubts about what we've heard (or think we've heard), God will often confirm his message.

Especially if we ask him to clarify it.

It may not be instantly comprehensible, but over time the photograph develops.

110.5 BACK TO THE SOURCE

In the previous chapter, we said things had to measure up.

Baby bread has to taste the same as the mother dough.

Anything God says now has to be consistent with what he has said in the past. If that's so, how can something old and ancient also be surprising and new?

Old and new at the same time.

Known and unknown in the same message.

Confusing, isn't it?

It's the *expression* that feels fresh, because his words are specific to our needs. Yet God's message doesn't change. He continues to communicate his grace, mercy, forgiveness, and love.

Can we quantify the mercy he extends to us?

How many times, and what offenses, will he forgive?

To paraphrase the Bee Gees, how deep is his love?

It is in the answers to questions like those, especially when the answers are specific to our situations, that his words appear fresh and surprisingly personal.

Remember Jan, who was frustrated because she couldn't become pregnant? She heard God say he loved her enough to let her hate him. That was a startling way of saying he loves her no matter what. His words to Jan were new and fresh, yet at the same time, they were consistent with his ancient words.

God's love isn't new.

But the expression of his love is new every day.

God will always be consistent with what he has done and said in the past. God is unchanging. Though at any given time he may choose to reveal to us a different part of his character, the whole is steadfast. It's likely that he's already told someone else the same things he's telling you—just in a different place, time, or context. The Bible can often be a guide to such examples. That's one reason it is important for us to know what's in it.

It would be comforting if we could reduce this down to a few simple formulas—listen here, show up there, or get holier to hear better. But it's not that simple.

Hearing God speak often isn't easy, or easily understandable.

It's messy, complex, and sometimes incomprehensible.

In fact, what *is* simple is to believe God *doesn't* speak to you.

110.6 SIGNALS

With the smallest grain of faith, the universe pulsates with meaning.

If we look, will we see God everywhere, all the time?

Does God speak through *everything*?

Even the most horrific events?

Like Hurricane Katrina?

Or the Holocaust?

Some preachers believe God spoke very specific messages through these events. That Hurricane Katrina was punishment for promiscuous sexual behavior—specifically, homosexuality—and that the Holocaust was payback for the Jewish people who rejected Jesus.

We don't drink their Kool-Aid.

Not every circumstance and situation is *caused* by God.

God doesn't *cause* child molesters to abuse. He doesn't *cause* little old ladies to lose their houses on Main Street to pay for the crimes of greedy executives on Wall Street. And he doesn't *cause* your spouse to have an affair.

But in *every* circumstance, God is willing to speak.

One of the best ways to understand this is in the words of Anne Frank. Before she was sent to a concentration camp, where she later died, Anne and her family were locked away in a tiny apartment. Eventually, someone she knew betrayed her family, resulting in the deaths of everyone but her father. Despite the horror in her world, years later her father read in her diary: "I still believe, in spite of everything, that people are truly good at heart."[4]

In other words, Anne sought out beauty, truth, and goodness, despite her circumstances. Somehow, amid all the darkness, Anne saw light. She saw goodness. And what she saw and heard, whether she recognized it or not, was God.

The Psalms say it this way:

Is there anyplace I can go to avoid your Spirit?
to be out of your sight?
If I climb to the sky, you're there!
If I go underground, you're there!
If I flew on morning's wings
to the far western horizon,
You'd find me in a minute—
you're already there waiting!
Then I said to myself, "Oh, he even sees me in the dark!
At night I'm immersed in the light!"
It's a fact: darkness isn't dark to you;
night and day, darkness and light, they're all the same to you.[5]

It seems even in the midst of natural disasters, violence, and wars,

God speaks.

Of hope and redemption.
Of restoration and renewal.
And of a goodness that can live on in the human heart.

Not every circumstance is caused by God,
but God is willing to speak within every circumstance.
Some just require more looking than others.

. . .

Jan, whose heart operation left her unable to conceive, went through a dark period. But her sadness turned to joy when she adopted her four children. When she later learned that a pregnancy could have killed both herself and her baby, she found confirmation that God knew best. God didn't *cause* that situation—the doctors did. Yet God spoke to Jan through her pain.

At the beginning of this chapter, we told you about Lyn and Larry, who just received the devastating news that the cancer surgery Larry had ten years ago left him sterile. Lyn told Jennifer that she didn't think God was speaking to them.

Jennifer couldn't help but think that God might be speaking to Lyn through Jan's story. The timing of the two conversations felt like more than a coincidence. Perhaps Jan's story was the encouragement that Lyn and Larry needed, to remind them that God was in control even though circumstances seemed hopeless. To Jennifer, Jan's story felt like a message of hope for Lyn and Larry—that God knows what is best for us, even when we're disappointed in our current situation.

After reading Lyn's e-mail, Jennifer immediately replied to Lyn and said, "God may not be speaking to you right now, but maybe he can speak through someone else's journey." And she shared Jan's story.

But Lyn didn't believe Jan's story was encouragement from God. Maybe she failed to see Providence in the timing of the correspondence. Or the hope prevalent in Jan's story. Lyn still believed God wasn't speaking to her.

Why does God speak to one person and not the other?

He doesn't.

He speaks to each of us.

Perhaps a better question is, Why does one person hear and not the other?

We don't have to perform in some way by going to church or doing good deeds to earn the right to hear his words. But to hear him, we do have to listen.

As we said earlier, listening doesn't mean we have to spend our lives in a Benedictine monastery, climb a mountain and meditate, or even wait for the pastor to speak during a church service. It does mean we need to stay tuned in to the channels where we hear him speak.

God has gone to great lengths to communicate with us. He created a world where the very idea of communication is possible. He created humans in such a way that our survival depends in large part on our willingness to commune. We have fine-tuned sensors that can, if we aim them correctly, detect his constant, subtle messages.

We really have no excuse.

If we want to hear God, we can. Maybe not *what* we want, *when* we want it, but God is always trying to communicate with us.

As we said in the opening chapter, there are electronic signals constantly swirling around us. There are specialized electronic frequencies for radio, television, cell phones, walkie-talkies, Wi-Fi, and satellite. We receive one signal and not another because of the decoder we use and the channel to which we tune it. A TV helps us pick up television signals; a radio, radio signals. And each has a variety of channels to choose from.

Perhaps *faith* is the detector that helps us tune in to God's signals.

If we say that we don't hear God speak to us,

is it because we don't have the ears to hear what he is saying?

Or the faith to believe he can?

Or maybe we're afraid . . .

of what we'll hear,

that we'll look like a fool,

or that no one will believe us.

Are we like the apostles, worried that God will ask us to do something we don't want to do—like step out of the boat or follow him somewhere we don't want to go?

Hearing God isn't only for those with great faith. It takes a mere drop of faith to believe God is speaking and a drop more to ask for understanding when the message is confusing.

But sometimes it takes more than just a drop to *act* on what we hear.

110.7 BELIEVING ENOUGH TO ACT ON IT

We *say* we want to hear from God.

But do we really?

No, *really* . . .

It seems like a cool thing. We'll be at a potluck or a church league softball game, and we just kind of toss it out there: "Well, yesterday God told me that—"

Somehow hearing from God makes us hipper, holier, or at least holier than thou.

But hearing from him has drawbacks.

What if hearing God's voice meant you had to leave your cushy little American life and move to Rwanda?

What if hearing God's voice meant you had to befriend thieves and murderers?

What if hearing God's voice meant you had to sell all your possessions, leave your family, and follow him?

Hearing God's voice may require us to do things we don't want to do. Instead of asking if we want to *hear* his voice, maybe we should ask if we're willing to *follow* his voice.

If faith is the detector helping us tune in to the various frequencies, maybe action is the volume control that brings everything to life. A radio tuned to the correct station can't be heard unless the volume is turned up. Maybe acting on God's Word is like turning up the volume. When we do something, we hear more.

• • •

Susan learned not only to hear God's voice, but also to act on what he said through lots of small things. Like the time she heard him tell her to stop at a garage sale, where she found the exact furnishings her son wanted for his room.

Hearing God's voice and being faithful in the small things helped her to hear him and respond in the big things—like guidance for her and her young sons when her husband was diagnosed with, and then died from, a brain tumor.

She explains her listening journey this way:

> It's like a snowball: you've got to step out and follow a nudge. When you do, and it's right, you gain confidence to keep following. You can take bigger and bigger risks over time because you've learned how he speaks to you.
>
> And as I write, I'll add this. . . . I didn't really want to write about this. You know why? 'Cause two years ago, I pretty much heard an audible voice from God. A newly widowed man from my church had smiled at me that morning, and I'd thought, *He's going to call.*

The widower was a great Christian man, but his wife had been gone for only a month. He was well-known in the church, and both he and his deceased wife were greatly loved by the congregation. That presented a dilemma for Susan.

> I walked in the rain for almost an hour that day, crying out in earnest. "God, what do I do? This could be good. This could be bad. Surely, he won't call me now. Why am I thinking he will? What do I do if he does? I don't want the hassle, the heartache, the grief. . . . What is going on? Why am I even thinking this?"

As she walked up the hill to her house for the fourth time, she heard God speak, "He's going to call and ask you for coffee, and it's okay." Susan described the voice not as an audible one, but as an inner voice. It calmed her.

Still, she wasn't sure, so she asked again, "Why?"

She knew that a relationship with this man, at this time, held the potential to upset a lot of people at her church. But God's answer to her was clear, "You've been alone a long time."

> I walked inside my home, dripping, and within five minutes my oldest son brought me the phone. It was the widowed man. We talked for two hours, and he asked me out for coffee. Trembling, I met him. We married fourteen months later.

Dating and then getting married weren't easy things for Susan to do. Though she knew it was from God, she also knew what others were thinking. Her church wasn't ready for this, and neither was her pastor. She left her home church of nine years.

The transition has been difficult for the whole family. Susan's new husband still grieves for his first wife, and though Susan has tried to help him through that grief, she also has to ease the transition for her two sons, now in the eighth and tenth grades.

> We're finally finding peace, after months of great turmoil in which it was easy to question whether or not I heard the voice of God. Lots of Christians couldn't imagine we'd heard the voice of God, and

I've wondered why he allowed all that. Could it simply be, "You've been alone a long time?"

So though I want to say, "Hooray! Listen to God! He directs and guides and it's grand," the truth is, it all has me shaking in my boots a bit lately. Hearing his voice led me to one of the most challenging experiences I've had.

Susan *knows* that hearing God's voice is dangerous. But that reward is often worth the sacrifice we make to receive it.

A roller-coaster ride is fun for the three minutes you're on it, but a white-water raft ride down the Colorado River is truly an adventure. They both stimulate the same thrill mechanism in the brain, but the river ride poses real risks that even an experienced river guide cannot totally foresee.

Tuning in to hear God speak is dangerous because it invites us out of amusement into adventure.

"What God says to me almost always pushes me in a direction outside my comfort zone," says Mark. "It's not that he's cruel. But he wants me to be a risk-taker just like him. When he talks, it isn't to hear his own eloquence. He wants a conversation, and then ultimately a response. He doesn't make suggestions. He gives directives. Occasionally, I flat-out don't want to hear him. Sometimes, I plug my ears and turn on football. But he runs me down. . . . I can run but never hide."

As Mark Twain once said, "It ain't the parts of the Bible that I can't understand that bother me, it is the parts that I do understand."[6]

It takes faith to live a life of expectation, to believe God is speaking to us, and to have the courage to act on it. Susan concluded her e-mail by saying, "But as we grow and solidify, and the hard times resolve, I'm certain my thanks and confidence will grow."

Her gratitude and her confidence in what she's doing aren't quite there yet;

she hasn't tasted the proof,

but she's got the faith that one day she will.

That's real.

That's authentic.

And that's all God asks from us.

Susan knows that hearing from God isn't all cookies and ice cream. Sometimes it's embarrassing, frightening, or demanding. Yet, she has the faith to act on it, to believe God's plan is better than hers.

Ultimately, the question isn't, Does God speak?

God does speak,

is speaking,

and *will continue* to speak.

The question is, What will you do when God speaks?

110.8 THE NINTH WAY GOD ALWAYS SPEAKS

So God always speaks through

> our circumstances,
> other people,
> history,
> nature,
> dreams and visions,
> emotions,
> our conscience,
> and his Word.

Hmm, that's eight. The title said, "*Nine* Ways God Always Speaks."

So what's the ninth way?

Before you go grab the receipt for this book off your kitchen counter, drive to the store where you bought it, and declare the authors chapter cheats, we want to tell you about the ninth way. Our goal in this book has never been to present you with a formula to replicate. Rather, we've tried to expose you to the various ways God communicates. God can use anything, anywhere, and anytime, but he doesn't always use the same thing, in the same place, all the time.

But it does seem that God requires a bit of action on our part. Listening alone is not enough to continue the conversation. Jesus said,

> "Not everyone who calls out to me, 'Lord! Lord!' will enter the Kingdom of Heaven. Only those who actually do the will of my Father in heaven will enter. . . . Anyone who listens to my teaching and follows it is wise, like a person who builds a house on solid rock. Though the rain comes in torrents and the floodwaters rise and the winds beat against that house, it won't collapse because it is built on bedrock."[7]

Listening isn't enough.

There must be a response.

In the first chapter, we said that a one-sided relationship isn't worth much. Every relationship requires two people who each speak and listen, hear and respond. But before a relationship can even begin, someone must initiate contact or it never will be a relationship.

Mark attended a meeting that also included Tim Pawlenty, the governor of Minnesota. After the meeting, and as Mark and a few others stood talking, the governor came over and introduced himself. Mr. Pawlenty knew that none of the others had a good excuse to start the conversation, so he did.

That's what God does. He speaks first, and then waits for us to do something in return. His words are an invitation to dialogue. He doesn't expect us to start the conversation. He knows we'd be too intimidated to make the first move. So he breaks the ice. He speaks first.

And then patiently waits for us to respond.

In an earlier chapter, we talked about tennis being a sin for Linda because she made tennis her god. But it isn't a sin if we play tennis *with* God. He serves a message; we volley it back with an obedient act. Or maybe we ask questions for clarification. Sometimes we even object to what he's asking.

When we respond, he'll speak again. His objective is to keep the action rolling and the game progressing. Like the rhythm of a good tennis volley, we stop thinking about what's happening and just fall into the groove of this give-and-take communication.

The ninth way God speaks?

It's in response to our action. Though he initiates conversation, he also speaks in response to our acknowledgment of his overture.

Don't you need to hear him at least once to be able to respond?

Ah, but you have. He *has* spoken to you already.

You may think, *Sure, in big, impersonal ways.* And that would be true. But he also intended his general messages to be specific to each human being regardless of time, place, or circumstances. Consider these general words as if they were meant specifically for you:

> He said to give to those in need. (How do you respond to that?)
>
> He said to forgive those who have wounded us. (Ouch.)
>
> He said to find ways to love our enemies. (How do you do that?)
>
> He said to be grateful to those who have shown his mercy to us. (Do we demonstrate mercy?)
>
> He said to tell our stories to others. (When is the last time you listened to someone else's story or shared your own?)
>
> He said to remember our sorrows and how he brought us through them. (Do you remember?)

God has said many things to us universally, yet he speaks to each of us personally. When we respond to what he's said, he says more. And we get better at hearing him. So there.

He's just spoken to you, too.

No excuses.

Now, what are you going to do about it?

Your challenge is to find a way to act on something he's already said to you. Maybe it's a message you've been brooding over for years. Maybe it's something you've been avoiding or something you read about in this book.

Whatever it is, the action of obedience will be a response. That response becomes an initiative for God to respond.

Then you will no longer wait to hear God speak.

Instead, it will be an ongoing conversation.

Go ahead.

We dare you to listen and then act on it.

Then drop us a note and let us know what happened.

In our first book, *Six Prayers God Always Answers*, we discuss how we talk to God. In this book, we discover how God talks to us. The books are interdependent. Neither speaking to God nor hearing from him is a one-sided activity. We must both speak and listen; and for that to happen, God must do the same.

Ultimately, it's all about an ongoing dialogue, a dialogue that is as fundamental to our relationship with God as communication is to any relationship we have.

So, for God's sake, do something.

The ninth way God speaks is in response to your obedience to what you last heard him say—in other words, the ninth way is the way in which you give him permission to speak. Chances are, you'll discover a tenth way in which God speaks to you, a fiftieth way, and many more.

. . .

In the first chapter we said we would be your guides on this listening journey, and we asked you to trust us as we traveled together. Now, as we near the end of that journey, it's only fair to admit that though we have been the leaders of this little expedition, we have also been the greatest students.

Each day we worked on this book, we were surprised by how frequently and how boldly God spoke to us. Well-timed e-mails with stories from people's own lives arrived just as we needed illustrations for relevant points. Hard-to-believe stories were confirmed by similar ones, which gave us faith that God speaks in unbelievable ways.

Occasionally, a difficult section of the book slowed us down. We'd become frustrated by our inability to keep moving ahead; but often, our delay meant that a clearer point, a more poignant story, or a funnier illustration (okay, not so many of those) was coming. Soon we learned that delays were to be welcomed, not disliked.

But the hardest part was

recognizing all these amazing coincidences and signs,

hearing his stories through others,

learning from our history,

experiencing new ways God speaks through our dreams,

seeing him in nature,

feeling him speak through our emotions,

understanding how he uses our conscience to speak,

comparing all that to what he says in Scripture,

and wondering if we as writers were communicating the sense of wonder and awe we felt every day as we wrote this book.

We are not the same authors who started with you on this journey. We have discovered new and more personal ways that God speaks to us. Our hope and our prayer is that you are not the same either.

He is our God and our Creator—we are so unworthy to hear from him, yet he wants to have a conversation with us. When you need advice, he's a career counselor, a locker-room confidant, a sage who says more with one well-placed question than Chaucer, Shakespeare, and Milton all together. He's the father who names you, the mother who coos over you, the artist showing you his wondrous world.

He is the attorney who defends you and the gentle watcher who sings over you through the night. He's the real hitchhiker's guide to the galaxy.

God is your biggest fan and your greatest lover.

There's no one more mesmerizing, more clever, generous, witty, or spontaneous. He's been to the most interesting places, knows the most fascinating people, and tells some amazing tales—and he wants to introduce you to all of this.

Our journey together ends now.

But your lifelong listening journey is just beginning.

At the beginning of this book, we said some things are almost too good to be true.

Hearing God speak to you is one of those things that may seem impossible,

but it can be true.

In fact, it's too good *not* to be true.

And . . . it's true for *you*.

May you not only hear him in fresh and personal ways, but may you have the courage to share with others what you've heard, so they can hear him too.

Acknowledgments

Writing the acknowledgements section is always the hardest part of writing a book. So many people have contributed to this book—some unknowingly—that it is easy to overlook a contribution and harder still to know where to draw the line on who to thank in the limited space provided. To all of you who played a part with suggestions or hours of work, please know that we value your contributions and we know that this book wouldn't be the same without your input.

Our greatest thanks must go to every reader of *Six Prayers God Always Answers*. The time and money you spent on our book, the blog reviews you carefully crafted, and the word-of-mouth recommendations you passionately made all helped to make *Nine Ways God Speaks* possible.

To everyone at Tyndale: You have been a dream to work with and we feel so privileged to have met so many of you and heard your stories. Our time with you has felt less like a business relationship and more like a family reunion. We are truly honored to be working with teams that live out their mission.

Carol Traver, thank you for your support, wise counsel, and prison stories. This book is better because of you. Ron Beers, we're sorry for putting chocolate in your shorts, but know that from our perspective you have assembled an amazing team. Maria Eriksen, thank you for bringing your creativity and insight to both books. Vicky Lynch, you are always willing to try new ideas and you respond to our phone calls and e-mails faster than anyone else in the business. Thank you to Cara Peterson for being patient while we ironed out the bumps; the book is stronger because of your tireless efforts. To all of the sales professionals at Tyndale, and especially Sharon Heggeland, thank you for personally representing us to booksellers and readers.

We are so privileged to have Beth Jusino from Alive Communications as our agent. Beth is smart, savvy, and always there when we need her. Thank you, Beth, not only for all your hard work on our behalf, but also for your friendship. You are a valued participant in our writing partnership.

There is no question that our books are strengthened by those who review them. We are fortunate to have friends and professionals who have invested hours in reading, critiquing, asking questions, and challenging us to refine our words. Daniel Aalberts, Marlene Dickinson, Julie Garmon, Adrienne Stuckey, Matthew Paul Turner, and Nan Thorsen-Snipes all reviewed portions of this manuscript, suggested ideas, or helped in other ways.

Teisha Moseley read and commented extensively on

our early drafts, helping give shape to our stories. Wayne Holmes and Patrick Borders made countless personal sacrifices to give us hours of their time, not only throughout the process, but especially in the last days and hours before the manuscript was due. Each of you who reviewed the manuscript not only improved it but encouraged us with your friendship, dedication, and thoughtful input.

Our children—Emily, Elizabeth, Matthew, and Michael Herringshaw; and Jordan Schuchmann—were patient while we spent hours writing about how God talks to us and perhaps weren't listening to them as much as we should have. Thank you for letting us tell more of your stories. Our spouses, Jill Herringshaw and David Schuchmann, were understanding, supportive, and encouraging throughout the process. Thank you—again—for the grace you extended. We love each of you more than you'll ever know.

Finally, this book wouldn't have been possible without so many people who were willing to tell their stories of how God speaks to them. We would like to list them each by name, but some preferred anonymity. There are also many stories we didn't use due to length, similarity to other stories, or deadlines. But please know that we learned from each of you who shared your stories with us, and the content of this book is wider and deeper because of your experiences. We were surprised at how often God spoke to us not only through the content of your stories, but often through the arrival or timing of your story, as well. We've recorded some of the "stories behind the stories" on our Web site, and you can read about them at www.sixprayers.com.

Most of all we thank God, who desires to communicate

with each one of us. He divinely orchestrated every story at the exact moment we needed it. He also knew from the beginning of time that you'd be reading this right now and which of these stories would speak to you. If your hearing improves half as much from reading this book as ours did from writing it, you will be blessed indeed.

~Mark and Jennifer

NOTES

101.0 Hearing Voices

1. Allen Williamson, "Biography of Joan of Arc (Jehanne Darc),"
   http://www.joan-of-arc.org/joanofarc_life_summary_visions.html.
2. Ibid.
3. World Book Encyclopedia, s.v. "Joan of Arc, Saint."
4. Ibid.
5. See John 1:46.
6. See Luke 1:2-4.
7. Luke 1:28.
8. Luke 1:30-33.
9. Luke 1:34.
10. Luke 1:35.
11. Luke 1:36-37.
12. Luke 1:38.
13. Luke 1:39-41.
14. Luke 1:42-45.
15. Luke 1:46-49.
16. Matthew 1:19.
17. Matthew 1:20-21.
18. Matthew 1:24.
19. Matthew 1:25.

102.0 Circumstantial Evidence

1. "Jesus Christ image sells on eBay for $1800," *News Limited*, August 11, 2007, http://www.news.com.au/story/0,23599,22224584-2,00.html.
2. "'Virgin Mary' toast fetches $28,000," *BBC News*, November 23, 2004, http://news.bbc.co.uk/go/pr/fr/-/2/hi/americas/4034787.stm.
3. Ibid.
4. Edwin Chavey, "Face of Jesus Appears in Pancakes and Toast," *Ezine Articles*, http://ezinearticles.com/?Face-Of-Jesus-Appears-In-Pancakes-And-Toast&id=159727.
5. Mark Schultz, "I Am," *Live . . . A Night of Stories and Songs*, Word Entertainment (2005).
6. See Mark 8:11-12; Matthew 12:38-39.
7. See John 4:48.
8. See John 2:11.

103.0 Prophet Sharing

1. See Matthew 18:1-5.
2. See Matthew 16:15.
3. See Matthew 16:17.
4. See Matthew 16:18-19.
5. See Matthew 16:22.
6. Matthew 16:23.
7. Hebrews 1:1, NIV.
8. John 10:3-5.

104.0 *His*-story

1. "Quotations about History," *Quote Garden*, http://www.quotegarden.com/history.html.
2. Jone Johnson Lewis, "History Quotes," http://www.wisdomquotes.com/cat_history.html.
3. Steve Herzig, *Jewish Culture and Customs* (The Friends of Israel Gospel Ministry, Inc., 1997), 124–125.
4. Matthew 26:26-29.
5. Matthew 26:30.
6. Steve Herzig, *Jewish Culture and Customs*.
7. Ibid., 125–126.
8. Luke 4:18-19.
9. Luke 4:21.
10. Isaiah 42:9.
11. Peter W. Stoner, *Science Speaks* (Chicago: Moody Press, 1979), 106.

12. Luke 4:23-27, author's paraphrase.
13. "Quotations about History," *Quote Garden*, http://www.quotegarden. com/history.html.
14. Luke 23:34.
15. 1 Corinthians 10:1.
16. C. S. Lewis, *The Silver Chair* (New York: HarperTrophy, 2000), 154.
17. Romans 8:28, NIV.
18. C. S. Lewis, *The Discarded Image* (Cambridge, England: Cambridge University Press, 1964), 176.

105.0 You Must Be Dreaming
1. See 1 Samuel 3:1-10.
2. Lee Ann Obringer, "How Dreams Work," *How Stuff Works*, http:// science.howstuffworks.com/dream.htm.
3. J. L. Saver and J. Rabin, "The Neural Substrates of Religious Experience," *The Journal of Neuropsychiatry and Clinical Neurosciences* (1997), http://neuro.psychiatryonline.org/cgi/content/ abstract/9/3/498.
4. Dean H. Hamer, *The God Gene: How Faith Is Hardwired into Our Genes* (New York: Doubleday, 2005).
5. Jack Hitt, "This Is Your Brain on God," *Wired*, November 1999, http:// www.wired.com/wired/archive/7.11/persinger.html.
6. Mario Beauregard and Denyse O'Leary, *The Spiritual Brain: A Neuroscientist's Case for the Existence of the Soul* (San Francisco: HarperOne, 2007), 271–272.
7. Ibid., 272.
8. Ibid., 37.
9. Ibid., 275.
10. Ibid.
11. "The Conversion of Constantine," Elpenor's Home of the Greek World, http://www.ellopos.net/elpenor/vasilief/constantine-conversion.asp; *Library of Nicene and Post Nicene Fathers*, 2nd series (New York: Christian Literature Co., 1990), 489–491; "Eusebius: The Conversion of Constantine," *Medieval Sourcebook*, http://www.fordham.edu/halsall/ source/conv-const.html; Shaye I. D. Cohen, "The Path to Victory," *Frontline*, April 1998, http://www.pbs.org/wgbh/pages/frontline/shows/religion/why/ legitimization.html.
12. *More Than Dreams: From Dreams to Reality*, http://www. morethandreams.org/dreamsofjesus.html.

13. Job 33:14-18.

14. See Genesis 15:12-18.

15. See Genesis 28:1-22.

16. See I Kings 3:5-15.

17. See Matthew 1:18–2:14.

18. See Acts 10:9-15.

19. See Acts 16:6-10.

20. Acts 2:17.

21. "Joseph and the Amazing Technicolor Dreamcoat," *Andrew Lloyd Webber's Really Useful Group*, http://www.reallyuseful.com/rug/shows/joseph/.

106.0 The Nature Channel

1. John Muir, "My First Summer in the Sierra—The Mono Trail," *John Muir Writings*, http://www.yosemite.ca.us/john_muir_writings/my_first_summer_in_the_sierra/chapter_8.html.

2. Luke 19:40, NIV.

3. John Muir, "My First Summer in the Sierra—The Tuolumne Camp," *John Muir Writings*, http://www.yosemite.ca.us/john_muir_writings/my_first_summer_in_the_sierra/chapter_10.html.

4. "Christian Teachings," *Re:Vision*, http://www.revision.org/content.asp?pl=482&sl=531&contentid=533.

5. "Legend of the Sand Dollar," *Shell Factory and Nature Park*, http://www.shellfactory.com/sanddollar.html.

6. "About the Author," *What to Expect*, http://whattoexpect.com/home/about-the-author.aspx.

7. Francis S. Collins, *The Language of God* (New York: Free Press, 2006), 6.

8. Wayne Martindale and Jerry Root, eds., *The Quotable Lewis* (Wheaton: Tyndale, 1990), 134.

9. "George Washington Carver Quotes," *Thinkexist.com*, http://thinkexist.com/quotes/george_washington_carver/.

10. Ibid.

11. Ibid.

12. Toby Fishbein, "The Legacy of George Washington Carver," http://www.lib.iastate.edu/spcl/gwc/bio.html.

13. "George Washington Carver Quotes."

14. Ibid.

15. Authors' retelling of Numbers 22.

16. "Fun Pet Facts," *Richmond Pet Lovers*, http://www.richmondpetlovers.com/pet_facts.php.

17. Elizabeth Barrett Browning, "How Do I Love Thee?" http://www.amherst.edu/~rjyanco94/literature/elizabethbarrettbrowning/poems/sonnetsfromtheportuguese/howdoilovetheeletmecounttheways.html.
18. Matthew 6:28-30.
19. See Matthew 14:24-33.
20. Psalm 29:7.
21. Romans 1:20.
22. See John 18:10.
23. Matthew 26:35.
24. Matthew 26:74.
25. Psalm 19:1-4.
26. Jeremiah 10:13.
27. "Christian Teachings," *Re:Vision*, http://www.revision.org/content.asp?pl=482&sl=531&contentid=533.

107.0 Infectious

1. Chris Tiegreen first sparked our thinking about this. He has a new book out on the subject: *Feeling Like God: The Emotional Side of Discipleship—and Why You Can't Fully Follow Jesus without It* (Carol Stream, IL: Tyndale, 2008).
2. Dennis Ngien, "The God Who Suffers," *Christianity Today*, February 3, 1997, http://ctlibrary.com/1027.
3. See Genesis 6:5-6.
4. See Deuteronomy 1:34, 37.
5. See 1 Kings 3:10.
6. See Zephaniah 3:8.
7. See Zephaniah 3:17.
8. See Psalm 17:4; 21:8; 28:5; 44:3; 91:13; 99:5.
9. "Theism for Our Time," in Peter T. O'Brien and David G. Peterson *God Who Is Rich in Mercy* (Grand Rapids: Baker, 1986), 16. (As quoted on http://www.spurgeon.org/~phil/articles/impassib.htm#19.)
10. "Memorable Quotes for *Chariots of Fire*," http://www.imdb.com/title/tt0082158/quotes.
11. Matthew 23:27-28.
12. Matthew 23:15, NIV.
13. See John 2:13-17.
14. Daniel Goleman, "Happy or Sad, a Mood Can Prove Contagious," *New York Times*, October 15, 1991, http://query.nytimes.com/gst/fullpage.html?res=9D0CE6D91131F936A25753C1A967958260&sec=&spon=&pagewanted=print.

15. Ibid.
16. Ibid.
17. H. L. Willmington *Willmington's Bible Handbook* (Wheaton: Tyndale, 1997), 381.
18. Philippians 3:10-11.

108.0 Pushy Little Weenie

1. C. S. Lewis, *Mere Christianity* (New York: HarperCollins, 1998), 3–4.
2. Ibid, 5.
3. Ibid.
4. Romans 2:14.
5. Genesis 20:5, NIV.
6. Genesis 20:6-7, NIV.
7. Donna Jordan, *Listening to God* (a self-published manual, 2002), 51.
8. "Confession Makes a Comeback," *The Wall Street Journal*, Friday, September 21, 2007, page W7.
9. See Romans 13–14 and I Corinthians 8–10.
10. See Romans 14:14-15.
11. 1 Samuel 24:5-6.
12. See Genesis 37:26-27.
13. "Homer Says," http://www.angelfire.com/home/pearly/homer/homer-quotes3.html.
14. Michelangelo Merisi da Caravaggio, *David with the Head of Goliath*, http://www.bbc.co.uk/arts/powerofart/popups/caravaggio.shtml; *The Columbia Encyclopedia*, 6th ed., s.v. "Michelangelo Merisi da Caravaggio," http://www.encyclopedia.com/doc/1E1-CaravaggMic.html.
15. Romans 7:21-24.
16. See Romans 2:14.
17. Luke 18:10-14.
18. Romans 7:24-25.
19. John 16:7-8.
20. Jeremiah 31:33.

109.0 Inhaling the Bible

1. *Readers Digest*, March 1993, 71. Revised slightly for readability.
2. Matthew 27:5.
3. Luke 10:37.
4. "God's Word Changes Lives," *The Gideons International*, http://www.gideons.org/Tgi.web/TGI.Web.PublicWebSite/pages/Changed_Lives_Video.aspx?source=video_ellio.

5. "Miracle from a Helicopter," *The Gideons International*, http://www.gideons.org/Tgi.web/TGI.Web.PublicWebSite/pages/changed_lives_text.aspx?source=MiracleFromAHelicopter.

6. "A Stolen Opportunity," *The Gideons International*, http://www.gideons.org/Tgi.web/TGI.Web.PublicWebSite/pages/changed_lives_text.aspx?source=AStolenOpportunity.

7. Text from "The Confessions of St. Augustine" (Book 8, Chapter 12) translated from the Latin by J. G. Pilkington, in *A Select Library of the Nicene and Post Nicene Fathers of the Christian Church* edited by Philip Schaff, Series I, Vol. I (Edinburgh: T&T Clark, 1882).

8. Steven Tomkins, *John Wesley: A Biography* (Grand Rapids: Eerdmans, 2003), 66.

9. Blaise Pascal, *Pensées*. A. J. Krailsheimer, trans. (New York: Penguin, 1995), 87.

10. "Section X: Typology," *Leadership University*, http://www.leaderu.com/cyber/books/pensees/pensees-SECTION-10.html.

11. John Maynard Keynes, "Newton, the Man," http://www-groups.dcs.st-and.ac.uk/~history/Extras/Keynes_Newton.html.

12. Pieter W. van der Horst, "Ancient Jewish Bibliomancy," *Journal of Greco-Roman Christianity and Judaism* 1 (2000).

13. Cited from Mark's personal conversation and also http://www.dmm.org.

14. Kathryn Jones, "Travel Advisory; Texas Museum with Bragging Rights," *The New York Times*, May 6, 2001, http://query.nytimes.com/gst/fullpage.html?sec=travel&res=9806E1DD1039F935A35756C0A9679C8B63.

15. "Elmore Family Lineage," http://www2.arkansas.net/~mgee/1elmore.html.

16. "YMCA Bible Belonging to Corporal Frank Richards," *National Museums Liverpool*, http://www.liverpoolmuseums.org.uk/online/exhibitions/faith/bible.asp.

17. "Book Review of *Nightmare on Iwo* by Patrick F. Caruso," http://members.aol.com/VonRanke/caruso.html.

18. "Bible Stopped Sniper's Bullet," *Newsmax.com*, August 9, 2007, http://archive.newsmax.com/archives/ic/2007/8/9/82730.shtml?s=ic.

19. Sharon Turco, "Mother's 911 Call 'Heartless,'" *News Press*, September 4, 2001, http://www.fact.on.ca/news/news0109/nwp010904.htm.

20. "Man Says Bibles Stopped Bullet," November 8, 2006, http://www.freerepublic.com/focus/f-news/1734860/posts.

21. "How to Smoke Marijuana," http://everything2.com/index.pl?node_id=1369958. Emphasis added.

22. William A. Dembski, "Cracking the Bible Code," *First Things*, August/September 1998), http://www.firstthings.com/article.php3?id_article=3549.

23. Hugh Ross, "Cracking the Codes," *Reasons to Believe*, http://www.reasons.org/resources/apologetics/crackingcodes.shtml.

24. William A. Dembski, "Cracking the Bible Code."

25. "Voltaire Bits," http://www.blinkbits.com/blinks/voltaire.

26. "Bestselling author worldwide," http://answers.google.com/answers/threadview?id=14.

27. Audrey Barrick, "Poll: Nearly One-Third of Americans Believe Bible Word-for-Word," *The Christian Post*, http://www.christianpost.com/article/20060522/22040.htm.

28. John 1:1-5, 14.

29. Matthew 5:17.

30. "Personal Promise Bible," http://personalpromisebible.com/wantbible.php.

31. See Ezekiel 2:9.

32. Eugene Peterson, *Eat This Book* (Grand Rapids: Eerdmans, 2006), xii.

33. "'Mother' dough dates to first Gold Rush loaf; San Francisco's Famous Boudin Bakery Celebrates 150 years of Fresh-Baked Sourdough French Bread," *Business Wire*, August, 26, 1999, http://findarticles.com/p/articles/mi_m0EIN/is_1999_August_26/ai_55565713/print.

34. "A Russian Murder," *The Gideons International*, http://www.gideons.org/Tgi.web/TGI.Web.PublicWebSite/pages/changed_lives_text.aspx?source=ARussianMurderer.

110.0 You Might Think I'm Crazy, But . . .

1. Job 5:9, *The Message*.

2. Job 9:10, *The Message*.

3. See Zechariah 1:8; 2:1; 5:1; 5:9, *The Message*.

4. Anne Frank, *Anne Frank: The Diary of a Young Girl—The Definitive Edition* (New York: Doubleday, 1995), 333.

5. Psalm 139:7-12, *The Message*.

6. "Mark Twain," *Quote DB*, http://www.quotedb.com/quotes/3290.

7. Matthew 7:21, 24-25.

ABOUT THE AUTHORS

Dr. Mark Herringshaw, Ph.D., is a pastor, leader, and teacher. He currently serves as a teaching pastor of the 7,000-member North Heights Lutheran Church in Roseville, Minnesota. He is professor of leadership at the Master's Institute Seminary in St. Paul. Mark is a writer, speaker, and seminar leader, having written more than 75 articles appearing in various periodicals, as well as *Six Prayers God Always Answers*, his previous book also co-written with Jennifer Schuchmann. His doctorate is in organizational leadership from Regent University. He is the founder and director of eEmbassy, an organization that develops interactive educational experiences for youth, families, and businesses. Mark and his wife, Jill, have four children.

Jennifer Schuchmann is an award-winning writer. She has contributed to several books, including *Six Prayers God*

Always Answers, also co-written with Mark Herringshaw (Tyndale, 2008); *Your Unforgettable Life*, with Craig Chapin (Beacon Hill, 2005); *The Church Leader's Answer Book* (Tyndale, 2006); and a couples' study Bible (Zondervan, 2007). Jennifer holds an MBA from Emory University, with an emphasis in marketing and communications, and a bachelor's degree in psychology from the University of Memphis. She lives in the Atlanta area with her husband, David, and their son.

1
Prayer Doesn't Work

Prayer Doesn't Work.

God works.

We often get that confused, don't we?

We think there is a certain formula we have to follow—a right way of doing prayer. If we do it right, God will answer. It's like using the correct postage after a rate change: the proper stamp ensures delivery. But when our prayers don't get answered, we believe we're somehow at fault. We "prayed the wrong way." There are lots of ways we could have screwed up—not having enough postage (read: good deeds); mislabeling the envelope (praying to Jesus when we should have prayed to God); or forgetting to seal it (with a promise to do better next time).

If that's how you think, this isn't the book for you. We don't believe there's a *right* way or a *wrong* way to pray. Yes, biblical literature, church history, and religious tradition present some great guidelines when we need an example to follow, but the truth is that prayer is nothing more than communication with God. Some of us prefer long, elegantly handwritten notes on premium stationery. Others prefer text messages with abbreviated words that aren't grammatically correct (and that parents can't decipher). But regardless of *how* we pray, it isn't prayer that changes things. *It's God who changes things.*

Sometimes we forget that.

We're so caught up in our own expectations of what prayer should look and smell like that when we look for God's reply, we limit our thinking to a #10 business envelope in the mailbox, when perhaps God is answering us with a marshmallow, an old lady's smile, or something else so completely unexpected that we miss it.

Consider the example of the Sunday school teacher who asked her young students to guess the answer to a question.

"Okay, class, I'm thinking of something brown and fuzzy that jumps from tree to tree. Does anyone know what I'm thinking of?"

No one in the class responded, so she tried again.

"Okay, it has a bushy tail, plays in your yard, and is very hard to catch. Now do you know what I am thinking of?"

Again the kids remained quiet.

Exasperated, the Sunday school teacher gave it one last try.

"Okay, it's a small animal that eats nuts. Does anybody know what I am talking about?"

Finally, Bobby raised his hand.

"Teacher, I know the right answer is Jesus, but it sure sounds like you're talking about a squirrel."

From our earliest experiences at church, we learn that it is more important to be right than to be authentic. So it's no wonder that, when it comes to prayer, we'd rather say the right words, follow the correct formula, and assume the designated posture, even when it feels phony to us.

LANGUAGES

We talk to God, but we don't all speak the same language. One person's prayer comes wrapped in a work of art, like Fabriano's *Nativity*, Handel's *Messiah*, or little Jimmy's finger painting, *Jesus Raises Stinking Lazarus*.

Another prayer might appear as a dramatic enactment, such as the Jewish Passover or a Native American rain dance. Prayer might waft above a city, sung from atop a mosque tower. It might tumble from the lips of a sniffling child, meander along the lyrics of a Kentucky bluegrass song, or conceal itself in the eloquent silence of a Benedictine friar.

Communicating with God takes many forms in its effort to express our common predicament. Our reach is never long enough, our fingers never nimble enough. We run out of time, stamina, and will. Our ambitions outpace our capacity, and the gap cannot be spanned by noble savagery or advanced technology.

And then?

We kneel down. We look up.

And when we don't get the response we're expecting, we look inside ourselves and ask, "What did I do wrong?"

WHAT PRAYER IS NOT

It is said that St. Catherine's Monastery near Mount Sinai, Egypt, still honors the final will and testament of three monks who lived there twelve centuries ago. One monk, who was a doorkeeper, wanted to keep his job forever. In honor of his request, his mummy still sits beside the door he guarded when he was alive.

Behind that door lived the other two monks. Each had taken a vow to devote his life to perpetual prayer. One would pray while the other slept. They never spoke to or saw each other. Their only connection was a chain that ran through the wall and was attached to their wrists. When one had completed his prayers, he would yank the chain as a signal for the other to begin.

When the two men died, their skeletons were laid side by side in caskets. And there they rest today, still united by the same chain.[*]

Some historians believe that rigorous monastic disciplines like the one practiced by these two monks helped to preserve civilization during the cultural deterioration of the early Middle Ages.

Perhaps.

But anecdotes like these, told as sermon illustrations by well-intentioned pastors, may unintentionally decrease not only the occurrence of prayer but also the number of active pray-ers. When the average twenty-first-century Westerner hears of such eccentric dedication, a typical response might be, "If this is what it takes to pray to God, count me out."

Prayer isn't accomplished by some divine formula. Its power isn't amplified if we assume some sort of ascetic or monastic posture.

---

[*] R. C. Sproul, "Chained Together for 12 Centuries," *Mission Gate Prison Ministry*, www.charityadvantage.com/missiongateministry/images/Acts7.doc.

Religion has a way of complicating prayer, making it self-conscious, rehearsed, and . . . well, awkward. We found through some informal research that although nearly everyone in church feels comfortable requesting prayer aloud in a small group, nearly eight out of ten feel uncomfortable actually praying aloud. In other words, 80 percent of the people we surveyed had no problem verbalizing their requests to a pastor, teacher, or small-group leader—even in front of their peers. But they became physically uncomfortable when asked to verbalize their prayers directly to God when others were listening.

Well-meaning prayer tutors often respond to this issue by teaching acronyms such as A.C.T.S. (Adoration, Confession, Thanksgiving, and Supplication) as a way of remembering what to include in a prayer. But the result is that we get hung up on the steps. *Did I spend long enough on the A? And do I really need more T before I can get to the S? How much C?* They seem to emphasize style over substance. Prayer techniques meant to teach us to look up often have the unintended consequence of making us look over our shoulders. *Am I doing this right?*

Prayer isn't work. Or at least it shouldn't be.

Prayer should be like communicating with a lover.

Sometimes words aren't necessary.

Regardless of what the magazines teach, a good kiss doesn't happen from good technique. It's not about how warm, moist, and soft—if so, we'd all be kissing cinnamon rolls.

It's not the how but the who.

Prayer, like a kiss, is best when it's about the *other person*. Especially if the other person is God.

WHAT PRAYER IS

Prayer is a conversation with God.

Real prayer has the same elements as a real conversation—bold questions, bursts of emotion, and room for silence. Think of the times when you've had a real, honest-to-goodness conversation with someone you love. It can happen at any time—when your teenager comes home from school, over the dinner table, in bed with your spouse, or in the middle of the night when your toddler wakes up from a nightmare. Conversation isn't rehearsed; it just bursts forth as a response to the situation.

Ellie bounces into the kitchen, where her mom and dad are finishing their dinner. "Can I go to a friend's house tonight and take the car?"

"Whose house?" asks her mother.

"What time will you be home?" asks her father.

"I'm just going to Sarah's. I'll be home by ten."

"Is anyone else going with you?" asks Mom.

"No, just me, but Cindy's meeting us there."

"Is there gas in the car?" asks Dad.

"I'll check," she says and runs out the door. A few minutes later, she's back in the kitchen with a report that the gauge is almost on *E*.

Her dad hands her some cash, tells her he loves her, and reminds her to drive carefully.

There is no formal presentation to this encounter. Nobody carefully planned their words. Ellie, in a hurry to get to her friend's house, asked the most direct question she could. Everything else that took place in the exchange was a result of that first question.

Ellie's conversation wasn't self-conscious or insecure.

Prayer shouldn't be either.

We don't carefully calculate our words into some sort of exploitative formula; instead, we're focused entirely on the person to whom we're speaking—to their responses, as well as our own.

Good prayer is like talking with children. We're more interested in hearing what they've said, or how they're reacting to what we've said, than we are in carefully selecting our words.

Sometimes prayer means we get naked—as with sexual intimacy—revealing parts of ourselves that no one else has ever seen. The only reason we can do this is not that the lights are turned off, but because there is trust in the relationship.

God doesn't ask us to undress in front of him, and then go off and share the details with his buddies. He doesn't betray us, even when we've shown him *everything*. Prayer, like a comfortable, intimate conversation, is a safe place to be vulnerable. And whether or not we get enough *A* and *C* before our *T* or *S*, God will still be there in the morning.

• • •

Whether on TV, in the movies, or in conversation, people thoughtlessly invoke the name of God into the mundane ("Oh, my God!") and the profane ("Jesus Christ!"). Believers are offended—convinced it is disrespectful, even blasphemous. Nonbelievers toss it up to a slip of the tongue ("Pardon my French") or simply give it no thought at all.

But what if these were really prayers?

Oh, sure, they're not the kind of prayers found in a

Baptist Sunday school class or at a Catholic Mass; they aren't led by a Lutheran minister or a Jewish rabbi.

Tim, a recent seminary graduate hoping to start his own church, asked, "Does a father stop listening to his child because the kid is swearing at him? Or is he able to see beyond the pain and the hurt that life has inflicted, to see it as a cry of a beloved child, wounded, crying out to Abba? Could Jesus see these outbursts as a cry of a wounded brother or sister? How do we know what is in the heart of those who utter such words? Do we even know our own hearts? We might just be condemning the prayers of a hurting child who is crying out, 'Lord forgive me.'"

God is the judge of these prayers.

And we believe God answers every one of them.

We pray.

God answers.

In the answers, we learn who he is.